Advance Praise for
Urban Meltdown

You'd better believe we will have to rethink the way our cities work as the West enters a new age of energy scarcity. We have to get serious about making other arrangements — for getting around, for manufacturing and trade, and even growing our food. Clive Doucet has been at the center of this issue as an activist, an elected official, and an author. *Urban Meltdown* is both an astute diagnosis of the problem and a visionary agenda for correcting things.

— James Howard Kunstler,
author of *The Long Emergency*

I know I'm going to enjoy reading it and learning from it. Every now and then I've been dipping into it unsystematically, and find it hard to put down.

— The late Dr. Jane Jacobs,
author of *The Death and Life of Great American Cities*
and *Dark Age Ahead*, in a letter to the author, 2005

Why are our cities so miserably prepared for the impending post-petroleum future, and what can we do about it? If you want answers informed by experience, look no further. Clive Doucet is the kind of local politician the world desperately needs an abundance of: he's realistic, forthright, courageous, aware — and a damned good writer to boot.

— Richard Heinberg,
author of *The Party's Over,*
Powerdown and *The Oil Depletion Protocol,*
and Research Fellow, Post Carbon Institute

Through Clive Doucet's poetically inspired kaleidoscope we get a clear picture of how our cities have rapidly and increasingly come under ecological seige and why politics as usual will not get us out of this mess.

— Tony Clarke,
author of *Inside the Bottle*
and co-author of *Blue Gold*

Clive Doucet writes powerfully — from the head and heart. In *Urban Meltdown,* he shows clearly and convincingly that climate change is not only the great global challenge of our generation but that it is also a local concern. He draws connections between the city and planet in a way that make us realize we cannot evade our responsibilities as citizens and, more importantly, as members of the human family.

— JOHN CRUMP,
Polar Programme, UNEP/GRID-Arendal,
Norway and Ottawa

Global warming is the issue of our time. Perhaps of all time. Clive Doucet has been on the front line of the struggle to understand the consequences of not governing accordingly. I highly recommend this book.

— DAVID MILLER,
mayor, City of Toronto

Poetic, insightful, and filled with hope, this book will open your mind, change your life, and liberate your soul. *Urban Meltdown* offers a new and valuable perspective on the world's most important issue — climate change — from an informed, practical, and passionate voice, Clive Doucet.

— DOUGLAS E. MORRIS,
author of *It's a Sprawl World After All*

URBAN MELTDOWN

Cities, Climate Change
and
Politics as Usual

CLIVE DOUCET

NEW SOCIETY PUBLISHERS

CATALOGING IN PUBLICATION DATA
A catalog record for this publication is available from
the National Library of Canada.

Cover design by Diane McIntosh.

Printed in Canada.
First printing February 2007.

Paperback ISBN 13: 978-0-86571-584-4

New Society Publishers acknowledges the support of the
Government of Canada through the Book Publishing
Industry Development Program (BPIDP)
for our publishing activities.

Inquiries regarding requests to reprint all or part of *Urban Meltdown*
should be addressed to New Society Publishers at the address below.
To order directly from the publishers, please call toll-free (North America)
1-800-567-6772, or order online at newsociety.com

Any other inquiries can be directed by mail to:
New Society Publishers
P.O. Box 189, Gabriola Island, BC V0R 1X0, Canada
1-800-567-6772

New Society Publishers' mission is to publish books that contribute in fundamental ways to building an ecologically sustainable and just society, and to do
so with the least possible impact on the environment, in a manner that models
this vision. We are committed to doing this not just through education, but
through action. We are acting on our commitment to the world's remaining
ancient forests by phasing out our paper supply from ancient forests worldwide. This book is one step toward ending global deforestation and climate
change. It is printed on acid-free paper that is 100% old growth forest-free
(100% post-consumer recycled), processed chlorine free, and printed with veg-
etable-based, low-VOC inks. For further information, or to browse our full list
of books and purchase securely, visit our website at: newsociety.com

NEW SOCIETY PUBLISHERS   newsociety.com

Dedication

There is always one singer that your wife would have left you for if only he would have asked; that singer is always nobler, more poetical, more talented than you ever could be. For me that singer was Phil Ochs and the girl is a freckle-faced, strawberry-headed, the-world-is-here-for-me-to-fix girl named Patty Steenberg. It's easy to understand her preference for Phil Ochs. Sometimes when I listen to Phil's songs today (forty years after he wrote them) hot tears stream down my face. They are not tears for Phil but for the vivid hope his songs evoke that a better world is possible. They are tears for the naiveté of youth and the kind of world we have today. We seem to have learned very little. The Iraq war has replaced the contra wars in Nicaragua, and Nicaragua followed Pinochet and Chile. The list of man's inhumanity to man in just a few centuries of New World settlement has been a long one founded on genocidal wars, slavery and ethnic cleansings. All that ever seems to change are the participants in the human folly.

They are tears born in hope.

To Patty Steenberg
who has been my comrade in arms
in all the ways that matter.

Contents

Acknowledgments

There is a worldwide movement going on as I write these words. It's a movement that has its roots in many places and in millions of people's lives. We saw it in massive, worldwide demonstrations against the war in Iraq, in the election of Lula da Silva in Brazil and the new power sharing that is occurring in that country via participative budgets. We see it in "Earth Day" and other new ways of celebrating our shared existence.

We sustain each other in this grand conversation for a better world. Some of the sustaining people in my life have been my wife Patty Steenberg who introduced me to complexity science, the concept of the fat tail rate of change and encouraged me to think of politics and societal change in the context of these new scientific paradigms instead of the old right-wing-left-wing political models. Murray MacGregor introduced me to the global conversation via the Internet, read and critiqued drafts. In my office at City Hall without the help of Stuart Lister, Donna Silver, Pierre Johnson, Tara Pearman, Sarah Lindsay and Cyndi Box I could not have done Hay West, the Connecting Community studies and the Ottawa Participative Budgets.

Rejections are often an author's best friend and they have been for me. I am very appreciative of publishers who took the time to critique earlier versions of this book. Ronsdale Press was kind enough to send me several thoughtful readers' reports; Doug Gibson suggested cutting a great deal which I did, and Jan Walters made me think harder about point of view; and Ramsay Derry who edited my first book and became a life long literary mentor.

Thanks to Val Ross and Patrick Martin at the Globe and Mail who published excerpts in their newspaper; to Elizabeth May, Jane Jacobs and John Ralston Saul who read early versions and encouraged me. Last but not least, I thank the people of Capital Ward who took the chance on electing a poet.

And most of all, I thank my publishers at New Society who met with me, talked with me and were able to see the connections between the poet and the politician. I had the sense from our first conversations that my manuscript had found a fine home.

All writing is vanity, and the vainest is autobiographical. A political life is also a tangle of conceits, ambitions and ideals, but as I wrote this book, I could not see how to untangle my own life's experiences from the more general experiences of politics and society. They were all mixed up. The personal gave meaning and emotion to the political, and the political gave the essential context of society to my individual experiences. Chris and Judith Plant of New Society had reservations about trying to mix a life lived with general conclusions about how society worked, but decided I was worth the risk and assigned Betsy Nuse to shepherd the words from manuscript to book. To all I am very grateful.

Prologue

There is a celestial order
which floats in still cobwebs
above clear water.
It is as timeless as mountaintops,
as splendid as spring flowers.
It weaves in evanescent nets
disappearing with the sun.
Forgotten for another day
the mortality of moments
the infinity of days.

— from "Canal Seasons"

THERE IS NO CELESTIAL ORDER to this story. The scale often defeated me. How do you connect for the reader the desaliniza-tion of the oceans, the temperature of the Gulf of Mexico or rain in January in Ottawa with the mundane tasks of a city councilor? My office gets 3,000 calls a month, and they are rarely about global warming. Yet the reality is that there are many very ordinary connec-tions.

Rain storms in January followed by profound flash freezes require new and expensive equipment to clear city sidewalks, otherwise they remain twisted and frozen like fast flowing creek beds that thaw and freeze, thaw and freeze. Summer heat now requires my city to air condition all of its buildings. We now consume more electricity in the summer than the winter — unheard of as recently as ten years ago, and the damage from ice storms, like hurricanes cannot be stopped, just endured.

Many constituents refuse to believe that torrential rains followed by flash freezes are connected to anything but poor city manage-ment. We just can't clear the streets properly anymore. City staff are incompetent. This is a comforting thought, but it isn't true. To connect the details of a city councilor's life and the broad currents of planetary change, you first need to understand that more than 80 percent of the greenhouse gases that are cooking the planet are created by cities.

The second and only other thing you need to know is that the greatest terror facing the world isn't some demented men willing to kill themselves blowing up buildings, trains and buses. As upsetting as this may be, it is trivial compared to the complex, immensely difficult struggle to stop climate change and ecological decline from overwhelming all governments' ability to govern.

Finally, this book isn't about success. I've been fighting against urban sprawl for 40 years. As a student, I began with the Stop Spadina Movement in Toronto in the 1960s. Then I went to work for the federal Ministry of State for Urban Affairs, the provincial Ministry of Municipal Affairs, citizens groups and now as a city politician.

After forty years of effort, urban sprawl has achieved dimensions that I would never have thought possible when I started. Toronto has been paved all the way to Hamilton. The 1960s strip mall has morphed into "Big Box" power centers with parking lots that you could land a jet on. These warehouse shopping areas are so vast, people drive from one end to the other. Estate lots now cover entire townships. Four cars in a driveway are not unusual.

The main streets of this new suburban landscape have evolved into perfect traffic sewers, totally devoid of any life except the automobile. Unlike a traditional main street like Bank Street in Ottawa, Queen Street in Toronto or Grand Avenue in Des Moines, Iowa, all of which generate millions of dollars in small business taxes, a suburban traffic sewer like its larger freeway cousin generates nothing but immense financial and environmental costs. This is the way Bill Bryson describes Grand Avenue in the 1950s. "In those days, it was adorned from downtown to western suburbs with towering, interlaced elms, the handsomest street-side tree ever.... But more than this, Grand felt the way a street should feel. Its office buildings and apartments were built close to the road, which gave the street a kind of neighborliness and it still had most of its old homes — mansions of exuberant splendor, nearly all with turrets and towers and porches like ship's decks — though these had now mostly found other uses as offices, funeral homes and the like."[1] This description of Grand Avenue in Des Moines could equally apply to Bronson or King Edward Avenues in Ottawa or just about any other city's main street in the mid part of the last century. They have all been butchered into traffic sewers.

Today, 25 to 50 per cent of every city's budget goes into road construction and reconstruction. The pollutants from this form of development have turned the most precious things human beings have — the planet's atmosphere — into an aerial sewer that is beginning to strangle us, as surely as foul water and urban typhoid did in the 19th century.

The reason for this failure is as complex as each and every one of our busy lives. I haven't been alone on the environmental podium. The chattering classes have been busy. David Suzuki has written and spoken eloquently for decades for less corrosive forms of urban growth. His Institute has written practical descriptions of how to get to a sustainable society — quickly. There's Elizabeth May of the Sierra Club, a powerful voice of eco-sanity. James Kunstler of New York State has described the toxic connection between burning the planet's supply of fossil fuels, climate change and ecological decline in powerful books like *The Long Emergency*.[2]

It's worth reflecting on why so much effort has achieved so little. I've come to believe that it rests on three reasons. The first: despite all the talk, books, UN conferences (Montreal, Kyoto, Rio), newspaper articles, TV programs, the exact nature of the worldwide environmental crisis still remains obscure to most people because it is so diffuse. It's polar bears that can't hunt on the ice anymore. It's the Rideau Canal in my hometown, which melts in the coldest months of the year. It's force five hurricanes in the Gulf of Mexico. It's…it's all too confusing to understand in any collective way. What does polar bears who can't hunt have to do with me? Or the Gulf of Mexico and New Orleans? Hence no common political vision has emerged to attack it.

The result of no common political vision is that national governments not only ignore the climate crisis but actively aid it without the slightest public sanction. Locally I've never seen a wetland win an argument with a road. Voting for a road, coal generation plants in the US and China or a pipeline always takes precedence. So while the weather may be on the front pages of your local newspaper with strange winters, it's never on the front page of your government's agenda.

And the fact that the accumulative effects of all these anti-environmental decisions are impossible to calculate except in the most distant and obtuse ways further confuses the situation. Consider this hard-to-comprehend factoid: currently greenhouse gases are about 380 parts per million compared with 220 parts per million during the last ice age. Climatologists postulate that 440 parts per million will create a climate tipping point.[3] Most people think "so what? It's all scientific gobbledygook." But 380 is not far from 440 parts per million, and we are on a fast elevator to it right now.

A recent Canadian example of the disconnection between environmental reality and political reality was the Canadian 2006 federal election. Nowhere should have climate change been a hotter topic than Calgary. Calgary rests in a semi-desert and depends on the Bow River glacier to provision the quickly growing city. Climate change is frying this glacier. It will be gone in 10 years; as we say in the political trade that's a done deal. No one can arrest the glacier's demise.

Thus, one would think a national political leader from Calgary who appears to suffer from asthma (an air quality-related disease) and whose home city is headed straight for a major water crisis would have environmental issues front and center. They never registered in the national election debates. Among the first things Canada's new prime minister from Calgary did on being elected was the same thing President Bush did: he cut the environmental budget by 40 percent; and to catch up with President Bush he withdrew from Kyoto.

How could he get away with such an inappropriate response to the great crisis of our times? Well, ten years is a microsecond on the biological calendar, but it's a long time on the human scale. For many, 40 years is a lifetime. When I was a young man climate change didn't exist. I was interested in the community and social consequences of bulldozing freeways through dense city neighborhoods. They seemed unreasonably destructive. The biological environmental consequences were more theoretical than real.

In less than four decades social consequences have been left behind by physical consequences. UV rays now require lotion for our skin and sunglasses for our eyes. Asthma (an unusual condition when I was young) is now the number one reason we admit children to hospital. When I was a boy "smog days" didn't exist in my clean northern city. Our summers now have as many air quality advisory days as clean air days. Someone dies in Ottawa every 36 hours from poor air quality.

In the winter, the City of Ottawa's greatest and most famous festival "Winterlude" — focussing on the longest skating rink in the world, the Rideau Canal — is more like waterlude. In the last five years we've only had one winter when the canal has stayed frozen for

10 weeks. Most recently we had only one skatable weekend during the festival in spite of enormous efforts on the part of the crews who flood the ice at night during the coldest part of the daily cycle.

Climate change is racing down upon us in biological terms but human governments don't react to biological clocks, which is the second reason human governments have been environmentally impotent. Four months is a long time in the life of a government. Four years is a complete mandate. In ten years, children can complete both their secondary and university education, marriages will begin and fail, politicians and governments come and go. In the meantime Calgary, the city of the Canadian Prime Minister, sits on a lake of oil. If you can't drink oil, you sure can sell it for a pile of money. So who cares about the Bow River glacier? It's far up in the mountains, and ten years is a long way off.

The third and final reason governments seem to ignore climate change is that most people are convinced there's a magic bullet that will arrive to solve the problem. We will invent a new kind of snow for our ski hills just as we invented synthetic rubber to replace natural rubber. President Bush clearly thinks the hydrogen fuel cell will save the day; if he does many others do also. The hydrogen cell is not a source of energy and like ethanol made from corn takes as much fuel to create as it produces. One of the reasons the Brazilians are burning down the Amazonian forest is to produce corn for ethanol, which they have embraced. In a nutshell, the replacements for oil commonly mentioned "for the future" won't work to arrest climate change. Nonetheless there is a generalized belief that something will come along to save the day, and it is not an irrational belief. Peace activists preached Armageddon during the Cold War. The Cold War has come and gone. The fear mongers were wrong.

Remember the 1970s oil scare? The end of cheap oil had arrived! What happened? The OPEC cartel crumbled. The oil price crisis of 1971 was just a blip; that's what people think will happen today with climate change. When the chips are down, people's intelligence and innate sense of survival will win out.

This is where I differ from my colleagues at City Hall. I believe we are embarked on daily local and global disasters that will not be fixable at the last minute because by the time the gravity of the situation is understood by enough people, it will be too late. Just as we cannot stop the Bow River glacier melting, there is nothing we can now do to stop the oceans warming at the rate they are now. At the moment, the Antarctic ice cap has shrunk to its smallest area ever recorded and is suffering a net loss of 36 cubic miles per year. This measurement is accurate to one micron.[4] The magnitude of this freshwater loss is impossible to comprehend. The largest cities on the planet only consume about one-fifth of a cubic mile annually.

Some of the long or short term consequences of climate change are ocean temperatures changed sufficiently to flip the Gulf Stream and cause annual force five hurricanes along the Gulf coast of the United States. But as grave as these environmental catastrophes will be, they are nothing compared to the earth's atmosphere turning sour. With carbon, oxygen and hydrogen shifts occurring at the rate and order of magnitude they are today, a souring or thinning of our planetary envelope could be triggered in any number of ways.

For example, if the planet as a whole ever begins to suffer a net loss in water vapor, i.e. more water vapor escapes or is lost from the earth's atmosphere than is replaced, the end of human life has arrived. This could occur if hydrogen cells (the building blocks of water) arrive at a new steady state that precludes bonding with oxygen as they do now. If this occurs, the great blue and white marble we call home will dry up into a version of our companion planet Mars.

Unfortunately, there is no Newtonian or Einsteinian law written in the science of a physicist's lab that says Earth must have a livable atmosphere for the human species. In fact the probabilities are against it. No other planet in the sun's solar system has the earth's atmospheric balance. The other atmospheres are either too thin like Mars or too chaotic like Venus to support life beyond bacteria. Only on earth do we find that curious situation where there is a balance between the vaporous state and the frozen one called water.

In the night sky, Earth is bracketed by Mars and Venus. They are similar to our planet in size and situation in the solar system. Venus is a little closer to the sun and Mars a little further away. Venus has a chaotic poisonous atmosphere and uninhabitable surface. Mars has a thin atmosphere and a waterless stone surface. The surface scarring on Mars that resemble the marks of watercourses has given rise to speculation among scientists that this neighbor once had running water.

Climate changes being created by mega-cities which depend entirely on a constant, carnivorous, planetary energy burn are moving the earth's atmosphere towards a different hydrogen/oxygen configuration with different consequences for the planet's surface, a configuration that is simultaneously creating a dryer, hotter planet and global dimming.

There are many speculations about the possible end points of climate change. But the general global picture is crystal clear. Climate change is "slow cooking" the earth like beans being baked in a ceramic pot. Carbon dioxide traps the sun's radiant energy on the earth's surface, but the carbon particulates block the sun's incoming rays with the net effect that there is less sunlight but hotter conditions on the surface. It's a slow, dim cook.

As dangerous to human life as this is, it shouldn't surprise anyone that governments have not been able to do much about the conditions which are driving climate change: human society has been built using the planet as an endless debit account. This is the way industrialized societies (which are now the principal society in every nation of the planet) work. They depend on more land, more minerals, more oil, more water somewhere — under the ground in great aquifers, in rivers that can be diverted and dammed, in great lakes. Why worry? The Atlantic cod fishery disappears, but the Arctic one opens. There are deserts like the Sahara, but aquifers to be discovered to pipe water to the surface.

It was devastating for the fishermen around the Aral Sea when it evaporated into a desert. It's been crushing for the peoples of West and East Africa as the Sahara has grown southwards — but globally it has never mattered. As long as there have been enough places like the Amazon River valley to counterbalance the H_2O deficit created in the planet's dry regions, the total global water bank balance remained positive.

But what happens to the global water account if the total withdrawals start to exceed the total deposits? This is not an unreasonable supposition. The planet's greatest reservoirs of fresh water (the Arctic, Greenland and Antarctic glaciers) are melting, increasing the volumes of the oceans. But once the glaciers have drained away into the oceans, the next step is for the oceans to begin shrinking themselves because the same climate change trends which have evaporated the glaciers will begin to work on the oceans. A coup de grâce would occur very quickly if an atmospheric chemical change resulting from carbon densities and atmosphere thinning ever compromised the H_2O bond.

This is only one of the possibilities of the end point of global warming and climate change. The disappearance of the world's oceans may seem absurd to contemplate, but the oceans of the planet, as magnificent as they appear to us, are nothing more than a thimble of water in the cosmic calculation. If every H_2O molecule disappeared on the earth's surface tomorrow, nothing would change in the solar scheme of things. The earth's oceans and all the life systems associated with them would just disappear as they appear to have disappeared from Mars. The great rhythms of the solar system would go on. Earth's mammalian communities would just not be part of it.

Fortunately this is all speculation. Scientists have tried to mimic the earth's atmosphere under vast, transparent domes stocked with water, fish, plants, bacterial, insect and mammal life (a kind of 20th-century Noah's Ark) and not been able to duplicate what happens in the course of every earth day. The atmosphere under the dome became poisonous. The scientists were not sure why it did, but the only way to preserve life inside was to cut windows in the dome, let the "normal" air in and let the poisonous air escape. In short, no one will have the faintest idea what a terminal ecological crisis might be until it happens; that is the nature of a non-analogue state or a biological phase transition. The only thing scientists are sure about is that the way we are presently living is changing the fundamentals of earth's biosphere more quickly than has happened in at least 650,000 years.

We lead exceptional lives in an exceptional place. Earth with its great forests, grand oceans and horizons of prairie grass are not the norm. Nowhere else in the universe have we been able to find a planet like ours with an atmosphere which gathers and retains the basic molecules necessary for water-based life under the thin protective shield of an atmosphere no more substantial than the rain which falls.

This is what is at stake: life itself.

Changes to the earth's atmosphere and ecology have been created mostly by our greatest achievement: cities. The only way they can be arrested is in the place they were created: cities. That means changing first how we govern ourselves and second how we live. Our present democratic electoral systems require governments to create public policies that advantage short term profits and disadvantage all public decisions for the longer term social and physical health of the commonwealth. Air quality is the most vital but is just one of them.

The problem is that there is no easy or quick way to change this in spite of the grave danger humanity is facing. Human governance has evolved over centuries in an erratic and eccentric fashion and changes very slowly. Chinese government has always been by central command and remains this way to this day. There is little difference between the emperor and his imperial bureaucracy and the Communist chair and his Beijing bureaucrats. The political labels and technology have changed but the fundamental imperial Chinese government paradigm remains the same. The European feudal system took more than a thousand years to be replaced by representative democracy, and democracy is still new and poorly understood in many countries.

National governments' principal preoccupation has always been defending their borders against the economic and military aggressions of other nations. In the First Great War which started the 20th century, every nation involved perceived itself fighting a "defensive" war against the aggressions of others. In much the same way as President Bush sold his invasion of Iraq as a defensive war against a hostile nation's weapons of mass destruction, the European governments in 1914 thought themselves to be honoring treaties and defending their authentic national interests, not aggressively attacking anyone. This is still the principal reason for national military actions. The irony is that President Bush governs a nation so powerful that he can't find any nation powerful enough to threaten his, so he has had to make do with a stateless enemy.

In terms of governance, nothing much has changed for cities either. Cities are about wealth generation and have been since the days of Troy, Athens, Rome and Renaissance Florence. In 2006 from Shanghai to London, from New York to Los Angeles cities remain as successful at creating wealth as their civic ancestors. City councils have always been there to ensure commerce is successful within their city walls and this is what they do today. City councils don't last long who begin passing local legislation that is perceived not to be in the immediate interests of their business communities — from the small shopkeepers to the great land developers.

Change comes very slowly for human governance. Unfortunately climate change has rewritten both the stakes and the time available to adapt to our changing circumstances. We no longer have centuries. We may not even have decades. Urban Meltdown is about this fundamental environmental change, the life of one city councilor and how he came to think that knowledge wasn't the problem, politics was.

PART I

A Poet Goes to City Hall

Yes, I remember Marietta.
She was the one from Sarajevo.
What's she doing now?

THE ROOTS OF THIS STORY are as long as my life. One is on a street in Sarajevo, where a young woman wearing a beautiful green loden coat lies dying on a city sidewalk. Another is on my grandfather's farm on Cape Breton Island in the village of Grand Etang. Then there were still thousands of small farms in Atlantic Canada; it was a time when factory farms and sonar fishing radar did not exist. Small fish boats went out before dawn and came back to the harbor the same day loaded with beautiful fish, their sharp skins glistening, iridescent. Then cod fish were so bountiful, they fed whole nations. A time that now seems to belong to another age. The story also has its beginnings 1,250 miles away from the sea in the city of Toronto with the struggle against the Spadina Expressway and discovering tattered little paperbacks like Tally's Corner and The Autobiography of Malcolm X. But there was one event without which not one page of this book would have been written, although all the rest remain the same.

On November 10, 1997 I was to everyone's astonishment elected to the City Council of the City of Ottawa in the province of Ontario and the country called Canada. I was up against the chair of the

Catholic School Board, a former city councilor, a successful businessman and an environmental activist. All were formidable candidates. I had never been elected to anything before. My best friends thought if I came third I would do well. I won by a thousand votes and became the first poet ever to be elected to Ottawa's city council. It changed everything.

Suddenly, I was in the privileged position of seeing how a city actually worked. I became intimate with both the gritty details of city life and the grind of national and global forces. Instead of watching through the peephole of the local newspapers or making judgments from the perspective of a single cause, I was catapulted into the complex center of how a large city and ultimately the nation functioned.

The first six months were terrifying as I struggled to make sense of hundreds of programs, thousands of employees and mountains of paper which came through the front door on electronic and paper conveyer belts. There were 300 worthy charities waiting in my in-basket; they were all — suddenly — most interested in my support. What could I do for 300 charities serving everything from emergency food in shelters for the homeless to programs for stroke victims? What could I accomplish with three employees and an office budget of $37,000? It was overwhelming.

But I grew to love the job. What was there not to love? Cities are the heartbeat of the human condition. They are our burrows. They are the places human beings create society with all its myriad powers and possibilities. British Prime Minister Maggie Thatcher once said, "there is no such thing as society; there are only individuals." I have arrived at the opposite conclusion: "there are no individuals; there is only society." Without society there can be no individuals: no professional hockey players, no rock stars, no filmmakers, no journalists. Society makes individuality possible. It is in our cities where the most complex expressions of society and individual accomplishment can be found.

Without cities, there is no western civilization. From Athens to Florence to New York, cities are the alpha and omega of western existence. Cities have distinguished the West from the East, the continent of Africa and aboriginal society. And it was through city politics that I came to understand how wrong headed and how destructive the course we have chosen to live on this planet has become, for since being elected I have been forced to see what I used to be able to ignore.

**Global Cities
and
Horse and Buggy
Nations**

*It is no longer "my country right or wrong,"
it is now "my planet right or wrong."*

— Mayor Manuel Tornare of Geneva,
on the phone to President George W. Bush
after the World Trade Center attack

IN 1905 PEOPLE IMMIGRATED to nations with names like Canada, Australia or the United States. In 2005 no one immigrates to
Canada or the United States. They immigrate to cities with names
like Toronto, Vancouver, Atlanta and Los Angeles. In 2005 nations
do not exist as they did a hundred years ago. A hundred years ago
immigrants came to Canada to farm or live in the many small towns
that dotted the national landscape. A hundred years ago more than
80 percent of the population lived and worked on farms and in small
towns. And the national government worried about providing
services which served these rural communities — rail, postal service,
national police, support for marketing and agriculture. Cities were
ornaments in the national fabric but not essential to it.

All this has changed. Industrial farming and globalization has
decimated rural Canada. Less than two percent of the population
now earns its living through farming, and the numbers are declining.[1] People buy blueberries and wine from Chile, vegetables from
California, oranges from Florida and chickens from battery barns.

Farm production has now been globalized. Oranges for example sell for the same price in Ottawa, Canada as they do in Dade County, Florida. Lobsters are the same price in New York as in Cape Breton. There is little financial advantage to being local.

Globalization has not only changed where people live and what they do, it has changed how things are produced. The whole globalized structure depends on oceans of cheap oil. You can't truck vegetables across the continent unless the cost of the gasoline to move them declines year over year in real dollars, which it has done. Relative to income gasoline costs less today than it did 25 years ago.

Carbon-based globalization has not just globalized agriculture, it has globalized cities. Cities have become nation states that belong to the planet. When a great city is threatened as New York was in the 9/11 attack the economies of many nations tremble. Argentina became a third world economy overnight when the banks of Buenos Aires could no longer pay their urban creditors. There is no Mexico without Mexico City, Britain without London or France without Paris. Even a little city like Ottawa no longer thinks of itself within a national matrix, but within a planetary one. Software companies in Ottawa compete with their counterparts in Toulouse, Denver, Calgary and New Delhi.

City councils govern with an eye to how they are doing against other cities in other places. No one wants their city to become the kind of place that business types fly over instead of towards. Globalization has created new and difficult power relations. In the name of giving private corporations the maximum room to advance profits, globalization has forced national governments to withdraw from funding familiar services in the name of creating a "more competitive environment."

In Canada we've seen the federal government reduce family welfare benefits and withdraw from funding affordable housing, unemployment and welfare benefits. Provincial governments have followed the national lead, downloading public health, transit and other social services onto cities. But the needs of citizens to be adequately housed doesn't evaporate because the national government has decided that decent housing is no longer a priority. In Ottawa we have 12,000 families without adequate shelter.

Another part of the new global equation is climate change, and it has affected everyone — even my clean little northern city. Recently Ottawa city councilors hosted Toronto city councilors in a friendly midwinter game of shinny hockey. In the sky above the canal, there was a mustard sheen on an otherwise perfectly sunny day in February. A smog advisory day in February in Ottawa had never happened before. It was a first.

In summer, smog warnings regularly tail all the way up and over Algonquin Park and the cottage lakes north of our city. Climate change has given a whole new urgency to old dilemmas like public transit versus more roads. Suddenly you're staring at a map of your city and realizing if you don't get that electric light rail system in place, you're going to be building four new expressways when you can't get clear air days with the roads and cars you've got now.

People are adapting as best as they can to climate change. In France, farmers are harvesting grapes at night when it's cooler and the grapes have more flavor than in the heat of the day. Since the North American heat wave and continental brown out in August of 2004, many American municipalities have developed buddy systems to ensure that when another one occurs, the elderly are able to seek help.

Another part of the new power relationship is that, while globalization has immensely strengthened international corporations, it has enfeebled national and state governments as they divest themselves of important public revenue sources like Canada's formerly national petroleum company Petro-Canada and tolled roads like Ontario's highway 407. On the other hand, it has empowered city governments in new and unexpected ways. Suddenly, citizens of cities are beginning to realize that their interests may be not only different from the interests of their own national government but inimical to them.

As a result today you have Mayors acting like statesmen, thinking more comprehensively than Presidents and Prime Ministers. Nuclear weapons in the eyes of many national governments are viewed little differently than the US 7th Cavalry once was: an arm to be launched at an enemy. This is nonsense. In the eyes of a Mayor or a city councilor, nuclear weapons so violate human rights that no government under any circumstances should be allowed to use them. They are weapons of lunacy not defence. Hundreds of Mayors and city councilors from around the world have signed on to Mayor Akiba of Hiroshima's Mayors for Peace movement calling for the eradication of all nuclear weapons, just as we eradicated the smallpox virus.[2]

After the 2002 Kyoto Protocol the Mayors of all the world's great coastal cities signed a letter petitioning President Bush to take climate change seriously and sign the accord. It said:

Dear Mr. President,
As Mayors, we would like to underline the dangers that our local communities, all located on delicate coastal areas, are facing due to global climate change caused by greenhouse gas emissions. Our cities will be heavily affected, not only by the raising sea level, but also by the probable intensification of extreme climatic conditions. The case of Venice and its lagoon is a prime example. A world cultural and environmental heritage of mankind is destined to suffer tremendously, because of the intensification of periodical flooding, by the effects of global climate changes. Consequently, international support that Venice is receiving for its ordinary maintenance, much of it coming also from private donors from the United States, is bound to be rendered useless…
   …[W]e need to feel that we are part of a global plan, which cannot pretend to be successful without the essential role of your Country. This is why we feel that we have to express our deepest concern about the position that your administration has recently assumed towards the Kyoto Protocol. We are convinced that the Kyoto Protocol should not be discarded but reviewed and improved…[3]

The signatures of mayors from around the world were then affixed to the letter: Paolo Costa, Venice; Cesar Maia, Rio de Janeiro; Abel Mounim Ariss, Beirut; Kari Nenonen, Oulu, Finland; Tarso Genro, Porto Alegre; Ken Livingstone, London; Russell Goodway, Cardiff, Wales; Job Cohen, Amsterdam; Marc Morial, New Orleans, Louisiana; Jerry Brown, Oakland.

   There is something both poignant and awful in seeing Mayor Marc Morial of New Orleans' signature affixed to this polite but clear plea for some bio-sanity from his national government. I wonder if he would have been so polite if he knew what was to come. During the years between when the letter was written, signed and sent and August 2005, the Gulf of Mexico heated up in an extraordinary way — close to blood temperature — and became the baking oven for Katrina and other hurricanes.

There is a profound disconnect here between city governments and national ones. City governments continue to act locally as they have always done, but they now think globally. Yet national governments continue to behave as if 19th-century conditions still existed and it was possible to wage physical and economic war — as if one nation could be insulated from the effects on another.

Suitcase nuclear bombs didn't exist in 1905. They do now, and they don't need an army or a nation to be employed. For the purposes of exploding a nuclear suitcase bomb, nations and their armies do not exist. Nations are not places, nor are their armies necessary to detonate a suitcase nuclear bomb. Nations have become administrative mechanisms mostly to raise taxes to feed their military/industrial complexes that President Eisenhower first identified more than 40 years ago.

A suitcase nuclear bomb will be used against the residents of some global city like Toronto or Chicago — a place of flesh and blood not lines on a map draped in the colors of a flag. If you think I'm being alarmist or irresponsible with these statements think about "the war on terror" waged by the national governments of the UK, Spain and the United States. One response to this war was against the unarmed civilian citizens of Madrid and London as they rode their city's public transit system. Yet these are the very cities where the most massive demonstrations against the war proposed by President Bush and Prime Minister Blair took place. The democratic disconnect doesn't get any more profound than this.

In this scenario it is entirely possible that a suitcase nuclear bomb will be detonated in a city which has declared itself to be "nuclear free" and strongly opposed to the foreign policies of its government. In short, we have a governance system in which cities have adapted to and accept the idea of global citizenship, but national governments haven't. National governments with their 19th-century constitutions have become problems for rather than partners of city governments.

Think about Canadian cities like Toronto receiving 100,000 new immigrants a year, a million in a decade. Toronto is now one of the most multi-cultural cities on the planet. But 92 percent of the financial benefits of those immigrants flow to the federal and provincial treasuries in the form of new income taxes, GST and land transfer taxes. For the federal government it's an immigration policy that is enormously enriching because 60 percent of the services that this growth requires must be delivered by city governments in and around Toronto — on their eight-cent share of every federal tax dollar collected.

This kind of inequity could be borne easily when cities formed a very small part of the national fabric as they did in 1905. But in 2005 with 60 per cent of the Canadian population in seven city-regions it's a recipe for urban meltdown as growth increases far beyond any city's ability to integrate people and services into a sustainable paradigm. The current paradigm is not sustainable because mall sprawl can't function without cheap fuel. People understand this instinctively; that's why there is a panic when gasoline prices begin to rise. The panic is entirely understandable. Right now, it takes 62 cents every mile an 18-wheel truck travels just to pay for the diesel fuel; the trucks and their drivers have become North America's new wage slaves.

One of the largest products of those slave hours is 11 millions tons of carbon dioxide being released into the air each day every day. Difficult to imagine, isn't it?

Think about a mustard cloud of pollution over Ottawa on a bright February day.

Think about the number one reason we admit children to our hospital emergency wards each day: asthma.

Think about the constitutions of nations written in the days of the horse and buggy, when national armies charged each other with cavalry, and foot soldiers ran with fixed bayonets carrying rifles like spears across grassy fields. What does that scene have to do with today's reality? Modern national constitutions are as outdated as these old armies. The horse cavalry has gone, but the constitutions remain.

The bio-sanity of the planet, the security of our greatest human treasures — our cities, the local and foreign trade between our planet's great cities are controlled by national governments that can't understand either the gravity or the urgency of the problems their horse and buggy constitutions are creating. We need to say goodbye to these dinosaurs and hello to a new era ruled by cities and loosely knit confederations like the European Union.

If we can't create new city governments and new confederations which can stop the environmental degradation of our present way of life, climate change and resource exhaustion will trivialize the ambitions of nations as Katrina and other hurricanes destroyed so much life in southern Louisiana. The pressing question is will we change the way we govern ourselves in time for a new world order to emerge which can attack real, not imagined problems?

The problem isn't knowledge. It's the political system — at every level.

City politicians remain the servants of an economic system that depends on money moving constantly from the center of the city to the edges to underwrite billion-dollar profits in sprawl development; as long as this relationship between money, political power and growth exists nothing will change for cities. We will continue to carpet the green landscape with strip malls, parking lots, arterials and residential pods as we have done now for more than half a century.

In this way Canada's capital Ottawa is no different than any other North American city. For fifty years, we have subsidized the most expensive, unsustainable form of urban growth and penalized the least expensive, most sustainable to make a tiny group of people very rich. And I have come to realize that this destructive growth has nothing to do with good planning or the lack of knowledge. There are thousands of books, essays and speeches available on the impoverishing qualities of urban sprawl. Yet it continues unabated.

If you can imagine growth and services on one end of a balance beam with M for Municipal in the center, the faster the city grows the larger the weight on the growth side of the municipal beam becomes — and the smaller the weight on the revenue side of the balance beam becomes. While for federal and state or provincial governments, it's the reverse. It's an accounting system designed to produce an unsustainable landscape.

None of this was obvious to me, but once elected to city council I began to connect the dots. I started to see how the economic and political threads of my city, national and international life were all strung together; that nothing happened in isolation. The world was no longer divided between federal and municipal, suburb and city, rural and urban; it was all braided together. Once surprised by this thought that everything was connected — from the front page of the newspaper to the city section at the back — it wasn't a long step to realizing the key to creating better cities was figuring out how the connections worked.

Once I understood this I began to discover them in the most unexpected places from the 19ᵗʰ-century constitutions of nations which are now used to hide from creating solutions for cities; to golf courses where geese feed on the waters and grasses of immaculate pesticide-fed lawns that corrupt their health for those in the north who harvest them; and above all the oceans which are fundamentally changing the planet's climate and threaten all of our coastal cities.

The more I lived the life of a city councilor, the more tentacles that appeared, the more difficult it was to explain to myself or anyone else the extent and breadth of the intersecting crises that were facing us. Katrina's devastation of New Orleans didn't surprise me nor did the federal and state government's slow and confused reaction to it. The extent of the disconnection between the real problems in the real world and any nation state's vision of the world is there for all who care to look.

In October of 2004, an article appeared in National Geographic describing with pictures exactly how tropical storms would start ramping up to category four and five hurricanes as they moved across the super-heated waters of the Gulf of Mexico, smash into the Gulf shore, ripping apart the Mississippi levees, and flood the suburbs of New Orleans.

Is it not all bizarre? Billions of dollars being spent on a war that was never needed; billons on a missile shield to protect us from weapons that shouldn't exist; billions to secure airports so air travel can continue burning the carbon treasure of our planet — and from this we create climate change disasters like Katrina. It's a world which fits the graceful lunacy of Kurt Vonnegut, more than any future for our children.

What the hell happened? How is it that my generation, the largest ever to grace the planet, which began with such high hopes for a better world with eloquent troubadours like Phil Ochs and powerful compassionate leaders like Martin Luther King, is leaving the planet at the edge of an entirely new and violent volcano called climate change? We live on a planet where deserts are growing, water reserves shrinking, the weather more violent, oceans over-heating, food sources diminishing, governments more fragile and human life itself is threatened. What happened?

Neighborhoods to Love

Catch the sun, Dad.
See there it is!"
I skate behind my son
And see the light
Playing on the ice
Just in front of us.
Julian skates towards and through it.
"I've got the sun! Dad.
I've got the sun!"
And we skate
into an infinity
Of moments,
The sun, the ice,
Julian and I.

— from Canal Seasons

PATTY AND I ARE VISITING our son Julian who lives in a run-down section of Montreal around Avenue du Parc and Saint Viateur. The pavement is cracked. The sidewalks tilt. The buildings sag. The balconies cling rather than hang to the sides of houses. There aren't enough trees. This neighborhood needs a green plan for their streets. A small fountain on a street corner would sure be nice, some street furniture. I tick off the many things that need to be done to bring the neighborhood up to scratch. The list is a long one. It would take a hard working city councilor ten years to make a dent in it.

I love it. I love Avenue du Parc from the second my foot hits the sidewalk. The sidewalks are alive with all kinds of folks. There are a lot of Hasidic Jews in the neighborhood who stroll along for their evening promenade in black suits, ear locks and black hats. A young man passes me with his wife pushing a baby carriage. His suit may be from another century, but the cut of it is perfect and the cloth looks so fine it could be black silk. I find myself staring impolitely, jaw agape. It's like watching a Quaker from the 17th century suddenly emerge through the curtain of time and appear before me, large as life. The young man glances at me and with one proud regard indicates his family is perfect before strolling on his way. His wife, on the other hand, looks a little tired which is understandable as she is pregnant and pushing another baby in the carriage in front of her.

Julian takes us down a narrow side street and we stop for supper at a tiny hole-in-the-wall restaurant. The tables are all jammed together. There is a rough plastic curtain around the inside of the door which allows the restaurant to keep the front door open for fresh air but also cuts the direct breeze from the street. The only table left is one right behind the curtain. We take it. The kitchen is open and about the same size or bigger than the eating area. The aroma of cooking food is delightful. It feels like we have fallen into a little piece of heaven.

The young woman who serves us does so in French but she speaks across the room to someone else in fluent, musical, rather wonderful Italian. She is a light chocolate in color as is one of the cooks, and I can't help but wonder where this restaurant has come from? How is it that the waitress speaks Italian like an Italian, French like a French woman and serves food that is flavored by Africa?

I order the Italian sausage, rice and something green. It is served quickly along with some wisecracks between Julian and the waitress whom I attempt to ignore, as older men in the presence of their wives are required to be modest in the presence of beautiful young waitresses. The meal is very simple and very tasty. I do my best to savor the experience and resist the impulse to hoover the fine food down as if I were a car backing up to a gas pump.

In the window seat a couple of homeboys sit wearing a good deal of heavy jewelry. If they aren't in the drug trade already they look like they want to be. At another table there is a woman who is reading her newspaper and does not want to be disturbed. The woman sitting at the table closest to me has no newspaper and is quite willing to exchange a few companionable sentences with our table so we do. Opposite there is a very handsome gay couple. Being the kind of person who delights in casual eavesdropping, I am anxious to overhear their conversation, but these two men are hardened café goers and have clearly mastered the technique of speaking just loudly enough to hear each other but not loud enough for anyone else. It's frustrating because I am sure their conversation is worth hearing. Are they talking about business deals? Perhaps some article in Le Devoir which has antagonized them? Or better, who is sleeping with whom? Always a favorite of mine. Every now and then I cast a beseeching regard their way to please speak up, unfortunately to no avail.

The cappuccino arrives and is so perfect that I can't help it, I order a second. Maybe there is someone in the world who can make cappuccino better than the Italians but I've never been able to find them.

Just before we go I am finally able to sort out where this restaurant has flown in from: it is out of the old Italian-Ethopian colony of Eritrea. The waitress is a refugee from the latest war to break out between Eritrea and Ethiopia. Our gain, their loss. The waitress smiles and for a fleeting second a shadow passes across her beautiful face.

Julian, Patty and I pay our bill and stroll out into the June evening.

We are going to walk across town to St. Laurent to hear my cousin's band Veal play, but we have plenty of time and we mosey along the busy streets taking in the soft evening air. The walk gives me plenty of time to reflect on why I feel so at home in this tumbledown neighborhood. I do because in its essentials it feels like my own. Although on the surface they could not be more different for one is rich, the other poor.

Patty and I live in the Glebe. As I write this it is the most desired neighborhood in all of Canada based on real estate demand. Every time a "for sale" sign goes up there are ten buyers at the door with fistfuls of money offering more than the sellers are asking. Our front door gets flyers pushed through the mailbox from real estate agents telling us that they are not soliciting "a listing," but our house fits exactly the description that a client of theirs wants. If we will just take the time to let the agent know, she or he can hook us up immediately with a client. We will be sure to find the sale price agreeable. Everyone would be so happy if we would just move out and let someone with more money move in.

But in spite of its upscale façade the Glebe and Avenue du Parc are both nothing more than old streetcar neighborhoods. They were built in the days when the streetcar was the principal form of urban transportation. Their main streets are not traffic sewers designed only to flush cars along to some other destination but places people live on, promenade, shop and chat with their neighbors. In 2003 Avenue du Parc may be a lot poorer than Bank Street in the Glebe but it wasn't when we moved in 30 years ago.

At that time Bank Street was in full decline: empty storefronts, lots of folks on welfare, lots of cheap housing and lots of destructive absentee landlords. The Glebe was built in the first decades of the 20th century as a substantial place with large brick homes, broad streets and a prosperous main street just like Avenue du Parc was, and it remained that way until the early sixties. At that time the popular mayor of the day, Charlotte Whitton, decided that streetcars around which the community had been built were old fashioned and ugly with their overhead wires and rails buried in the street's surface. Besides they were old and badly needed to be replaced. All in all it was easier to simply trash them for buses as had already been done in other cities across North America.

In 1960 Ottawa had over 300 miles of electric streetcar lines which served the city quietly and efficiently from distant West End beaches to the French-speaking neighborhoods in the east. It was one of the oldest electric systems on the continent. Tearing the streetcar rails up changed the entire face of the city. The principal commercial streets of the city — Sparks, Rideau, Bank and Wellington — went into a precipitous decline from which they have never recovered while the car-dominated suburbs exploded.

In the old streetcar neighborhoods, cars began to flood along what used to be quiet residential avenues. Each driver was anxious to use the streets to get quickly through to the downtown or to escape the downtown to the distant neighborhoods. The car privatized the streets, turning the city's greatest asset into private traffic sewers. "Get the fuck out of my way!" was the attitude of most drivers. Turning lanes went in on every corner. Sidewalks were narrowed. Informal public squares became interchanges for cars and trucks. People and businesses quickly began to abandon the old parts of the city.

The Glebe's schools which dated back to the 1890s went unrepaired. Their dark brick sides started to take on the grim look of old factory buildings. By 1970 a third of the children at First Avenue Public School were from families on social assistance. The housing itself reflected the schools. In the 1930s and 40s the houses had the hauteur of the bourgeois: solid, respectable and comfortable. By the 1970s they looked dilapidated, dour and sour. Street after street of sad brown homes stood on small, grubby urban lots. The houses themselves were owned more and more by pensioners or by absentee landlords interested in rental profits and depended on young tenants who didn't complain about shoddy maintenance.

Bank Street, the principal commercial street, was caving in on itself with empty storefronts. The ones that had survived didn't offer much. There was some talk at City Hall of filling in and paving over the Rideau Canal to provide a convenient expressway downtown. The future of the city was out in the green, pleasant and prosperous suburbs. It was slash and burn in the oldest parts of the city. The oldest industrial neighborhood in the city, Lebreton Flats, was simply expropriated from one end to the other and torn down. Over 150 acres of brick row housing, small hotels, bars and warehouses were flattened by bulldozers and turned into a snow dump. The downtown neighborhoods had become a discard zone.

Patty and I moved into the Glebe for exactly the same reason other young couples did: we had no money, no car, and rents were cheap. It was convenient. We had no plans to stay. It was just a stop on our way to a better place. We had no idea the neighborhood was about to begin a long climb up from Sorry Town into one of the most desired neighborhoods in the country.

It began with the most unlikely of ideas, a skating rink. Doug Fullerton was appointed the chair of the federal government's National Capital Commission. He was an imaginative and iconoclastic man, a most unusual choice for a position which is usually reserved for compliant party hacks. In this capacity he was able to do something that people had talked about for years but no one had been able to pull off.

Ottawa was founded around the Rideau Canal built by the British engineer Colonel John By to give Canada an alternative communication route to the St. Lawrence River between Lake Ontario and Montreal. The canal took five years to complete at great human and financial cost. Thousands died in the mosquito-invested swamps much of it went through, and Colonel By himself died in disgrace for "overspending" on the project. But even in 1832 when it was completed it was quickly recognized as one of the world's engineering wonders linking the new towns of Kingston and Ottawa via canals and wilderness dams with a series of waterways along a 99-mile route. The Rideau Canal became the means by which the entire eastern part of the province of Ontario was opened to settlement.

But by 1970 the Rideau Canal was regarded as more of an eyesore to Ottawa city council than an asset, and if the federal government hadn't by chance owned it, the city would have long ago drained and paved it over as has happened to other canals in urban areas. Rochester, New York did exactly this to its eternal regret. Many other cities let their canals fester into fetid industrial lagoons. Fullerton had a different idea. He saw the possibilities of turning an eyesore into an asset by creating a recreational corridor around the canal that would attract thousands of people winter and summer. For the winter he proposed a five-mile skateway from Carleton University to Confederation Square in the heart of the city.

The mayor of the day and the city council exercised their usual capacity for vision and complained it would be too expensive to operate. They refused to co-operate. It was rumored this project would cost at least $50,000! It was clearly a waste of taxpayers' money. The practically inclined complained that it was impossible. How could you flood a rink that large? You'd have to truck the water in from city hydrants and wait until the ice was thick enough to drive trucks on to clear the snow. By that time the winter would be over.

Fullerton found the money from his own budget and said you didn't need to wait for the ice to thicken naturally to get trucks on the ice. He accelerated the freeze process by using small snow blowers to clear the initial snow from the natural ice. He then drilled holes in the ice and began flooding — not by trucking water in but by pumping water up from beneath the ice using small gas compressors dragged on a sleigh. This small equipment very quickly developed a thick layer of ice that could support heavy equipment. Then he rolled the trucks out. In one extraordinary week he had the entire length of the canal from Dow's Lake to the National Arts Center open for skating.

Skating on the canal was an immediate, spectacular hit. On the first weekend 50,000 people came out to use the longest skating rink in the world. Old folks, teenagers, families with babes in arms — there seemed to be no one who was immune to the canal's winter charms.

The effect on the old streetcar neighborhoods like the Glebe, Old Ottawa East and Old Ottawa South which bordered the canal was equally spectacular. It galvanized them almost overnight from has-beens into places that were interesting. In winter the canal which separated Old Ottawa South from the Glebe and had been regarded as nothing more than an inconvenient ugly ditch was suddenly transformed into something beautiful. To have a house close to the canal in the wintertime suddenly became a desirable thing. For the first time since anyone could remember, house prices along the canal started to climb instead of fall. Families instead of absentee landlords began to buy.

And the Glebe began to shift from a decaying and dismal collection of streets dominated by absentee landlords and police sirens into one of the most valuable pieces of real estate in Canada. Doug Fullerton began this transition with his skateway, but the people who lived there did the rest by investing in the old housing stock. There is an old joke that the most important place in the community is the hardware store because that's where everyone spends their money and time buying equipment and supplies to renovate their old homes.

The principal public schools, First Avenue and Hopewell, were renovated instead of being torn down. When these old schools emerged from behind the construction hoardings they no longer looked like decaying warehouses. First Avenue emerged as a swan, a graceful and welcoming school on the edge of a green park and a small pleasant inlet of the canal. First Avenue became a French Immersion school, which parents decided they liked. Hopewell became a robust and interesting combination of the old and the new next to a busy commercial street. Both schools began to look like the kind of schools where parents wanted to send their children. The welfare rolls began to decline.

At the same time Doug Fullerton was creating his skateway, his chief planner John Leaning had been doing some thinking about how the cut-through traffic in the Glebe could be reduced. The first step was to kill the city's plans to tear down eight blocks of houses and expand Glebe Avenue into six comfortable commuter lanes which he accomplished with an energized community behind him. The second was to close off most of the east-west streets to cut-through traffic by making them exit only. Leaning's plan, which was in part implemented, made it much harder to traverse the community from one side to the other. Cut-through traffic did decrease dramatically, and young people instead of moving out as soon as larger paychecks arrived started to buy the old houses and fix them up.

◈ ◈ ◈

I disliked the house Patty found for us from the start. It was boring. It had absolutely no panache. You could drive by a million times and never remark on it. It had been built in the 1930s and not changed since. The original owners still lived in one side; their daughter-in-law and grandchildren lived on the other side. We bought the daughter-in-law and grandchildren side. Nothing had been done to the house since it had been built fifty years previously. The basement floor was cracked and decomposing from the spring floods which regularly invaded it. There was no plumbing for a washing machine.

Entering the front door I felt nothing but the creeping panic of being old before my time. Three bedrooms upstairs and bathroom at the head of the stairs; kitchen, dining room and living room downstairs: it resembled the house that I had grown up in. I didn't want to buy it. I didn't want to be old before my time.

Unfortunately for my sense of panache the house had two inescapable virtues. We could afford it and the walls were straight. With me whining all the way to the bank we cobbled together $5,000 for the down payment and mortgaged ourselves for $45,000. It was not a happy day for me. I had visions of a long and ugly servitude in the interests of normalcy.

What happened to our house over the next 25 years has become an extension of what has happened to the neighborhood and ultimately much of the Ottawa downtown.

Over the years we found the money to tear the crumbling basement floor up, put a new one down and lay proper drainage tiles around the edges of the house. Suddenly the house didn't flood in the spring; instead the water was swept out to the city storm sewers. We had a dry and useful basement area. The back of our house had a wooden shed leaning against the house; it overlooked an apartment parking lot and Bronson Avenue. The constant stream of cars from Bronson threw an enormous amount of dirt, pollution and noise our way. The previous owners had used the garden area to park their car. I decided we could park the car at the front and buried the gravel with clean earth and planted trees. The idea was to create a tiny urban forest: a solid green mass between our back door and the roar of Bronson Avenue.

I planted a hawthorn and a small McIntosh apple on either side of the back door. Two crab apple trees along one fence line, a magnolia at center stage and then a big basswood right on the fence line so that it would spread its great spatulate leaves over onto the adjacent parking lot. No one was especially happy with me planting all these trees on a postage-stamp-sized lot because there was no place left for flowers, but I insisted. When you have thousands of cars rolling by a short distance away from your back door you need all the green screen protection you can get, and flowers just won't do it. The small yard at the front was reserved for flowers where they could get the morning sun.

It has turned out well. We now have a small but vital urban forest in the backyard which forms a dense private bower of green all summer long. You can see neither the apartment parking lot nor Bronson Avenue.

◆ ◆ ◆

I had somehow managed to conserve the old image of the Glebe in my head as it had been when we had first moved in. In my mind it had not much changed since Fullerton had first flooded the canal. It had just been "spruced up." But it is not the same. It has become rich.

Houses on the Glebe's principal avenues now sell for half a million dollars. Bank Street now has "destination stores" like the Gap, and local stores themselves have become "destination stores." Old parking lots have sprouted new and impressive homes. The "loft" apartment, that ubiquitous signal of urban success, has arrived. The front yards of the Glebe's streets are still small, but they are now resplendent with flowers and trees of all sorts. Peer down a Glebe street and you will be struck by how green and leafy a place it seems. The houses behind the gardens gleam instead of sag with new windows, doors, sunny additions, bright porches and so on. The canal is used not just in the winter but all year long — to jog beside, to paddle on, to in-line skate and stroll beside, to contemplate the flowers. The Glebe has become a very desirable address.

The thing I like best about visiting my son's neighborhood in Montreal is that it reminds me of my own youth and of the enduring vitality of the old streetcar neighborhoods. Even battered and poor, they retain a sense of vitality, civility and interest that comforts me with the thought that when we started building cities in North America, we did a lot of things right. Each one of those old neighborhoods has a Rideau Canal in it somewhere. I'm sure that there's one in Avenue du Parc. Perhaps it will be the planting of trees and the creation of some recreational paths that can be used summer and winter. Perhaps it will be nothing more complicated than the replacing of the old sidewalks, narrowing the streets and planting some trees. But I am sure there is something, somewhere that will trigger the regeneration of this old neighborhood and then private money will begin to flow back into it just as it has in the Glebe. The houses will be repaired; windows, balconies and curving staircases on the old townhouses will be replaced and refurbished. New stores will open and soon real estate agents will be pushing offers for sale into mailboxes.

I'm not so confident about the modern communities that we've built around the car, malls and parking lots. When the houses begin to sag and most of all when gasoline prices finally begin to rise, how will they regenerate themselves? When I look into the future what I see is the cities of South America translated into the Northern hemisphere. In the center of the city are rich comfortable neighborhoods, but at the periphery are miles and miles of desolation: empty malls, vacant parking lots, weeds growing between the cracks, with miles of impoverished housing. Our suburbs will become North American versions of the shanties above Rio di Janeiro.

At the moment most North American suburbs are fine well-situated places to live, but look into the future. In Los Angeles the rich live in the hills above the city, but in South America it is the poor. It is the poor because the commonwealth — the city — cannot provide adequate roads, water, sewage, police, transit, schools and community centers. These are the public amenities that Canadian taxpayers and citizens now take for granted as their "right." But what happens when the Municipal Price Index, the cost of providing city services, begins to rise much faster than taxes can be collected to provide those services?

The Municipal Price Index (MPI) tracks the cost of running a municipality like the Consumer Price Index (CPI) tracks the cost of living for a family. The MPI is rising 2.5 times faster than the CPI. This is because cities must buy a different basket of goods and services than a family household. Running a city is not the same as running a family house. A city budget is much more energy dependent — on petroleum and electricity especially. Asphalt is made from petroleum; bus fleets, police cars, ambulances, fire trucks, snow plows, graders and backhoes run on petroleum. City buildings are large and expensive to heat, light and cool.

Citizens complain bitterly when the people that they elected are taxing them more but providing less. That's exactly what's happening now. To make ends meet every city — in spite of taxes increasing faster than the CPI — is having to cut back. Cities are providing less snow clearance in the winter; less street cleaning and repair in the summer; fewer wading and swimming pools; fewer libraries. The reality is there's not much anyone can do about it except grow the city differently. The old way of growing is too expensive to operate.

Everything is determined by trend lines. Are things gradually getting better or gradually getting worse? If the trend lines for climate change and oil exhaustion are correct our very survival will depend on wasting nothing and building smarter, more efficient cities. If we do we may escape the worst of the South American shanty town scenario. If we don't it's a surety.

◆ ◆ ◆

The time to skate is about ten o'clock at night. The heat of the day seems to gather along the ice surface in a warm bubble before the nightly flight to the stars. Skaters fly by like wood sprites, silent and graceful. I come around the corner at Fifth Avenue, and the starry arc of the sky curves above me in a great bell. Under my blades the creak of the ice seems to mimic the sound of space and infinite hope of the sky in a great white arc curving above.

I never skate at night without being filled with a sense of wonder at the imagination and improbability of humankind. Here I am — a two legged creature attached to these improbable boots, which are attached to these improbable steel blades, which are cutting quickly over the surface of frozen water, specifically frozen for me, my boots and my steel blades. What curious inventions we humans are. How we love to imagine! How clever we are!

In the distance, on the south shore, there is the United Church which raises its sturdy spire stuffed with prayers to the heavens, and beside it rises the delicate, elegant curves of the Bank Street Bridge. On the north shore is the football stadium at Lansdowne Park, which sits, reminiscent of Roman times, like some cavernous, ghostly sculpture waiting for crowds. And above are thousands and thousands of stars winking their cold bright light.

I look up at the bright heavens and they seem to warm me too, and I have to remind myself that space is dark. It is not bright. Space is as black as a mineshaft. Light from our star only becomes light when it hits the atmosphere of our earth. Starlight and sunlight become the thing we call light when it finds a receptor — us. The starry sky only becomes an arc of lights when it traverses our planet's atmosphere and we ourselves turn it into that image we have named the night sky. We the people of earth are a necessary piece in God's jigsaw that is what the night sky says to me.

I skate home reminded once more that our planet is more beautiful, more filled with wonder than any poet could ever describe. How lucky I am to be one of these curious lumbering creatures called humans alive under the starry sky.

This is the reason I am a city councilor: to be part of helping my city continue to be a beautiful place. It should be that simple but I cannot detach myself from the feeling that this is no longer enough, that there are great forces at work which are closing around the city. I feel it in the summer smog stinging the eyes on what should be a clear and pleasant summer day. I feel it in the gyrations of winter's cold that yo-yos up and down between thawing and freezing. There is no longer any regularity in the seasons. 2002 was the warmest winter in the century; 2003 was one of the longest and coldest. The temperature yo-yos around from season to season, and between night and day so much no one can be sure if the winter will be warm or freezing or what to wear outside on a summer night.

Our famous canal was only skateable for three weeks in 2002, yet in 2003 it was the longest, coldest winter ever for skating. These violent seasonal gyrations cradled within a constant warming trend are a trend line which is not sustainable. Unless stopped sooner or later, drought and the failure of crops will be the principal problems humanity faces. It is not nostalgia that makes me look back to the past for models of more sustainable urban and rural environments. It is practical observation.

I sit on various city committees like a minor satrap with my fellow councilors and listen to pleas from the public: pleas for money to keep the daycare centers going; pleas for decent home care for a husband who has had a stroke; pleas for better ambulance services; pleas for transportation for the handicapped; millions for a new hospital and new schools. The list goes on and on. It is not all dreary news. We have some successes. We cobble together a financial agreement that will keep a heritage school functioning as a public space for artists. We cobble together a new light rail service by leasing the rights to an old freight line.

But the harder I work the more it seems to me we city councilors are nothing more than well-dressed butlers in a mansion that is falling down around us. Like the butler in the novel *The Remains of the Day*, the better we do our jobs the more we camouflage the reality that the system itself is rotten. Governing a city well in this time of carnivorous globalization has become just another "good cause," because the larger political and economic system within which we exist and which we depend on isn't working to make the planet a safer happier place.

**The
Barbell Society
and Just-in-Time
Delivery**

Our achievements have become our atrocities.

— Diarmuid O'Murchu,
Quantum Theology:
Spiritual Implications of the New Physics

I HAVE GRADUALLY REALIZED that as much as I would like to
simplify things and blame everything on "development money"
and compliant politicians for paving over North America, that's only
a part of the story. Our urban problems are also a result of the centralized production system that has evolved in North America. Just-
in-time delivery was introduced in the early seventies as a way of
reducing manufacturing and distribution costs. The animating idea
was that it was a waste of time and money for manufacturers and
consumer retailers to have warehouses for storing large inventories of
parts and food. It would be much more efficient if they just ordered
the components as they needed them and then had them delivered to
the door of the factory or store just-in-time.

With just-in-time delivery, they could cut out city warehousing
and all the space and staff needed to staff these warehouses and organize the transfers of materials from warehouse to store or factory.
This was the final nail in the railroad's coffin. Railroads are a cheaper
and much less polluting way to move goods long distances but they
can't turn around at the mall. Railroads need transfer areas with some

warehouse capacity to store the goods that aren't needed immediately. Just-in-time delivery changed the landscape of cities and of North America. Highway construction and the trucking industry exploded. Warehousing and railroading collapsed further.

Companies organized along the old lines, competing against just-in-time companies, went out of business or changed their own operations to just-in-time very quickly. Just-in-time was a cheaper way to deliver products to the sales floor. Just-in-time was the magic hand of the competitive marketplace determining the highest and best use of resources and production techniques. North American corporations got leaner, consumers got cheaper products, and stores started to look like warehouses. On the level of producing cheaper goods for the consumer and bigger profits for those who survived (Walmart is now the richest corporation on the planet) it was a win-win situation.

Just-in-time delivery has been a disaster for city governments, national governments and the planet. The reduction in corporate production costs was achieved by downloading the cost of warehousing onto the environment and the public sector. Somebody had to pay for the warehousing. Governments have. National highways and city streets have become publicly funded, incredibly costly, rubber-tired warehouses. Everything now sits in truck stops or rolls on 18 wheels on just-in-time highways. One train can move the equivalent of 100 18-wheel trucks or bulk tanker trucks. Warehouse districts gave cities flexibility and security of supply. Just-in-time killed all of this less costly, less polluting, flexible activity. I use flexible in the sense that warehouse districts can serve small stores as easily as large.

Just-in-time delivery has been a key component in the accelerating degradation of the biosphere through global warming. In the five-year period between 1995 and 2000 in Canada, there was a 44% increase in truck traffic from 100 billion tons to 180 billion annually. My city takes 3,000 trucks through its downtown core every day. Just-in-time has successfully downloaded corporate costs onto the environment, onto the taxpayer's pocket, and has degraded the quality of life everywhere even in rural villages, because all these trucks needs roads, bridges and the fastest possible routes. Every minute counts. So if the fastest possible route is through the center of your village or city center, that's where the trucks roll and nothing can stop them because there is no alternative.

Most people have absolutely no idea of how great a burden roads are on their tax dollars. We are presently rebuilding 4.8 miles of urban highway in my city, which will add two lanes of road capacity.

It will cost taxpayers $67 million to add these two extra lanes, and this is cheap because there is no purchase of land needed. The $67 million is strictly a construction cost. If land must be purchased urban roads can cost $25 million for ⅔ of a mile.

To put this $67 million in perspective, the total cost of all the money spent for new community infrastructure in Ottawa is $19.3 million. That's right — two lanes of 4.8 miles is costing more than three times the entire budget for parks, community centers, swimming pools, ice rinks and daycares for 800,000 people. This is typical for every city large or small in North America. The city of Timmins in Northern Ontario, for example, spends half of its entire budget on roads every year and no one looks at it twice. But god help the Mayor if she tries to build a new library. She did and lost her re-election.

And once you have built the road in a northern country like Canada, road maintenance costs accelerated by the annual snowfalls, freezes and thaws kill you. In my city, this cost is $8,000 for every ⅔ mile of two-lane roadway. The unhappiest result of all is that road construction never solves the problem of road congestion as the congestion just moves down the road to where the capacity is four lanes instead of six lanes or six lanes instead of eight. At the point the road narrows, the cycle of failure will begin all over again. People will begin to complain about the bottleneck, and the road will be widened at tremendous cost to push the cycle of failure a little further out.

To put those costs in perspective, one four-lane, signalized city intersection costs between two and four million and every year, a single red light costs about $150,000 to install with $45,000 in yearly computer maintenance for the electronics. Year in year out, the Canadian province of Ontario spends a billion dollars on just the inter-city roads.

Just-in-time delivery has accelerated all these new road and maintenance costs by generating a constant pressure to expand roads everywhere. Thus, the road system grows in a tyranny of small decisions, which ultimately absorbs an ever greater proportion of city tax revenues. It is the roads which start to run the city, not the city which runs the roads.

To make just-in-time work successfully, it needs truckers capable of off-loading at a consumer warehouse. You can't drive an 18-wheeler from small store to small store. Enter the Big Box Mall. The Big Box Mall is the consumer end of the just-in-time factory. So the advertisements that say "from us to you" are correct. What they don't explain is that the simplification of just-in-time production, distri-

bution and consumption has turned North America into a barbell
society. At one end of the barbell is the production factory and at the
other end is the big box consumer warehouse. Connecting them are
the roads of North America. The triangular pivot in the middle,
which holds the two boxes up, is the public sector. Cities, federal,
provincial and state governments build, maintain and secure the arterial system on which the entire economy of the barbell society now
depends. Understanding the destructive capacity of the connecting
arterial road system is difficult to grasp because superficially it looks
efficient. How. could all those truck drivers working 16 hour days be
wrong?

To feed just-in-time production and consumption, cities must be
privatized. Urban and suburban landscapes are now designed exclusively for the truck and the car. Without easy parking lot access for
the producers and retailers, just-in-time can't function. So cities have
subsidized mall construction everywhere by assessing mall property
taxes at warehouse levels and by permitting mall parking lots to operate "for free." We are now building warehouse districts, not cities.
Do you see any real difference between the local "business park" and
the local strip mall and housing subdivision?

There is nothing free about parking lots at all.

The only reason that parking lots have any value is because they
are connected to a complex and costly urban street and highway
system, built and maintained at public expense. Cities literally give
parking lots to the mall and trucking industries. If the land was taxed
to reflect their real cost of operation, the competitive advantage of
malls would disappear tomorrow.

But it isn't the mall or the airport authority or the hospital or the
university's balance sheet which directly bear the costs operating local and national road systems, so why should they care? The parking
lot profits go to the institution which owns the parking lot, not the
public purse. Thus the public pays for the roads but the institution
profits from the parking charges or lack of them — so bring on the
parking lots! The more parking lots an airport has, the more revenue
it generates. In Ottawa parking is the second largest source of revenue for the airport. It's a toxic relationship for the taxpayer because
the more a mall, airport or a hospital depends on parking lot revenues, the greater the pressure on the commonwealth to feed those
profits by building more roads. In this way the public purse is constantly pressured to feed individual corporate interests. It's a never
ending hand-out that eviscerates cities' ability to do much else but

build and support road construction. It's a world in which there are billions to build freeways under the city of Boston but never enough for public transit or community centers for kids.

◆ ◆ ◆

Healthy cities and healthy nations should mimic trees. Cities should have many kinds of transit possibilities, many small producers, many farms on the edges of the city, many shopping streets, many warehouse and factory districts. There should be lots of roots and branches, lots of redundancy in the system. Duplication, diversity and complexity in the human urban world like in the biological world create stability because if one system breaks there's always another to take its place. But just-in-time delivery has worked against all of this by sucking all of society into a stick thin model where all the milk is trucked in from the cheapest possible factory farm, the apples from the cheapest possible orchards and so on. Don't you ever ask yourself why it is cheaper to eat apples from China than apples from down the road? And no, it's not just because labor is cheaper in China. It's because, among other things, the diesel fuel which powers the ships and trucks to transport the Chinese apples is publicly subsidized and the wages of the workers are depressed through flags of convenience. There's not much sustainable environmental logic to it except to feed and sustain international corporations.

During the ice storm that ripped into Ottawa in January 1998, what became very clear was that our city would run out of food very quickly because there were no local warehouse districts and no alternative to the icy, closed roads. The railway system has been largely put out of the transportation business. There was less train capacity in Ottawa in 2001 than there was in 1950. The train yards, rail lines, warehouses and repair shops that hummed along in the 1950s no longer exist. In most cases they have been literally paved over. The city's most extensive train yards are presently being converted into an enormous mall area and acres of parking lots. The development has the ironic title of "Trainlands." Ottawa's major east-west line is now an eight to ten lane expressway. The downtown railway tracks have been paved over and the station closed.

This story is repeated in other cities across the continent. So when a five-day ice storm hit Ottawa there were no inter-city trains to take the place of the trucks which couldn't navigate the roads, and there were no local warehouses to go to for food. The stores emptied of goods with just-in-time speed and were not replenished.

Calls to shut down the Canadian-American border after September 11 was an understandable circle-the-wagons reaction, but in a just-in-time North American economy it can't be done. Without trucks rolling down highways and endlessly criss-crossing borders, commerce of all kinds will freeze and people will literally start to go hungry. Two planes flying into two large buildings in one city should not have thrown North American society into catalytic shock. Some 350 million people live in North America and less than 3,000 people were killed in New York. The effect should have been minimal.

But global vertical and horizontal financial integration made the World Trade Center attacks a body blow. What the destruction of that office complex exposed was just how vulnerable North American society has become based on centralized production (in this case it was financial centralization) and a just-in-time society. Interrupt the just-in-time delivery system be it for moving money, food, computer or auto parts and suddenly the whole economy is in dire trouble.

Just-in-time production results in a rural-urban supply chain more analogous to a conveyor belt than a tree, and it is this conveyor-belt vision of society which is now pre-eminent. All North American governments have bought into the efficiency myth of just-in-time production and are attempting to model public services on the private models of efficiency. And what works for Wal-Mart must clearly also be good for hospitals and schools.

It's been a disaster. The drive to reduce wages by creating a public sector version of a Wal-Mart with poorly paid, part-time, just-in-time work force has simply driven nurses out of the profession and made it difficult to recruit new ones. It's one thing to not be able to find the clerk to help you purchase a garden tool; it's a whole other order of problem when your IV drip is jamming and you can't find the nurse.

Funding only hospitals where every bed is occupied and schools where every desk and every room is occupied hasn't been efficient either. It's been the opposite. In Canada this has been a formula for closing hospitals and schools that were cheap and worked while people stack up in six hour waits in just-in-time emergency rooms. Running a hospital and school system like this is the same as trying to run a transit system on 100 percent occupancy. There is no such thing as 100 percent occupancy on a bus line because to achieve 100 percent you have to leave people at every bus stop. Leaving people stranded is a failure. Turning away patients and students is a failure.

Hundred per cent occupancy of a school or hospital is the equivalent of 100 percent lane use on the highway. It doesn't work. It's gridlock. You need at least 15 percent give in all systems at all times for them to be efficient.

Ten years ago many inner city schools in my part of the city were down as low as 80 percent occupancy. The oldest school dating back to 1898 had fallen to about 70 percent occupancy. So the provincial government using its muscle funding formula began to force these "inefficient" schools to close their doors and to sell off the property for useful, tax paying re-development as they have in Britain and the United States. The problem is that children are not just-in-time widgets coming off a production line at a steady rate. Communities like individuals have youthful periods, mature and elderly stages. They wax and wane. At the elderly stage there is a steep drop in the number of children attending neighborhood schools. But if you close the primary and secondary schools during this phase there won't be sufficient space when the older folks move off to smaller homes and are replaced by young folks with growing families. Closing neighborhood schools creates inner city rot because no young family will move into a community where their children can't attend local schools. Why would anyone make that decision?

And once a city neighborhood school and its adjacent play yards disappear, they are gone forever. They are too costly to replace. Schools are the lungs of the community. They give it breathing space and vitality. Fortunately in my neighborhood those lungs are now filled with children. We are at 90 percent capacity in all our schools; some of them have spilled over into portables. The age pendulum has swung again and we managed to fight off — not all — but most of the school closures by defeating at the polls the school trustees who were for them. This happened across the province in sufficient numbers to irritate the provincial government; it moved in, disbanded local school boards and appointed provincial supervisors to impose school closures in major cities.

There may indeed be some small short-term savings in closing a school at 70 percent occupancy. Unfortunately the long-term costs of creating just-in-time schools are incalculable. Community stability, greenspace, generational revitalization, property values and the neighborhood quality of life all tumble. Everyone who has children in school knows just-in-time education isn't cheaper. It's bad news for students, bad news for parents and bad news for the community. But this is the model that has been shoved at the public throughout the 1990s. Over 150 vital, historic small schools have been closed in the province of Ontario. A few have been saved through what has been nothing less than a local guerrilla war against the Education Ministry on the part of parents and city school trustees.

On the hospital side, the idea was to concentrate the health services in single, "efficient" industrial hospitals where there was no "wastage," i.e., no unoccupied beds, no downtime for doctors and nurses. The small, community hospitals were all closed. The immediate upfront costs of these hospital closures are so staggering it beggars the imagination. Two thirds of all patients do not need "tertiary" (most complex) care, but the costs of keeping these patients in a just-in-time tertiary hospital are twice that of a community hospital. The state has, in effect, closed the cheap hospitals and expanded the costly ones. The bizarreness of these decisions can only be appreciated when you look at the actual costs. At a community hospital in Ottawa like the Salvation Army's Grace Hospital ward beds were $349 a night; at the new Ottawa General (a tertiary hospital) the costs per bed are $829. Guess which hospital has seen a multi-million dollar expansion? Guess which one was torn down?

The $829 a night, General Hospital was expanded and the $349 a night Grace was shut down and then demolished in the name of economy! The only people who have prospered from these just-in-time hospital closures are the consultants and hospital administrators who have won the contracts to work on the just-in-time expansions. They have made millions.

Unfortunately, bed charges are only the start of the just-in-time hospital costs. A major element of hospital costs is getting people, patients, visitors and staff to and from the buildings. A just-in-time factory hospital means that the normal city infrastructure, sewers, waterlines, roads and transit are not sufficient so special roads, special transit connections and special city services must be built. A small community hospital like the Grace fitted like a glove into the community and could exist on the various city services that were there to serve the neighborhood. Community hospitals have few extraordinary costs for the city.

The greatest failure of the just-in-time factory hospitals has been medical. Emergency rooms serve every kind of patient from highway carnage to flus. Wait times everywhere have ballooned from minutes to hours. And factory hospitals are so rife with bacteria and assorted viruses that doctors routinely send patients home if they can urinate. If there are any bacteria or a flu virus in circulation in a factory hospital, the virus just works its way through the entire building complex. This is exactly what has happened with the Norwalk and SARS viruses. The virus seats itself in these factory hospital operations and then spreads quickly through the buildings.

Small hospitals that are peppered across the city have the natural insulating factors of distance and different travel patterns, different staff, different accommodations and cleaner premises. Further, in an emergency they can be shut down if some really toxic bacteria or virus seats itself in the hospital without compromising medical services of the entire city. Efficiency, flexibility and creativity have been driven out of the system as hospitals have centralized into ever larger units. The Ottawa hospital is now so large it is more like a city within a city.

The provincial and federal governments of Canada have collectively managed through the just-in-time business model to trash what was just a few years ago the finest public health care system on the planet. Nurses from France now spend time in Canadian hospitals the way Canadian nurses visit Africa. They get a chance to taste a nation and a life which is a little different from the old continent, but these visiting nurses don't want to stay. The hours and working conditions are too difficult, the responsibilities too onerous. The hospital environment is too unpleasant. They want to go home when their year is up.

The fragility of North American private sector has been compounded by the collapse of the public sector. For North Americans, their pensions, their savings and their aspirations have been tied to the marketplace, and when it collapses they have no place to turn. France remains the one western nation that has maintained the most consistent and successful opposition to the globalized, just-in-time economic model. French citizens are reluctant to invest in the stock market; it is regarded as little more than gambling. The bulk of the French stock market is owned by non-French citizens. The French have their pensions locked up in the public system, public services and local investments, i.e., family run businesses, small scale industry and farm production. Stuff that you can see, feel, touch and visit; hence there is a feeling of solidity to French civic life that just isn't present in North America.

The North American and British governments have steadily withdrawn from providing all the key components of national infrastructure: airlines, train systems, energy, water and health while the French have fought a long and passionate rearguard action against virtually the entire west. This struggle has led them into alliance with the nations of the south by insisting that the "biens communs" should not be privatized, i.e., water, energy and national transit services should be held in common by the public for the public. The French have stood pretty much alone.

But cracks are appearing in the dominant ideology and some of them have been large and scary enough to get people's attention. Enron was one. The August 2003 electrical failure that blacked out 50 million people was another. The attack on the World Trade Center was another. The incidents are beginning to add up. People are beginning to understand that 50 years of unparalleled consumerism hasn't made the world a better place. It hasn't even made the majority of North American people richer.

In Canada the Vanier Institute of the Family reported in its 1999 Annual Report on the family that the 1990s recession recovery has been an "incomeless recovery." Poverty rates actually increased during the decade. The "recovery" was funded largely by record low savings and increased borrowing. Personal debt hit record levels. Taxes did not increase, neither did incomes but the cost of living did.[1] The percentage that taxes take from family income has increased, so newspaper headlines which scream "REDUCE TAX BURDEN" are not incorrect. Taxes do take more from the family's income. But it's not the tax burden that's the problem, it's the income that's the problem.

In the just-in-time, factory-to-mall society we've built, reducing taxes has proved to be a particularly pernicious way of increasing disposable income for the middle class and the poor because tax reductions reduce cheap public services. Inevitably, they are replaced with more expensive private services, special levies or simply making do without.

The ugly truth is that in spite of record levels of consumption things are not getting more stable or more comfortable. Both the modal (what most people are earning) and the mean (the dividing line between those above the modal and those below) income are getting worse. Mean incomes were less in 2004 than they were in the 1970s. We have now had 30 years of more people earning less and a larger and larger gap between the richest and the poorest.

Beyond the consumer delights of the internet and the DVD horizon, society is less balanced and less capable of producing real security for people than it was 50 years ago. And once these thoughts begin to insinuate themselves into the public consciousness, there is a secondary, more seditious thought that another war or more consumer spending aren't going to make the world a better place either. But this is the way the dice have been rolled by President G.W. Bush. He has made it very clear that it is unpatriotic if not treasonous to suggest that anything else but terrorists are North America's principal problem; that the patriotic response to September 11 is to keep on shopping at the mall and bunker bomb the "evildoers."

He's got the paradigm dead wrong. State and personal consumerism is the problem, not the solution. Consumerism organized around the urban barbell is not a sustainable development formula for anyone, rich or poor. These consumerisms are tickets to impoverishing the planet. State consumerism of missile shields, nuclear aircraft carriers and submarines combined with the personal consumerism of the barbell society is suffocating humanity. No wonder so many people are anxious no matter how rich they are. They instinctively realize that it doesn't all add up and that society as a whole is becoming less stable.

In Canada, the corporate income tax scarcely exists anymore. Corporations which export are essentially tax-less. They don't even pay value-added taxes (GST) on their products. Only those products produced for domestic consumption pay value-added taxes, yet the fabrication of products for both domestic and export markets equally require public support. A worker producing software for the US market requires the same health care, education and public transit as a worker producing software for the Canadian market, but only one form of production pays taxes: the domestic one.

Corporations have virtually disappeared from the credit side of the tax ledger. Commonwealth costs are now shouldered principally by individuals out of personal income and sales taxes at a time when the median income has declined; no wonder we do not have adequate resources to pay for public services. And no wonder people are screaming about taxation levels. Yet because of globalization and the persistent blackmail threat of corporations to move if taxed, the discussion of what constitutes a fair share of the costs of providing for the commonwealth is never even on the table. It's been years since corporations received anything but a tax cut. Anything else is seen as irresponsible.

Just-in-time production and delivery has created a black hole for public expenditures by forcing cities and states to assume massive capital and operating costs for a spaghetti road system. Corporations have not only off-loaded their just-in-time storage and delivery costs

on the public sector; they don't even assume their share of these costs.
Corporate taxes have become "unpatriotic" — so it's heads the public loses, tails the corporations win.

A few days after the New York attack, Mayor Giuliani said "hate
and intolerance" were the authors of the World Trade Center explo-
sions. It was these problems that needed to be addressed. Those
problems won't be addressed by putting a bullet through Osama bin
Laden or Saddam Hussein. It will take something a whole lot harder.
It will take re-thinking why we are the way we are. We need to trade
our barbell society for one that it is based on sustainability and social
justice from the street up, from the factory up and from the government down. We need to do what Mr. Bush has said he won't do —
put the North American lifestyle on the table and change it to one
that is more just, less polluting and less avaricious.

4

From Mont Tremblant to Ski Tremblant

A slave is he who cannot speak his thought.

— Euripedes 480–406 B.C.

THE GREAT NORTH AMERICAN divide at the beginning of the 21st century is not between religions, races or languages. It's the divide between those who believe in a political culture and public spaces that are inclusive, and those who believe in a political culture which advantages private space and just-in-time consumerism. The second group assume everything is just fine the way it is and advocates that the best response to terrorism is to crush the "evil doers" as one would noxious weeds. This is the ascendant side. I believe it is these attitudes which animate terrorism and environmental degradation. President Bush is good for terrorists and terrorists are good for President Bush. They feed off each other.

It is not military might which is the best way to combat terrorism, but creating a world in which everyone has a fair say and everyone has a stake. Then it becomes very, very clear what a violent act against unarmed and unprotected people is: it's not a statement about anything but criminality. As a cardboard sign carried by a protester during the lead up to the Iraq war said: "justice starves terrorists, exploitation feeds them."

This is the same basic conflict that animated and defined the 1960s. In this way, nothing has changed. The conflicts are still here;

they have just taken on a harder, more impenetrable carapace. The sides have been digging in for 40 years. The edges of the conflict have become more brittle, more fanatic and it has moved off shore. The image of the most powerful nation on the planet bombing the poorest is a statement not about justice or revenge. It's a message from the planet's most powerful Corporate Culture. That statement from the bombers is "our vision of society will prevail and if you're not a believer — just watch. We will bomb you into the Stone Age." It is a message directed at Martin Luther King and Jack Kennedy as much as Osama bin Laden. It is another message from the winning side — a message that is so bankrupt of humanity that it can turn mass murders like Osama bin Laden into a hero for millions of the world's poorest.

Consumerism in North America has become a way of life. Money is what malls are all about. Malls do not have a problem with homeless folks as city streets do. The unwanted can be ejected from the mall because it is a private space. Mall neighborhoods don't need sidewalks. They are not interested in welcoming visitors but dissuading them. That notion of keeping people out extends to government. A successful democracy for the mall-consumer culture is one which is the least intrusive on private spaces, keeps taxes down and keeps society "growing." The one thing consumerism can't tolerate is a reduction or stabilization of demand and population growth.

Would North America have evolved differently if Martin Luther King and Jack Kennedy had not been murdered? Would we have foreign policies based on building something more than a global financial platform for corporations? Would we have taxed automobiles so that gas-guzzling SUVs would be less popular? Would we have taxed parking lots to make it less attractive to lay more asphalt? Would we have created city and national rail systems that served the majority of the population, not just the poor? In short, would we have created the kind of society which was less rapacious of the planet's resources? The questions are all moot. Neither Canada nor the United States went down that route. History is about what happened, not what might have happened.

What you see is what you get, and what we've got is Malls, Money and Ski Tremblant. Whenever I want a single metaphor for the closing decades of the 20th century, I think of Ski Tremblant. Ski Tremblant is an international ski resort owned by Intrawest, which owns among other baubles the Whistler-Blackcomb ski resort in British Columbia. I never visit Ski Tremblant without a feeling of wonder.

The quaint cobbled streets of the ski village are jammed with folks from all over the world. It wasn't always like this.

It wasn't very long ago that Ski Tremblant was a place called Mont Tremblant. There was no real village on the mountain. There was just a church, a couple of ski lodges and a pub. Further away from the mountain were some small hotels and bed and breakfasts. Tremblant is a translation of the Algonquin name, the Trembling Mountain. If you look at the mountain from a distance, you will see the distinctive oval volcanic cone at the summit where the ski lifts disgorge their passengers. As you would expect from the rim of an old volcano, there is a very steep initial pitch followed by a broad, long outrun towards the base of the mountain.

In my racing days, there was no Ski Tremblant, or annual winter flights across the continent to the ski resorts which speckle the Rocky Mountain chain from British Columbia to Utah. The mountains were still there, but they were different. Mont Tremblant was the great mountain of eastern Canada. It was "the" mountain that we all turned towards, the place to test the skiing skills we had honed on smaller local hills like Camp Fortune. If you could win a race on Mont Tremblant's Flying Mile, you could win a race anywhere in the world. I'll never forget the day when two classmates of mine, Currie Chapman and Heather Quipp, won their races on the Flying Mile and each became Canadian Junior Ski Champions at sixteen years old. My awe at their early accomplishment has never evaporated. What finer moment could there be than to be sixteen and win the Canadian Junior Ski Championship on Mont Tremblant's Flying Mile?

We used to sleep at the foot of the mountain in an old barn, which had been insulated in an erratic way. The chairlifts were not high-speed quads; they lumbered up the mountain giving you plenty of time to freeze while pondering the origin of mountains and the color of a girl's hair. The people that we skied with were mostly from a few hours drive away, Montreal or Ottawa; you rarely met people from further away. Mont Tremblant was just a larger version of the smaller ski hills which ringed both cities.

In 1960, Camp Fortune, a ski hill a 30-minute bus ride from Ottawa was home to Canada's first Olympic Gold Medallist, Anne Heggteveit. It was the largest ski club in North America. It was owned and operated by its members. It had over 10,000 members, and skiing was cheap in every sense. I never had a new pair of skis. I bought secondhand skis at the autumn ski sales at Camp Fortune. I learned to ski in the public school ski program. I never raced in anything but jeans and the same ski jacket I wore to school. I know it is ridiculous for it is a long time ago now, but I still take great pride in the knowledge that I once raced with the best of my generation on nothing more than second hand equipment. It can now take $15,000 to $30,000 (more than my father's annual salary in 1960) to put your child into a racing program at Ski Tremblant.

Mr. Harrison, the father of a school friend of mine, operated the Co-Op ski lift at Camp Fortune (now privatized and called "Ski Fortune", a kind of mini Ski Tremblant). In summer, Mr. Harrison ran a fishing camp, and in winter he worked as a liftee and general maintenance man. I always regarded the ski lift as "his" ski lift, which I was borrowing for a ride with my ski pass. I could not imagine Mr. Harrison deigning to address me with something like "have a nice day" or "no problem." My job was to get on the chair with a minimum of fuss and say "thank you" for any assistance he might render me. That was it. The men who operated the lifts were not called "service representatives" or "associates;" they were called "liftees," and I cannot imagine even in my wildest dreams any of them ever saying to me "have a nice day." Mr. Harrison was typical of the kind of man ski hill owners then employed. They were mature men employed for their outdoor skills. They wore battered coats — sometimes with the ski hill's name on them, sometimes not. How they addressed the customer wasn't in their job description.

Mr. Harrison was a tad on the intimidating side, because he was a big man with a weather beaten face and large, strong hands. If he had reason to speak to me he would, and if he did not, he would not. I behaved in the same way. In its own way, it was a comfortable, respectful relationship. I love to ski but I find that I no longer have the same easy relationship with ski center employees. Instead, I find myself cringing at the thought of some "associate" approaching me in his or her impeccable matching ski suit to check my pass, smiling and telling me to "have a nice day." Nor do I think that I ever will stop cringing because if slaves could talk they would just as easily parrot "no problem," "have a nice day" and "how can I help you?"

The UK government has come up with what seems to me a bright idea: a gap year between finishing high school and commencing university where kids are obliged to go out into the world and work at something, to develop a little more maturity and experience before commencing university. It makes a lot of sense to me; the idea of children staying in school continuously until they are in their mid twenties before they ever get a taste of the real world seems foolish.

If their parents are rich, children can ski the gap year. The parents buy twelve months of ski instruction for their children around the world, the idea being that at the end of the year, their offspring will be qualified level-two ski instructors. The children go to the best ski resorts and ski with the best instructors. At the end of the year, they have learned a trade — an upscale trade — but a trade nonetheless. To quote my younger self, it would take "a shit load of money" to buy such a year of such instruction and travel. But these youngsters wouldn't feel out of place at Ski Tremblant because everywhere you look you see money. There are fine hotels, restaurants, expensive shops, an aqua center, a ski elevator to take you over the village from the parking lot directly to the gondola, which will take you up to the top of the mountain. Everything is most comfortably arranged.

I can't get used to the millions which now wash around Ski Tremblant like so much loose change. I can't help doing additions on the ski suits, skis, boots and so on, that I find standing beside me in the line. You could finance a meal program for an entire daycare for a year on the back of one customer. On the ski line itself, the daycares of an entire city are carried.

◆ ◆ ◆

Since this divide began to open in the 1960s, Canada has been steadily moving towards the same income gap between rich and poor that there is south of the border. In Canada now, 50 percent of the personal wealth is held by ten percent of population. The trend is steady and clear. We're headed for the American model of ten percent of the population holding ⅔ of the personal wealth.[1] At the same time, Canada is seeing a rapid diminution of all aspects of the public sector, from public schools to public health, and the corresponding growth in private police forces, private schools and private health care.

I see this reflected in an intimate way around my ward.[2] When I was first elected there were two private schools in my ward. Today there are eight. Three public schools have been closed and sold, and the ones left standing are dirty and overcrowded. People raise money for them as if they were private schools — by renting out the school yards for parking, filling the school gym with second hand book sales and so on. In the winter, churches in my ward now host soup kitchens and come-in-from-the-cold afternoons, when before there were none.

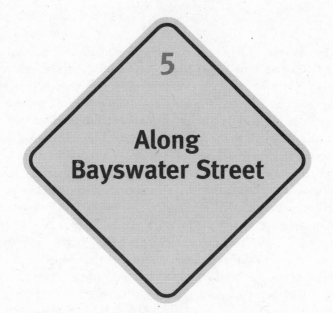

5

Along Bayswater Street

I think often of the terrace at Rousset overlooking the valley of the Arc. The light so limpid as if ordinary light had been filtered into a crystal purity, the vibrant colors of the fields reflecting radiantly from the earth in the valley below.

I was thinking these thoughts on the little deck that we built behind our old house in Ottawa. Hawthorne and apple trees had grown to completely cover it so that the deck itself was buried beneath a deep, green bower of leaf and branch — and it suddenly, belatedly, occurred to me that this also was a beautiful place.

— from *There Goes the Pension*
an unpublished mansuscript

Yesterday, i gave a speech at City Hall to kick-off Poverty Awareness Week. This is a week in which social activists try to sensitize the general public to how many poor people there are in the city. The center of Poverty Awareness Week is the "poverty challenge." This is where about 100 non-poor people try and live on $37 a week for food and transportation. I am not taking the poverty challenge. I know I can't make it. I spend about that much each week on coffee, which I am mildly addicted to and refuse to drink any other way except as espresso or café au lait. I know it sounds wimpy in the extreme but I need that coffee-café fix to get me through the day.

I dressed very carefully for the event. I wore my best suit and best tie. I did not want to convey the impression for a second that I was poor because I am not. I've never been poor, and it would have been phony to have conveyed that impression in any way. On the other hand, I feel profoundly that the gap between those who have and those who have not has become far too wide. I tried to convey this in my speech as clearly and passionately as I could in both official languages. The room was crowded with hopeful faces, and I was very conscious of the honor that the organizers had conferred on me by asking me to speak.

Afterwards, I sat down in my office and replayed the whole event in my head. I was overwhelmed with the feeling of how little words mean. To make a difference, you need more than words. You need higher salaries. You need affordable housing. You need cheaper and more comprehensive public transit so that everyone has access to jobs and recreation. You need decent work benefits like paid holidays, tangible things that make the physical part of life easier.

I began to think back on my own childhood and wondered if things were any better then? The more I thought about this, the more difficult it seemed to compare the winter of 2004 with the winter of 1965. They are worlds apart. Yes, there were poor people in 1965. Bayswater Street where I lived in the 1960s is an old city street about eight city blocks long. At the north end, the poor people lived. They tended to rent their homes and apartments and not own cars. They walked or took the streetcar to work. In the middle of Bayswater, the middle class people lived. These folks owned larger homes and a secondhand car. At the southern end, next to Sherwood Drive and not far from Dow's Lake, the richest folks lived. These folks had large, well-appointed houses and brand new cars in the driveway. They tended to be doctors, lawyers, senior civil servants. We lived in the middle of Bayswater but I went to school at the north end, first at a little school called Devonshire and then Connaught.

The children of both the south end and the north end of Bayswater Street went to these schools. We played in the same yard together. We played hockey together, chased girls together, got in some teenage scrapes together. In high school, many of the children from the north end would choose to enroll in the technical or commercial streams whereas the sons and daughters of the south end went into the academic stream and took erudite subjects like Latin. But we still walked the same halls together, went to the same school dances together, played on the same school teams together, listened to the same bands.

The south end kids on Bayswater clearly had advantages and circumstances that the north end kids did not, but the differences were marked by city blocks, not by universes. There were no GAP stores. Rich or poor, our school clothes tended to be similar. Jeans were jeans. A check shirt was a check shirt. This has changed. Forty years of government policies promoting consumerism have done more than crank up people's desire to buy things. Consumerism has changed the nature of life in the city — not just the clothes on our backs but the manner of conducting our lives.

I can't think of anyone in the 1960s who worried about the family's mutual funds or watched television ads assuring them that "their money was working for them around the globe." People's pensions were Canadian and usually locked up with the government or the company they worked for, and that was the end of it. Doctors and lawyers were different. They tended to own land and have "investments." They were the exceptions.

My city, like the world, has changed. The old city where I still live has become the domain of the well-to-do and the very poor. The middle class has shrunk into the car-based suburbs. Kids have been streamed into French Immersion or high-performance public schools which have become public school versions of private schools. The poor kids end up in different schools where they don't get French Immersion or "enriched" courses. This is regarded as a good thing. Excellence in public sector schools is being rewarded. I see it as just another way to disadvantage the poor. The poor kids don't even get a chance to go to a public school with the same advantages as the privileged. Excellence and merit have become excuses for further privileging the already privileged.

The gulf between the rich and the poor has grown so wide that you can scarcely see the folks who live next door to you, let alone at the other end of the street. And what you can't see, you fear. People don't want to be caught for a second on the wrong side of the rich-poor divide. Our interactions consist of platitudes like "no problem," "how can I help you?" and "have a nice day."

For those not familiar with *Tally's Corner*,[1] in 1965 a PhD student in anthropology, Elliott Liebow, decided to spend a couple of years hanging out with Negro street corner men. His book about that experience changed the way I saw cities and anthropology. I learned in just a few hours of reading *Tally's Corner* that men standing around on a city street corner led complex, interesting lives and that they were there — not through choice — but because getting out of the ghetto was a Herculean task that depended on luck as much as talent. Liebow's book changed forever the way I imagined the connections between society, the city and the individual.

At the end of his life, Dr. Liebow wrote a second book called *Tell Them Who I Am*.[2] At that time, he was dying of cancer. After the cancer diagnosis, he left his job and chose to devote the last two years of his life hanging out in a couple of women's shelters doing volunteer work and talking with homeless women. When he died, he was a tall gangling man in his fifties, about the age I am now. Eliot Liebow remains a great inspiration for me.

He never says in any of his books that it is monstrous so many people live such physically impoverished lives. He lets the homeless women tell their stories and the stories speak for themselves; just as 40 years before he let street corner men reveal themselves by being themselves, not by preaching from his own pulpit. But I am not shy. I believe that it is monstrous that we allow people's lives to be stunted when we have the wealth and resources to make it otherwise — that it is monstrous that a young woman should be shot in the back as she walks down a street to work. These things deserve our rage. But rage by itself benefits neither the living nor the dead. Liebow understood this, and let his life speak through what he did and how he behaved.

Anger must find a direction that can help us to move forward in a way that benefits people, not destroys, and to do that anger must be overcome by love. It is this mix of emotions that animates each chapter of *Urban Meltdown;* jostling each other, competing against each other are love versus anger, hope versus rage.

I believe that real freedom doesn't come from money beyond having enough to feed and house yourself decently. Real freedom comes from a community, which supports and loves all of its parts: the north end, the middle and the south end of the street. When you feel that kind of inclusiveness and caring, you don't need gated communities or thousands of investment dollars to "protect" your lifestyle, because your life already has security and style. It is a life and a style that endures and is filled with unexpected pleasures. I have no cottage, no deuxième residence. My back yard is a postage stamp — but each day the front door of my house opens on a great and wonderful world waiting for me to explore, where I am the most fortunate of men in the best of all possible worlds.

6

Urban Villages

The original polis, as Aristotle described it, was based not on trade but on a self-sufficient and self-governing group of villages in a narrow and closed region lying around an urban center.

— Sir Peter Hall, *Cities in Civilization*

THE VILLAGE OF ROUSSET is in Provence in the valley of the Arc. Patty and I cashed in our pensions and lived there with the children for a year. The entire Mediterranean basin is so beautiful that in a perfect world, all people should be allowed to live at least for one year somewhere along its shores. Life along the Mediterranean changes you for the better. We all came back a little more understanding of our own lives.

I saw with new, more appreciative eyes my old neighborhood and realized for the first time that the city that I had grown up in had become two cities. The old streetcar city, a series of urban villages, is the one that you see in the postcard scenes from Canada's capital. The cyclists along the canal, the flower stalls in the Byward Market, the sailboats on Dow's Lake, the nightlife on Elgin Street — all these photographs are taken in the urban villages of the old streetcar wards.

My district is an old streetcar ward composed of five urban villages, each one distinct from the next, each with its own shopping street, its own community centers, its own character. The ward stretches from Dow's Lake and Carleton University along both sides of the Rideau Canal. It is the part of the city where tourists gravitate for the many festivals that take place along the banks of the canal and for its lively city sidewalks, cafés and stores. The curious thing is that these villages operate much as if the streetcars still rolled along their streets although there haven't been any streetcars on them for 40 years. But people still walk to the main avenues to catch the bus downtown, to shop, drink coffee, visit the local pub.

The amazing thing about these urban villages is how robust they are. They are four times as dense as mall communities, yet they rarely have anything significant invested in them except patching. The sewers on the Main Street of the Glebe go back to 1910. Sometimes in extremely cold weather they break, damaging businesses and clogging up the street. Rich and poor, the residents of the Glebe pay more taxes per capita to the city than any other Ottawa neighborhood. Their tax money flows out to the suburbs to pay for brand new roads and brand new sewers which these lightly populated areas cannot afford themselves. Yet in spite of these gross inequities, the older communities remain remarkably livable, remarkably resilient despite the rapacious appropriation of their property taxes.

The Ottawa that you don't see on postcards is miles and miles of big, black box office parks, malls, parking lots and housing tracts serviced by "arterials." It's a different world. Sometimes, I drive out just to remind myself what it is like to sit in a traffic jam on a hot day on a traffic sewer, unable to get off, unable to go forward, unable to go backward. It makes you crazy. The development pods that edge these traffic sewers are all squat, shiny boxes set down in pans of asphalt capable of parking hundreds of cars. The roads to these development pods lead nowhere but back to the traffic sewer. You can't drive through them to some other place. They are islands of asphalt, office buildings and/or warehouses. It is the larger and more powerful part of the city.

My suburban colleagues frequently say, when I argue that we need to bring the streetcars back, that this "European idea" would be great if we had the same densities as European cities but we don't. Therefore it is impossible. Therefore I am being unreasonable. I don't agree. Population density is driven by how you build the city and above all, by how people travel. In 1950 Ottawa had ½ the present population. So if total population was the problem, Ottawa should be twice as dense today as it was in 1950 because it has more than twice the number of people living in it. It is the reverse: the city has twice the population and there are 50 percent less people living per square mile. In 1950 Ottawa had 186 miles of streetcar lines. Today it has none.

Urban densities are the result not of a city's total population, but of how people travel. If you move people around by car, urban densities will be slight because cars require so much space. On average, single occupant vehicles need four private and another four, on-street, shared parking pads or stalls. Not surprisingly, every person in a single occupancy vehicle (SOV) takes eight times as much road space as eight people in a bus and 16 times as many people in a tram or a train. The long and the short of it is, you can't build a smart, energy efficient city when the predominant form of transportation is an SOV.

I don't worry about gridlock. I worry about people getting killed or maimed. In my ward, I've had two students killed crossing Bronson Avenue in front of Carleton University; a woman lose her leg while she sat on a bench and a car rocketed through the intersection and jumped the curb; a nine-year-old girl bubbling with life killed while crossing an intersection; two SUVs driving one after the other through a café window (difficult to believe but true). These are the more spectacular examples; most of them are less compelling. Someone hit in a wheel chair. Someone hit at the corner. Broken bones. Broken wheelchairs. It's a rare week that goes by without someone being hit or hurt by a motor vehicle.

This is not news that is special to my city. Cities abandoned their streetcar lines and constructed car-based environments all over North America, but the extent of the social and environmental destruction this generated is still little understood. Ottawa's electric streetcar system was one of the oldest and most complete systems in Canada. Its only rivals were Toronto, Montreal and perhaps Winnipeg. In my childhood it was possible to hop onto a streetcar and be taken all the way to Britannia Beach at the furthest reaches of the city, some fifteen miles away. It took about twenty minutes on a dedicated, tree-lined rail route, which ran quickly beside a main street. It takes longer by private car or public bus today.

Electrified streetcar systems draw communities tightly together. Businesses and residences cluster around streetcar lines of their own accord. The electric streetcars were quiet, efficient, safe and long lasting. Unlike a bus which operates on the street like a large truck, a streetcar's trajectory is entirely predictable. Streetcars also don't dump a diesel residue over everything they pass. The streetcar's final gift to the community was that they worked to calm traffic as drivers were hesitant to take on a streetcar in an intersection duel.

The damage from the automobile is incalculable; how do you calculate the loss of livable environments? Bronson Avenue — named after a great 19th century lumber baron Edgar Bronson — used to be one of my city's premier addresses. Bronson was a gracious north-south boulevard lined with grand homes and magnificent trees which cast a shady arch over the street's entire length. Streetcars whisked quietly up and down each side of the trees. The sidewalks were broad. People strolled along the avenue on a summer evening.

Bronson has been steadily "improved" by the traffic engineers. Improvement has meant removing the trees "to improve sightlines," narrowing sidewalks "to improve road lane widths" to the point they are not much more than wide curbs that no sensible person would walk on unless there was absolutely no other choice. When I try to campaign on Bronson Avenue, the noise is so intense I can't hear what people say at the door. I notice double winter windows are left on all year long. Intersections have been "improved" with traffic turning lanes. Edgar Bronson would not recognize his gracious boulevard.

Today, Bronson Avenue is a broad, four-lane strip of asphalt lined with battered boarding houses, parking lots and small odd businesses looking for low rents. The houses that have hung on have done so by turning away from Bronson so that they are entered from a side street. High fences have been added to protect the property facing the Bronson side. These fences mimic suburban noise barriers along the traffic sewers we have built in the suburbs and give the street a shuttered, blind feeling. The trees have gone.

The transformation of Bronson from boulevard to traffic sewer is just one of many. King Edward Avenue less than a mile from Parliament Hill was once the centerpiece of the entire city, the grandest city street the city owned. It has been turned into the ugliest and most dangerous truck route imaginable — 3,000 trucks roll down it every day. It's lined with flophouses and soup kitchens.

As the extent of the damage began to penetrate, I began to search out old streetcar drivers — men in their seventies and eighties — and ask them for their stories. And I began to connect the larger dots, dots that led all the way to Iraq. The overwhelming importance of crude oil and the single occupant vehicle to the North American economy has been growing for a very long time. It began in the 1930s and 1940s with the destruction of North America's electric streetcars and inter-city train services. They were destroyed because there weren't enough profits to be made from them. Their destruction was about corporate greed. The same motivation drives foreign policy today. It's all about profits and market share, and enormous corporations who want to mazimize both.

Ironically, electric streetcars were "too cheap." They moved too many people too easily and were maintained at too little cost. An electric streetcar including the tracks with a little maintenance can last 60 years, and two tracks can move 16 freeway lanes. Automobiles to be useful, on the other hand, require billions in annual road construction and re-construction: cement, asphalt, truckers, graders, welders, designers, engineers, laborers. Best of all for vehicle manufacturers, a car or a bus lasts only seven or eight years without a major rebuild. Roads in northern climates especially have staggering maintenance costs. In my city, it's $8,000 per lane per kilometer (⅔ of a mile). The car and its many support industries constitute ⅓ of the Ontario economy. To imagine Canada in 2005 without the automobile at the center of the nation and city life is to imagine an entirely different place. This task defeats most people and all politicians.

Nonetheless, Ontario like the rest of North America wasn't always like this. In the 1920s, convinced of the efficiency and effectiveness of the electric streetcar, prominent Canadians like Sir Adam Beck and his American counterparts lobbied governments hard to extend city streetcars into a nationwide system of electric inter-city trains called inter-urbans. Some of these inter-urbans trains were already functioning between cities in Canada and in the American northeast. Combined with city streetcars, the inter-urbans were a clean, sustainable alternative to paving over the countryside with asphalt. To put this in a Canadian perspective, today four rail lines could replace the entire 401 commuter highway — 33 lanes of traffic, the largest in the nation. But as influential as the hydroelectric developer of Niagara Falls was, Sir Adam Beck lost his battle against the private vehicle and died watching his dreams of a network of inter-urbans powered by electricity succumb to the advance of the automobile.

The automotive lobby was successful in persuading both local and national governments to assume the entire cost of constructing inter-city highways without which their products had no chance of competing with the inter-urbans, and at the same time convinced governments to withdraw any financial support for rail corridors. The lobby successfully characterized public investment in rail as an unfair subsidy — a concept that endures in the public's mind to this day.

This favoritism forced rail companies to compete with roads, trucks and cars in impossible circumstances. The rail companies were obliged to pay for their own rights of way, construction, maintenance, policing of the rails, pay property taxes on the land they owned for the lines along its entire length, while the car manufacturers had the roads given to them. Not surprisingly, passenger rail service and freight lines collapsed all over North America. They couldn't compete with the billions in public subsidy to roads.

In a handful of cities — New Orleans, San Francisco, Toronto — electric streetcars managed to survive. Everywhere else from coast to coast, the automotive industries bought the streetcar companies up and then closed them down, leaving the public no choice but to buy cars or take rubber-tired buses which the same industries also manufactured.

The fruits of a century of asphalt are now with us. Our highways and city streets have become the single largest source of greenhouse gases and the principal drain on city taxes. For cities, between 25 and 50 per cent of the municipality's annual budget is now devoted to road construction and maintenance.

Ottawa spends about 26 per cent of its budget ($600 million every year) on roads. This $600 million doesn't include snow clearance. To put that $600 million in perspective, we spend about $20 million total on community and cultural infrastructure — that's all of our rinks, parks, community centers, theatres.

The $600 million is only the direct costs. In my city 30 people are killed each year by motor vehicles and about 2,500 are seriously injured. To put faces on those deaths and injuries, imagine a young man running for a bus. He's 21 years old, in his third year at university. He's popular and hard working, and his life is snuffed out by a car going the legal speed. The driver had timed his crossing of the intersection "just right" to reach the light just as it changed from red to green. The young man seeing the cars stopped at the intersection was running for the bus and never anticipated a car reaching the intersection at full throttle. What price do you put on this death?

Think of a young man standing on a street corner waiting for a bus. He and his wife have a three-month-old daughter. An SUV jumps the curb and crushes his spinal cord. He will spend a year in and out of the hospital. He will not walk again. This is just one of the deaths and one of the injuries that occurred in my ward last year.

Nationwide, 3,000 people are killed on Canadian roads every year and 220,000 injured. This is "normal." No one pays it much attention. Deaths and injuries from car accidents are like bad weather. People just accept them as part of life. In the United States, it's about 50,000 deaths each year (more than the number of Americans killed in the Vietnam War), and about three million are injured.

It's all connected. If city councils had not collapsed in front of the automotive lobby and kept their electric streetcars; if national governments had funded inter-urbans instead of interstate highways or had at least provided rail companies with rail lines as they have provided the car companies with roads, North America would be a different place today. Our cities would be configured more like European ones. There would be less mall sprawl. The air would be cleaner, global warming less threatening, highways and urban arterials fewer; Middle East oil less important and Saddam Hussein just another, distant tin pot dictator.

It's all connected and the connections come together in the political arena — at the City Hall Council Table, in the federal, provincial and state assemblies. It's complicated and it's not complicated at all.

City councils set land development policies, and the federal government sets oil and drug policies. That's why you never see oil or pharmaceutical money funding municipal political campaigns, and you never see land developers funding federal campaigns. The corporations put their lobby money where it buys the influence required. It's got absolutely nothing to do with supporting the democratic process and everything to do with increasing profits for mall sprawl, pharmaceuticals, health care and oil companies by ensuring that government provide direct public subsidies, protected access to markets and various insulations against competition.

The climate change message coming from the many activists in the environmental movement hasn't penetrated the corridors of city hall, parliament or congress with any real force because there's no advantage to the oil, forestry, pharmaceuticals or developers, and they're the folks who fund the political process. On the other hand, war is good business. Bell Helicopter made billions on the Vietnam War as Haliburton is doing on the Iraq, and developers make billions from malls.

◆ ◆ ◆

What does the future hold for our old urban villages? There are both hopeful signs and fearful ones, and the signs are in about equal proportion. On the hopeful side: after years of neglect developers are building downtown again, and much of it is high-end housing. It's always been my feeling the best protection for the downtown was high property values. Expressways don't cut through neighborhoods with million dollar homes. These road "improvements" are reserved for poor neighborhoods.

We are all born into the world alone and we leave it the same way. Whether one finishes one's days with the serene discipline that Pierre Trudeau did by simply repeating the Lord's Prayer or one dies on a street from the savage impact of a careening car, one exits alone. Nothing changes the separateness of one's departure. But between those bookends of birth and death, the kind of community in which a life is lived will have a great deal to say about the quality of individual life, the city and ultimately the planet. Life in an urban village is very different from one based on housing tracts, vast parking lots and big box stores.

The purpose of government has not changed since Aristotle first said it should enable members of society to live a full life, individually and collectively. This notion captures the meaning of both our short lives and the longer run of the human race. Athens was a place where the life of the individual and the life of the city were not split into separate places. Theater, sculpture, music, poetry, business, athletics and philosophy were part of the city's life and part of the individual's life. A great temple like the Parthenon belonged to each citizen and to the city as a whole at the same time.

Aristotle's Athens was not privatized. Men made money in the rough and tumble of the marketplace — contracting, buying and selling shares just as they do today — but the activities of the marketplace did not act to disconnect them from the public domain. Rather it was the reverse. Great success in business enabled them to be more vigorous citizens of the Republic of Athens. Like two legs of a human being, a city and a society need both the public leg and the private leg to walk straight. They are different and apart, but attached to the same trunk. The city of Athens was that trunk. It was a place where eccentrics like Socrates had the leisure to be cranky and brilliant, where polymaths like Aristotle could prosper as schoolmasters, where playwrights like Aristophanes could write and perform, where politicians like Pericles could cobble together the fragile alliances necessary to drive the public agenda and canny businessmen could conduct the commercial life necessary for individual and collective prosperity.

Urban villages clustered around old streetcar lines are not classical Athens. There is no magnificent Acropolis at the center, but there are still agoras — places where public life and public spaces still have priority. In an urban village it's possible to walk to a café, to run in a park, to see a film, to visit a library, to attend a play, to go to a church, to sit in a pub or open an office door without first opening a car door and driving. In an urban village the life of the individual and the life of the community constantly, naturally intertwine.

The liveliness of a streetcar ward, the liveliness of Copenhagen (voted Europe's most friendly and humane city) and the liveliness of ancient Athens are all connected by their urban landscapes which in their essentials have not changed in 2,500 years. It isn't very complicated — a series of mixed use urban blocks, spiked with small formal and informal village squares at intersections, with the principal commercial streets forming the ribs of the entire city. This is how Pompeii worked, how Athens worked and how the Glebe where I live works. Small neighborhood-scale development is combined with a few grand, public places which are the focus of the entire city. The grander place in Athens was the Acropolis; in Pompeii, it was the Coliseum. The "coliseum" in my ward would be Lansdowne Park, a stadium seating 35,000 people.

Whether this is accomplished in a planned way as it has been in Copenhagen where it is required that residences and businesses are built in close proximity and small public squares must be included in each block, or whether it occurs by accident as it has in the streetcar wards of Ottawa, the effects are the same. These are the kinds of neighborhoods that rest easy on the soul of the individual and the planet. For in their quiet success, you can find one of the keys to a more sustainable planet. In an urban village individuals can lead diverse and interesting lives with very little financial means. And urban villages are cheap to run because almost every inch of space pays some sort of tax: on-street parking fees, multiple unit residential taxes, small and medium sized business taxes and entertainment taxes. They generate tax-to-service ratio surpluses year after year. Unfortunately, these surpluses get creamed off and funneled out to the mall-sprawl communities, which generate deficits each year because they don't have the densities necessary to pay for the services they require.

It ain't Planning.
It's Politics.

They see Spadina as a corridor for cars. That is the problem
with planners. They can't see the people.

— Elizabeth Block,
resident of Washington Avenue in Toronto,
a street that intersects with Spadina Avenue

THE OBVIOUS QUESTION that arises is, if these urban villages are so fine why did we stop building them? Why do malls, parking lots and urban "arterials" dominate the city landscape everywhere? If city planners now subscribe to the social and economic advantages of small scale neighborhood life, why do we continue to build traffic sewers to parking lots for malls? Why do we keep the service costs to taxes equation always in the red? It is now more than 40 years since Jane Jacobs wrote her immensely successful book *The Death and Life of Great American Cities* describing in wonderful detail the efficiencies and the joys of old streetcar neighborhoods.[1] It was based on Greenwich Village in New York, a neighborhood which functions like the central neigborhoods of Toronto where streetcars still roll down the streets and where 40 years ago, Elizabeth Block spoke the words cited above.

What happened?

The argument is often made that the answer can be found in good planning versus bad planning. If lack of good planning was the problem, we would have at least some cities where the city planners had had sufficient understanding to not girdle their cities with miles of freeways, big and bigger malls and parking lots. Such a city does not exist. All that exists are variations in scale. Manhattan is the largest urban village on the planet — still based on the old streetcar lines. Like Ottawa, it also began as a series of streetcar wards. It is now surrounded just as Ottawa is by malls, parking lots and miles of suburban carpet — but because Manhattan is on an island, a ring of water protects it instead of a ring expressway.

The same can be said of the city centers of San Francisco, New Orleans, Toronto and Montreal and any other 19th/early 20th-century city you might want to pick. All that differs between these great cities and my own smaller one is the size and extent of the inner villages versus the outer sprawl. The size of Ottawa's old central city neighborhoods hasn't changed since 1960 when the streetcars were ripped up. Like every other city's central area it has gotten progressively smaller and more fragile relative to the suburbs and exurbs belting it. Each year, the cityscape becomes less dense and more sprawling. Each year more books are published on why this is not a good idea, but the bad idea continues. It continues because people are looking in the wrong place for the solutions.

Knowledge is not the problem; the political system is.

Here is a little development story from Ottawa to illustrate how sprawl politics works, but it can be transferred to any other North American city. There are thousands of acres of still undeveloped land relatively close to our city center. They aren't very prepossessing: mostly low wetlands fit for cow pastures, bird life and slow-running streams. That's about it. Several large developers have owned the wetlands and cow pastures behind the airport for years paid for by the rents and profits from their city properties. These lowlands were bought up for a few hundred dollars an acre years ago in anticipation that sooner or later they would be serviced with city sewer pipes because they are quite close to the city center.

But in this case, unlike other green fields around the city and in spite of pressure from the developers, the city council delayed and delayed on getting the sewer hookups installed. They had good reasons to delay. The federal government had an old and very toxic chemical waste dump in the area, which could only be contained from migrating its toxins by installing a filtration plant right over the site to constantly filter the toxic ground water as it welled up. Further there was some evidence that the dump's toxins were migrating along underground channels in spite of the remedial measures the federal government had taken.

Several expensive studies were completed and the evidence was not overwhelming that the toxins were migrating, but it was also clear the site was loaded with dangerous carcinogens that would migrate more easily once sewer pipes were laid because pipes provide natural gravity-fed underground pathways. There was also an argument that once the water table was lowered by the proposed housing developments, that it would be more difficult to prevent the toxins from roaming. It took many years to get this sorted out, and for many people it never was.

The environmentalists led by the Sierra Club continued to argue against the development for these and many other good reasons. There was a Class I bog in the area which contains, among other things, a large heron rookery, endangered plant species and is the eastern part of the province's premier carbon sink, i.e., an area that both stores a great deal of carbon dioxide and absorbs carbon from the atmosphere. It was the Sierra Club's contention that urban development by lowering the water table would cause the bog to dry up and release carbon into the air aggravating greenhouse gases and reducing the quality of the air for the entire city.

And there were other problems more directly linked to the city's pocketbook. The land, although close to the center of the city as the crow flies, was jammed behind the airport and pinned between a river and the bog with very few roads to serve it. It was clear there was no easy way to build new roads as the routes were blocked by both the airport and the bog. Furthermore, there was zero public transit. To make it work, the city would have to build a light rail line and widen rural roads at great expense, which would inevitably dump into city roads that were not possible to widen. So it was a costly, environmentally challenged development situation.

It was also the last green route out of the city for cyclists.

The nail in the coffin should have been that there were plenty of tract house alternatives elsewhere around the city. We weren't out of space for housing.

So what happened?

Developers aren't stupid. It was clear that a strong, popular coalition of environmentalists, transit advocates and fiscal conservatives were starting to form around the idea of not developing this area. Unless something was done quickly, city council might not be manipulated to vote in the normal way — which was to approve the developers request to provide the area with sewer and water pipes. Unless they moved fast this decision might be delayed indefinitely, leaving them stuck with their original investments in cheap bog and scrub pasture. It was not a happy thought.

The principal developers began to work city hall corridors quietly and diligently to convince city council to bring forward "an early servicing agreement" to fast track city services to their green fields behind the airport — before a new Official Plan was in place. Time was of the essence, they said. The city needed more cheap housing. This was the perfect place, "so close to downtown." The developers also worked the media.

Everything was fine. Dykes would be built to protect the central bog area so that it wouldn't drain toward the housing. Brand new studies showed there was no evidence of toxic migration. It was pointed out no farmers or local residents had ever been reported sick in the area from waterborne pathogens.

The developers would even be handing over "free of charge" some of their land to maintain the central bog that had been designated as "protected," just to be absolutely sure the "core wetland" area was protected.

Their traffic studies showed that the present road network was perfectly capable of carrying the traffic. What more could reasonable people do?

The pressure was ratcheted up. I had a pleasant young man in my office pitching the development. He explained to me very earnestly how the present road system wasn't at capacity and would be just fine for the foreseeable future. The city wouldn't have to invest in any new roads or public transit. And all this stuff about migrating toxins was hysteria. He was a very amiable, pleasant guy.

Result? The vote for the early servicing agreement was 19 councillors for, three against. It was probably just a coincidence that the three councillors that voted "no" to the early servicing agreement didn't accept money from developers for their election campaigns.

City sewer and clean water pipes are all a developer ever needs to make vast profits. It's not the cost of the local pipes to hook the houses up to that's the cost problem: that's peanuts. It's access to the city filtration plants which are billion-dollar operations no developer can bear. Once the developer has access to a city's filtered water, who cares if the ground water is toxic? The water is piped in clean from elsewhere. Besides if anything goes wrong such as flooded basements or invasive toxins it will be the public who will be liable not the developer — because it was the city which approved the development in the first place. It doesn't matter if all the studies and pressure were developer-driven. If the city didn't trust the developer's reports, they shouldn't have approved the development.

And once the developer gets their approval for the pipes, they're gone. We never see them again. They get all the gravy, and the city gets all the costs and the liabilities. It's a win-win-win situation for the developer and a lose-lose-lose situation for the city.

It will be the city who will face the new homeowners when they march on City Hall demanding they receive the adequate roads, schools, transit, policing, paramedics and recreation facilities that their new community requires. After all, they are taxpayers! It will be the city which has to deal with any public health issue over migrating toxins.

This is the way North American cities have always grown. My Ottawa example is small change compared to what has happened in California, where versions of the same process have carpeted much of the state with housing and made millionaires out of land specula-tors who bought up orange groves.

And where are we now with our brand new development south of the airport? City council is busy approving $75 million in immediate local rural road expansions and $200 million in light rail. Remember how there was plenty of road capacity when we approved the fast tracking, a scant six years ago?

And that's just on the road and transit side of the green field equation. The bills for new schools, community centers, parks, police and fire haven't even been calculated yet. The tax–to-service ratio here is right off the scale. In this case, for every dollar we collect in the green field area we've got to find ten elsewhere. The flooding basements have already begun although the underground toxins haven't reported in yet.

Welcome to city politics.

◆ ◆ ◆

I will never forget my first "development charges" debate at city council. Development charges are the taxes a city bills a developer to build on land which has been zoned urban. Developers are charged for the money required for local roads, sewer hookups and some con-tributions towards the larger roads. The idea originally came from the development industry so they could "pay for" the costs of devel-opment. It was the great racehorse owner and breeder E.P. Taylor who first pitched development charges to Toronto City Council when he came asking for city pipes to his farm outside of Toronto, now called Don Mills. His pitch was exactly the same one developers make today. Nothing has changed. Just give me the city water pipes, and I'll pay for the local roads, house hook-ups to city water, and I'll throw in some money for a community center too. "The city won't have to pay a cent".

Fifty years on, most city councillors still choose to believe this no-cost pitch.

The reality is that 70 percent of cow pasture growth is funded by taxes from the developed parts of the city where the services have been paid for, but the residents have kept on paying their water taxes, their energy taxes, school taxes, and so on creating a surplus. The oldest parts of the city pay the most because the tax surplus they generate is only fractionally re-invested in their neighborhoods. In this way, the bulk of the city surplus is rolled out to the green fields while the old city is left to rot.

◆ ◆ ◆

In city politics, there are long and passionate debates over tiny issues like wading pool hours for kids in summer, traffic bumps on public streets, and that perennial favorite "arts funding." It's all peanuts, but it makes great headlines. The big stuff blows through very quickly and very efficiently. Sometimes, it is not even debated. It gets carried in the consent part of the agenda with the usual suspects dissenting.

In the debate over development charges that I was involved in — but which is typical of thousands of others across the continent — the city staff had just completed a quarter of a million dollar study in which they concluded developers should pay development charges on a sliding scale depending on where they were building their houses and malls so that the charges reflected the real cost of the development to the city. What this sliding scale meant was that cow pasture development would have the highest charges because it was the most costly to the city. and development in the older parts of the city should have the least because it cost the city the least. A sensible idea.

I have never seen so many lawyers in one room before. The public stands were black with expensive, dark blue suits. The new sliding scale would cost developers $220 million more. This amounted to $220 million worth of pressure on the mayor and the councilors to vote against the staff report. The developers worked the press, and the press complied with stories about how development would stop if we imposed real cost accounting on developers. We would be chasing development away to cities that treated developers reasonably.

Three guesses how the council voted (and the first two don't count).

Council gave the developers what they wanted. We spent about the same time debating development charges as we do on debating summer wading pool hours. Whatever those dark blue suits cost the industry, the investment was cheap.

The city signed on for five more years of subsidizing urban sprawl across the entire region, and more of the endless race to feed transit, police and community services out to the bulging edges of the city. The developers walked out with $220 million in their pockets, and the city continues stumbling from budget year to budget year in a race that can never be won because developers can throw up tract housing faster than cities can ever pay for the services they need. Over the next five years, we would have to fire 500 city employees and slash and burn our way through public health, paramedics and library budgets to finance this $220 million shortfall.

Welcome to city politics.

Until city councils are prepared to push the development industry out of funding city elections, developers will continue to control how cities grow. No matter how many wonderful books Jane Jacobs wrote about the economies of cities.

How we build cities is a statement about the way city elections work, not any environmental, planning or fiscal logic.

The same rule applies to national and global priorities. The foreign, cultural, environmental and trading policies of nations have more to do with the millions that the oil industries, pharmaceuticals, agribusiness and manufacturing corporations invest in political campaigns than the wishes of the electorate. For example, it is impossible to believe that when the Canadian federal government financed an east-west natural gas pipeline for private American interests in the mid fifties and then handed the delivery and profits from this massive natural resource to a Texas company that this had anything to do with the wealth and health of Canadians.

Nor does it matter much what government is in power. In the 1950s it was the Liberals who gave away Canadian natural gas and made Canada a servant of an unregulated North American market that has consistently moved prices for natural gas up. This government at the same time made it impossible for there to be a coherent "made in Canada" energy policy. A "made in Canada" policy could have balanced electrical and natural gas supplies, instead of allowing them to destructively compete as they do in the US. Welcome to the national version of city politics.

Thirty years later another federal government (this time it was Conservative) removed the government's ability to regulate prices at the wellhead and signed NAFTA, which now makes it impossible for the Canadian government to limit natural gas exports.

The profits which natural gas and waterfalls generate makes the wealth of the Pharaohs look like a hot dog stand. Clearly, drinking water is the next great North American battleground, and it is just as clear that any national government which is serious about interposing itself between those profits and the private interests who wish to control them will not remain in power. My prediction is simple. If we don't get corporate funding out of all election campaigns, city, provincial and federal, Canadian governments will sell off our water and hydroelectric resources. In fact, it's already begun. Three Ontario hydro dams built and managed by the public for decades and their associated electrical generating stations were sold by the province's previous Conservative government.

There is no western interest or significant military presence in Burundi, Malawi or Rwanda because there are no oil or minerals in these countries. In contrast, there are oil, diamonds and other natural resources in Nigeria, Iraq and Saudi Arabia; hence the western military and corporate structure is present to ensure that compliant national governments are in place so that the resources may be controlled and extracted at prices congenial to corporate profits.

If you harbor any doubts about what inspired the Iraq invasion, check out the pristine shape the Iraq Ministry of Oil has remained in after hundreds of missiles have been launched at every corner of the country. Compare the oil industry's condition to Iraqi museums, electrical generating stations, hospitals and civic buildings that the invasion forces either blew up or couldn't find the time to protect. It was the oil wells, pipelines and refineries that were described in the western press as the "crown jewels" of Iraq and which the "Coalition Forces" raced to protect — and did. The rest of Iraq was collateral damage. Thus Iraqi guerrillas attempt to blow up their own refineries and pipelines because they know they are the only things the invaders value.

If you are still unconvinced that the electoral donations by private interests don't control how cities grow and determine the policies of national governments, then I've got some shares for a bridge in Brooklyn to sell you.

8

Citizenship versus Faithship

> *Children are our terrorists-to-be because they are so obviously not our citizens-to-come. How can this starkly asymmetrical globalization, one that entails such slow suffering, such deliberately paced violence be anything other than fertile ground for recruiting terrorists?*
>
> — Benjamin R. Barber,
> *Jihad vs. McWorld*

AFTER ENGLISH AND FRENCH, Arabic is the most frequently spoken language in Ottawa. New Canadians from all over the Arab world are an important part of our new city.

This week of 9/11 I was invited with Howard Hampton, the leader of the provincial New Democratic party and another city politician to a mosque. It wasn't one of the grand mosques that Ottawa can now claim as its own, but a humble one in the suburbs of the city. You could drive by it many times and never know it was there. I had never been in a mosque before so it was all new to me. On entering, I removed my shoes. The women worship separately, in this case downstairs and the men upstairs. Much of the ceremony was in Arabic so I had plenty of time to reflect on the service and what it meant to me.

What struck me most of all was how universal the basic elements of religious worship are. The imam held his hands flat, palm out when he was praying, just as a Catholic priest does at the altar. There was a familiar sense of humility people always have when gathered to think about their own small place in the universe. Sitting on the floor and bowing seemed simple and graceful to me and not that much different from Catholics gathered in straight pews, standing and kneeling on their prayer benches as the mass and prayer requires. The imam referred to "brothers and sisters in Islam" just as the Catholic priests refer to "brothers and sisters in Christ."

I was attending not as a religious person but as a secular political leader, and I listened attentively to the imam's sermon. He talked about the need for balance in mind and words, to be careful not to say anything inflammatory either in private or in public. The World Trade Center was never mentioned, but the images of those flaming buildings were in everyone's inner eye. The tension in the room was palpable, and it was clear when the imam referred to "our brothers and sisters in Afghanistan" that there was a powerful connection for the congregation.

I was glad that this congregation had thought to invite us to worship with them. These are not easy times for anyone, but they are the hardest for Canadians of the Muslim faith. In our city a young boy was beaten to death by his classmates because he was seen as an enemy; another is in intensive care. At least two men in the congregation felt they had just lost their jobs because of who they were, not what they could do.

At the end of the service, as it came my turn to speak, I found that I could not say anything. I was caught by so many different conflicting emotions that I did not know how to make sense of them. And so I minded what the young imam had said and thought it best to keep quiet, thinking it was better not to speak if what I had to say was not very carefully considered.

I am a secular city leader. I am not a religious leader. There are no brothers and sisters in Christ or Islam for me. My congregation are just "citizens." I was elected to defend the rights of all the citizens of my city. No group comes before any other. No group is more or less important than another. The citizens who elected me, be they Arab or Italian, French or English, matters not. It is their citizenship in my city which counts first for me, not their religion. But as I stood at the front of the mosque, I remained silent because such was the emotion of the moment that I was uncertain how to put this thought into words without offending people. So I said nothing.

The one thing that I am confident of is that neither the Taliban nor Osama bin Laden can defeat the United States. Only the United States can defeat the United States. It is the most powerful nation that has ever existed. With the push of a few buttons it can destroy entire continents. But what "terrorists" can do is provoke the United States into creating conditions in which civic, civilized discourse is no longer possible and the world becomes a place where people's religion comes before their civic attachments.

There is an enormous divide between the sacred and the secular. Secular democratic nations have always been founded on the principle of citizenship, not religious or ethnic allegiance. The day that religious leaders no longer invite their local politicians to worship with them in their mosques, churches and holy places will be the day that the common foundation of civic engagement crumbles. Democracy will no longer be possible, leaving the thugs and terrorists to reign.

The peoples of Europe have seen their cathedrals, their most handsome buildings and their populations destroyed by religious and ethnic violence many times. Religious wars went on for decades in both Germany and France and killed millions. Fifty million died in the Second World War. Fortunately, life in the larger sense went on. Wars are as old as time, but what has resulted from the World Trade Center attack is more than one nation or one ethnic group trying to conquer another. It is about something more fundamental: religious versus commercial values, the role of religion and the relationship of the citizen to the State. This is far more than one nation invading another. Such contests of values require no submarines, no tanks, no conventional armies. And with every cruise missile launched, with every picture of a child burned and bleeding in a hospital, with every innocent person killed no matter where or on whose side, that eternal enemy — chaos — comes a step closer.

For no city, no nation, not even the most powerful, can survive a populace where large numbers of people are convinced that religious attachment trumps citizenship. This is what bin Laden wants, and this is what the western leaders will give him if they do not turn their attention to creating a world government and local democracies which represent the popular will instead of armed coalitions backing special interests. A renegade Saudi millionaire hiding in a Himalayan cave is not someone to be feared, but what he can persuade others to do in his name is terrifying. We can feed his call to violence or take it away by reacting with courage, conviction and justice for all. Bombing an impoverished country from great distance is none of these things. Bin Laden has orchestrated billions of dollars in carnage and with a little help from America's military ruined millions of lives. The psalmists were right. Violence begets violence.

The Persian Gulf War turned Osama bin Laden from an ally into an enemy of America. Without the Persian Gulf War, Osama bin Laden would have remained just another disconnected veteran of the Afghan-Soviet war. The Persian Gulf War precipitated the World Trade Center attacks, and 9/11 triggered an invasion of Iraq. None of it would have happened if President Bush, the First, hadn't seen it necessary to protect the oil pipeline from the Middle East to the gas pumps of America and for that job President Bush had plenty of allies. Richard Nixon found a sympathetic response when he wrote in the New York Times that securing America's oil interests abroad was sufficient reason to go to war. But securing oil interests has created a domino effect none of these worthies ever anticipated. Instead of security, it has created massive insecurity.

It was all about oil. Without oil, Iraq's invasion of Kuwait would have been a Middle East version of Indonesia invading East Timor, little lamented and much ignored. Every time I take another look at the costs of the care and feeding of the automobile, I find another surprising piece in the massive jigsaw of public costs. We are building an old folks home in my ward. A single parking place in the basement costs $22,000 a slot to build; that's about the same as the down payment on one of the apartments the car will serve and yet, it's taken as a perfectly normal thing to do. In fact, city bylaws require developers to build parking slots for every apartment in their buildings. How can any form of public transit compete with this kind of subsidy? What if apartment builders were required to contribute millions for the construction of public transit? I imagine that subsidy would cause outrage, but this auto parking subsidy is regarded as perfectly normal.

This is what Eric Schlosser in *Fast Food Nation* says about the trashing of the American light rail system. "General Motors eventually persuaded other companies that benefited from road building to help pay for the costly takeover of America's trolleys. In 1947...GM, Mack Truck, Firestone and Standard Oil of California were all found guilty on one of the two counts by the federal jury.... The executives who had secretly plotted and carried out the destruction of America's light rail network were fined a few dollars each. And the post war reign of the automobile proceeded without further challenge."[1] This may sound like ancient unrelated history, but here is the connection to terrorists in 2003. If the public interest had been placed first in 1947, North American cities would be denser, more pedestrian friendly and much less reliant on oil. The World Trade Center horror had its roots in a great deal more than "good guys" versus "bad guys." People willing to end their lives for a cause don't just erupt out of the ground like dandelions after rain. They come from a place that has its own logic and its own raison d'être. There are clear connections between how we live and the reactive chains which led to the violence of the World Trade Center. President Bush, the Second, may not like the message that millions of people find the voracious consumption of the planet's resources by the richest part of the world objectionable, but that's a reality whether he cares to face it or not.

At the mosque that day, the worried men sitting in front of me, row on row of anxious faces, wanted me to explain what was happening. They wanted someone to make sense of the fear and community rejection they were feeling. In my head, I saw again the man and woman holding hands plunging feet first down the face of a New York skyscraper. The photograph caught them so that it looked like they were walking on air and succeeding, but the man's tie flying straight back gave him away. The couple were seconds away from eternal silence.

The disappearance of electric streetcars from North America and the emergence of global oil cartels to serve automobiles are not an easy thing to connect to the spiritual life of mosques when images of men and women falling to their deaths are dancing in your head. So that day I followed the imam's advice, kept my peace and prayed. I prayed that the young imam would always feel he could invite city politicians into his mosque to pray with him. I prayed that politicians would always humbly and gratefully attend. I prayed for democracy.

PART II

The Idea of Progress and Why We Got it Wrong

Every great city is a world treasure, not a national treasure. So the destruction of any one of them is a planetary catastrophe.

— Kurt Vonnegut,
Fates Worse than Death

FROM SAN FRANCISCO TO VENICE, from Dakar to New Orleans, from Toulouse to Ottawa, the cities of the world are all in the same global soup. This was both liberating and unnerving to discover. Liberating because, as a city councilor, I began to grasp that local solutions — if shared by other cities — can have a grand global impact. Unnerving because bringing enough people into the same idea tent to make a difference is difficult to imagine.

The Italian urban ideas of "slow growth" and "slow food" can have a global impact, but how do these new ideas overcome entrenched ways of fast growth and fast foods that have been part of the fabric of sprawl growth for generations? How can the Mayors for Peace movement led by the Mayor of Hiroshima unbuckle the vested interests of the international military-industrial complex? No one has been able to accomplish these things so far.

It began to be clear that the starting place for creating secure and sustainable cities was something so basic that it had to do with reformatting the way we think. We need to redefine what we think of as "progress" because without a new consensus about what progress is, mall sprawl will just keep rolling out across the countryside like a carpet. The principal way people now imagine living is making money, getting a big house in the best suburban neighborhood possible, owning a couple of SUVs and flying south for a winter holiday. This is the mentality that drives all urban growth, and as long as it's the dominant view of living, trying to contain it is like trying to put a halter on a wild elephant.

We need to change the elephant, not find a new halter. Part II is about thinking differently about life and about progress. We need to do this because we can't change the sprawl growth formula without changing the way we think the good life can be attained.

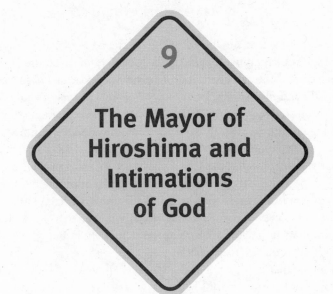

9

The Mayor of Hiroshima and Intimations of God

*Saddako died a long time ago now. If she had lived, she
would be the same age as I am now. She left us a few years
after the bomb was dropped of cancer caused by radiation,
and now all of the survivors are beginning to leave us. Soon,
none will be left. One of the things that I promised to do
when I was elected was that I would take their message
around the world; that they did not want to see any people
go through what they have been through. That is why I am
here today. They don't think the world should have nuclear
bombs and I don't think so either.*

— Mayor Akiba, Hiroshima, Japan

*Man is quite insane. He wouldn't know how to create a
maggot, but he creates Gods by the dozen.*

— Montaigne 1533–1592

WHEN I WAS IN ELEMENTARY SCHOOL living in St. John's,
Newfoundland, B-52s from the American bases would regularly rumble across the sky over the town. Newfoundland was at the
time one of the American staging grounds for an air attack on the
Soviet Union. I have vivid memories of looking up from playing
marbles with my little buddies and watching the planes' dark forms
growling across the sky like vast mechanical moths.

Looking back at the distant image of the little boy gazing up at the sky, I can remember that he understood very well that these great planes carried the same kind of nuclear bombs that had obliterated Nagasaki and Hiroshima. I can remember the tremors of fear at the idea of our own little town being blown up in some unimaginable exchange of bombs. But most of the time the little boy ignored the B-52s and the possibility of imminent extinction. B-52s, the Cold War, the Soviet Union, the US — they were just part of the way life was composed. A little boy could do nothing about these constellations of power any more than he could affect the arrangement of the stars, so he accepted them and got on with playing marbles with his friends, playing hockey, singing in the school choir and all the fine things that made life worthwhile.

This is what human beings have always done when unspeakable horror invades ordinary life. This is what Plato and Socrates did about slavery. Neither of these philosophers could imagine life without slavery and consequently neither of them spent any time thinking about it. Slavery had been around for a long time. Civilized life depended on the work of slaves, and the great philosophers both turned their faces and sensibilities away from it. Yet slavery is an unspeakably ugly diminution of humanity both for the enslaved and the enslaving.

We have now lived with the unthinkable — the destruction of entire cities and perhaps the planet itself — for more than half a century. The collapse of the Soviet Union and the end of the Cold War has changed nothing. In fact, there are many who believe the extraordinary proliferation of nuclear weapons has increased the possibility of someone, somewhere pushing a nuclear button and triggering millions of deaths both in the initial attack and the even more terrifying response. And we all accept this possibility tranquilly as part of the price of our modern existence just as that little boy did staring up at the sky over St. John's.

Nuclear weapons and the rape of the planet are regarded by most people as the price of our collective existence. Just as Aristotle and Plato could not imagine civilized existence without thousands of human beings in chains to keep the mines, farms and cities humming, we cannot imagine modern life without millions of men and women devoted to "protecting" our lives by being prepared to destroy the lives of millions of others or in the simple, everyday assault on the planet's ecosystems. The rapid exhaustion of our underground aquifers, the exhaustion of oil, natural gas, forests and prairies continue because we cannot imagine it otherwise. We accept all this because we think civilization and modernity require it.

It's all connected to the ordinary lives that we lead in my city. We have become dependent on a global production line which discounts costs to the health of the planet from the point of origin to the point of sale. But someone or something, somewhere, is always paying a nasty price for our "deep discounts."

As the sun goes down on my life, it all seems remarkably clear. There are two concepts of God that people have decided to accept. One is God as a gatekeeper, the God of Abraham and Isaac. This God is standing on guard for us against godless behavior such as homosexual relationships, cursing and apostasy. The Gatekeeper God creates rules, and if you play well by them you should become honored on earth and then happy in heaven. This is the kind of God that fundamentalists of all types worship. This God divides the world into good and evil; into those who are "saved" and those who are not; into those who follow God's verbal rules and those who do not. This is the world of the "rule enforcers": the priests who with tears in their eyes burned heretics during the inquisition to "save" them from polluting others with their refusal to believe and act in the right way. This is the world of the patriarchy where men have one set of rules and women another. This is the world of lawful and unlawful sexuality.

Then there is the concept of a God who doesn't stand at heaven's gate waiting to separate the "saved" from the "damned." This God is more like a verb, a verb of creation. In this intimation of God, it is impossible to imagine discriminating against someone because of a different religion, or who they are sleeping with, because in a world that is governed by the idea of God as a verb, humans are all connected to the essential creative force. We are all part of it. The old porcupine who lumbers across the road on a warm summer day, looking hot and cranky, is part of it. The rocks which thrust up from the earth weathered and impenetrable are part of it. The smell of fresh basil in a salad is part of it. This God leaves no one and nothing out.

It is impossible for the followers of this intimation of God to imagine treating someone poorly because of their skin color because to do so would be to discriminate against yourself. This is a concept of God which makes love very easy, but it doesn't make everything suddenly comprehensible. How could the world be easily comprehensible when it is entirely possible there is not just one world, but many worlds? When one looks up at the vastness of the sky on a summer night with its unimaginable distances, its billions of stars and planets, it seems ridiculous to think that all creation is limited to the life that we see around us on our little planet. Surely, God has more imagination than that.

In this intimation of God, how do malignant cancer cells fit? I understand things eating things. In the end, everything eats everything. Plants eat sunlight and carbon dioxide and from this create oxygen which mammals in their turn consume. Wolves eat lambs to create wolf cubs. Lambs eat grass which eats sunlight and carbon dioxide and so on. But malignant cancer cells destroy their hosts entirely. Where do the malignant cells go once their hosts have disappeared? Where is the eternal round here?

Does it have something to do with Verb God liking change? Killing the host entirely is a clumsy way to accomplish change, but change can be forced simply by destroying what exists. Change has always been part of God's world.

We live as our imaginations permit us. What we can't imagine, we can't accomplish. As Einstein once said, "imagination is more important than knowledge" because without imagination, you can't use knowledge. We create ourselves as we imagine we can be created. This is the world of the Verb God. It is a safe and comforting God because it is an inclusive God. It is an intimation of God that belongs to all of us; we can all share this God in the rituals of our different churches and religions. This God has one rule: "love thy neighbor as thyself." The rest we have to invent for ourselves.

The Gatekeeper God is a much harder God in the short term. This notion of God requires constant vigilance that God's gate is being attended to. It requires supervision by rule keepers and promise keepers, and it is filled with fear, because like a trip switch that may be inadvertently set off, you never know when the capricious forces of "evil" are going to be unleashed by someone not attending to God's rules.

The Gatekeeper God has no problem with cancers that destroy their hosts or nuclear weapons that destroy those whom they are supposed to protect. Armageddon and climate change are fine because the "saved" will always be fine. So while difficult to attend to in the short term, the Gatekeeper God and his inscrutable purposes holds great comfort in the longer term, because in the long term the "saved" will be gathered together happily on God's shore.

When Mayor Akiba of Hiroshima came to Ottawa on his whirlwind tour across North America looking for support for his Mayors for Peace initiative to ban all nuclear weapons by the year 2020, he did not speak using the language of any God, of the saved or the damned or rules that must be followed. He spoke simply on behalf of the survivors of the Hiroshima nuclear explosion. He spoke on behalf of the dead like Saddako, the little girl who made a thousand paper cranes in the hopes that her wish might come true and she might not die from the "atom bomb disease."

I listened to him speak to a classroom of school children in my ward. I was very proud to be with him and proud to be a Canadian. Canada had had the capacity to develop the nuclear bomb almost as quickly as the United States. Canadians could have been easily swept along with the US enthusiasm for this new weapon and developed a well-stocked nuclear arsenal. Instead, after seeing the monstrous consequences in Hiroshima and Nagasaki, Canada was the first nation to say "no," to say we didn't want nuclear weapons. We would make do with a conventional military force to defend our nation, and that decision did send a message around the world that many nations heard and heeded. South Africa is the most recent example of a nation with the capacity to build nuclear weapons which has also said no.

We need more local leaders like Mayor Akiba and more world leaders like Lester Pearson and Nelson Mandela to repeat with steady conviction that the use of nuclear weapons is a human rights issue, not a military one. No government has the right to kill millions of people "to defend" its boundaries. A nuclear bomb is not a defensive military weapon; it's an instrument of worldwide terror.

We need more people to say that nuclear weapons will not protect us from anything. Armies of every kind are mostly about safeguarding the privileges of elites; the bigger the weapons, the bigger the elite. Real security and real protection from disaster requires the kinds of powers that cities cultivate every day: the power to provide abundant clean water, electric power, to store and deliver food, to deliver public health and medical services. These very ordinary things are what people need in their daily lives and when disaster strikes, not nuclear weapons. Our greatest weapon against terrorists is social justice. Social justice starves terror, injustice feeds it.

We need less people praying to God to "save" us and more people imagining God has already given us the keys to paradise. It is called earth — our cities, our farms, our lives — and we're here to cultivate and care for them together. God won't do this for us or save us from our own destructive impulses. It's up to us.

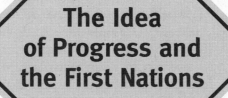

**The Idea
of Progress and
the First Nations**

*The basic premise on which this book is constructed – is that human beings
exist wholly within nature as part of the natural order in every respect.*

— Jane Jacobs,
The Nature of Economies

*When I raise my eyes to the morning sun.
Let me not forget my Grandmother Mi'kmaq.
Let me not forget that all the bruises,
defeats and humiliations of the Mi'kmaq people are my defeats,
my humiliations, that I wear them like rags around my soul.
Let me not forget that all her grace, her beauty, her courage are also mine.
Let me not forget to honour the memory of my Grandmother Mi'kmaq.
Let me not forget that without her I am nothing
but the movement of the wind that brushes the earth.
Let me not forget to honour her in the conduct of my days.*

— "Grandmother Mi'kmaq's Spirit Song"
from *Soul Stones,* an unpublished manuscript

MY CITY LIKE MANY OTHERS is named after a First Nation, the Ottawa, which is an English corruption of an Algonquin word "adawa" meaning trader. When the Europeans arrived the Ottawa people controlled the north-south movement of trade goods in the northeast as the Mandan people controlled the north-south trade in the center of the North American continent. From their headquarters on Manitoulin Island in Georgian Bay, the traders traveled each year over a vast territory stretching from present day Lake Michigan to Montreal. Every summer and fall, flotillas of traders' canoes would glide eastwards through Algonquin territory on the Ottawa River. When the French asked the Algonquin what the name of "their" river was, they were told "adawa" after the people who used it for trade. In English "adawa" became Ottawa.

The Ottawa people showed an amazing resilience in the face of the European onslaught. Unlike the Iroquois who were essentially based in towns and agriculture and the Algonquin who were organized around strongly defined hunting territories, the Ottawa cared less about ownership of a territory. They were used to adapting to the quirks of other nations and at the same time remaining resolutely independent. They met the French and began trading with them as they did with others, treating them no differently, and for the French also the Ottawa people quickly became synonymous with trade.

The Ottawa first stepped into the European's awareness in the summer of 1660 when 300 Ottawa traders came paddling down the Ottawa River in a flotilla of 60 canoes laden with a king's ransom in furs. It was valued at 200,000 French livres or about one million dollars. It was this Ottawa flotilla that ignited French interest in the immense wealth of the Canadian interior. The Ottawa themselves, though shrewd and successful at trading among First Nations, had no idea of the immense value Europeans would put on their cargos of furs and literally gave them away for interesting trinkets.

The French used the Ottawa to teach them trade routes and to make the connections that they needed to participate in fur trading directly, and the two peoples became trusted allies each of the other. But towards the end of the 17th century, the traditional trade routes became increasingly difficult to use for the Ottawa. Armed by the British, the Iroquois had begun a long, genocidal war against their traditional Algonquin and Huron enemies. Travel on the old trade routes became perilous. Then, for reasons that remain clouded by the passage of time, the Ottawa decided to abandon not just their trading routes but their villages on Manitoulin Island.

The Ottawa established new communities on the Blanchard River southwest of Detroit, on the shores of Lake Huron and Lake Erie and in northern Ohio where they switched from being traders to becoming successful farmers, but their journeys were not over.

The Ottawa left their name in at least three places, Ottawa, Canada, Ottawa, Ohio and Ottawa, Kansas and have two universities named after them.

In 1830 the Ottawa were forced to leave their land on the Blanchard River. The new settlers from Europe wanted it, and the United States federal government forced them to move west where the land had not yet been appropriated by Europeans. The government promised them land on the Marais de Cynes River in Kansas.

On September 19, 1882, an advance group of 72 men, women and children began the trek by pony and on foot, taking their worldly goods with them. Dogged at first by white traders who wanted their tents and ponies for liquor, they refused the "deal" and stubbornly kept going. It would take two and a half months. It is around 750 miles from Ottawa, Ohio to Ottawa, Kansas.

Happily the Ottawa people discovered that the land assigned them was verdant, the valleys wooded and alive with deer, turkeys and quail. Five years later, another group from Ottawa, Ohio joined them, and for 22 years they made a successful home in Kansas. Another group seems to have returned to Manitoulin Island.

The Ottawa were successful as farmers in Kansas also, but were forced out again when more Europeans caught up with them. Their reservation was appropriated and part of it re-named Ottawa, Kansas. But before they left they struck a "deal" for 20,000 of their reservation acres: Ottawa University promised their children free tuition. This arrangement still stands.

This time, the Ottawa people moved just over the Kansas state boundary into what was then Indian territory and is now Oklahoma. There, they founded another town called Miami, and this place remains the home of the Ottawas of Oklahoma to this day.

The story of the Ottawa experience with the European, including their great rebellion when they came closer than any other First Nation to driving the European flood back, is worth remembering because nations are composed of stories. Nations are nothing more than creations of the human imagination. The physical thing they most resemble is an iceberg. Eighty percent of the iceberg is below the surface forming the platform on which the iceberg stands. If the iceberg platform is not solid, the beautiful flutes of ice which rise towards the sky will turn over and disappear beneath the waves. If a nation's stories are not honest and true and inclusive of all the people that compose it, the national platform is immeasurably weakened. If a nation's platform contains more half truths and absences than honest accounts, then like the iceberg's bold skyline, the nation will not last long before it turns over and disappears into the ocean of time.

◆ ◆ ◆

Unfortunately, it is the European stories which have formed most of the platform on which Canada and the United States stand. One of the most potent stories was first told by the Scottish economist Adam Smith in the 18th century: that individual advantage should come before the collective advantage of aristocratic oligarchies. It was an idea born of its time and place and received a great welcome among both progressive thinkers and ordinary people struggling to make a living against the great estate owners of the day. Adam Smith's story is distinguished by its enduring nature. It has become one of "the" dominant stories of western nations. It is an uplifting story. In a nutshell it says that every individual should have as good a chance at the brass ring as the landed wealthy. Smith's story has become part of the civic and economic canon of western nations. It was this story that made it entirely reasonable for newcomers to simply appropriate aboriginal land, technology and knowledge as the native population was perceived to have an unreasonable share of the wealth of this vast continent.

Bill Gates has made billions not by appropriating Indian land but by appropriating ideas that were once in the public domain spawned by open, freewheeling nonprofits like the Home Brew Clubs in California. Gates realized it wasn't the product that mattered so much as controlling its distribution. His company has been built on controlling the access to and the distribution of software ideas ever since. Microsoft has become the Monsanto of the computer world.

As Gates appropriated Home Brew software ideas, corporations like Monsanto have appropriated "free" biological material from the universe by creating legal patents around the material and then defending those patents in very expensive court cases. They thus control the distribution of what formerly belonged to us all.

Nothing has changed. Oligarchies of all kinds have always tried to limit personal opportunity by appropriating the capacity of individuals to make individual profits. The rich did it in the days of Adam Smith and they do it today. This part of the Smith story remains as true as ever: when individual opportunity becomes too restricted the progress of society itself is compromised.

Today Adam Smith would be arguing against Bill Gates and the Monsanto approach to controlling economies just as in the 18th century, he argued for removing the protective tariffs around corn which favored the largest landowners so that the ordinary tenant farmers would be able to compete on more equal terms. With a more equal competitive field, all of society would benefit from lower prices and more equitably shared profits. Smith was absolutely right in his time and place.

But it is a long jump from this sensible 18th-century idea of fair economic competition to the idea that corporations are also "individuals" and that governments should behave like private corporations. The landed gentry of the 20th and 21st century (the corporate aristocrats) have cleverly managed to use Smith's call for fair competition between individuals and tenant farmers to provide enormous advantage to corporations by putting them on the same legal footing as an individual. This quite brilliant sleight of hand eviscerates the intention of Smith's original idea and has mortally damaged every government's ability to govern by limiting its ability to tax and regulate. It's a very neat psychological reversal of Smith's original idea. It retains the original idea "competition must be as free as possible" while applying it differently and thus reversing its outcome, returning economic and political power from individuals to corporate and political oligarchies.

The political disciples of this modern twist to Adam Smith's original story include Margaret Thatcher, Tony Blair, the Bush family père et fils, Stephen Harper, Mike Harris and Ralph Klein in Canada. Madame Thatcher summarized it most aggressively with her famous adage "there is no such thing as society, there are only individuals." This is nonsense: even bacteria need society. Humans are no different. The hallmark of successful societies and governments is efficient inclusivity: society gets what it needs at a reasonable cost. The hallmark of successful private corporate activity is efficient consumer exclusivity: you sell to those who can afford to buy. These social and consumer worldviews are radically different, operating from different paradigms.

In the social worldview, Athens made Socrates possible. That is why when he was exiled, Socrates considered it a death sentence. Athens could go on without Socrates, but Socrates could not go on without Athens. Without the democratic, tolerant, productive society of Athens there was no stage for Socrates and his discussions, which were the staff of his life. Through the same view, Wayne Gretzky was made possible by Canadian municipal rinks. Cancer cures, radiation, chemotherapy, doctors, automobiles, the entire panoply of services and creative spirits possible in any middle-sized modern city are dependent on people thinking and acting together in a sociable, organized and occupational way.

In the consumer world vision, towns and cities are the result of wonderful individuals and families working hard for their daily bread in individual shops as their parents did, espousing supportive family values. In the consumer worldview, everything can be reduced to "consumer value" and thoughts like "did I get my money's worth?" at the store or from my tax dollar.

In the consumer paradigm, cities are a product you purchase, and when that "product" — a city — isn't working out you move. This consumer model applies to neighborhoods as well as cities. When the neighborhood decays the solution under a consumer worldview is to move another part of the city where the grass is literally greener. And if this suburban edge also declines, you move on out further where things are quieter, cleaner and more orderly. Ultimately the cleaner, more orderly parts of the city become so distant from the original city that the person has effectively changed cities entirely.

◆ ◆ ◆

At the end of the day, nations and cities are just a collection of stories that people use to justify how they lead their lives. Neither the nation nor the city exists like a tree which pushes up from the ground as part of an inexorable biological round. In comparison, cities and nations are ephemeral. They are something we make and unmake together in the course of a few years. Sometimes we get it right and sometimes we don't. The glory that was classical Athens bloomed and faded and bloomed and faded again in the space of a few hundred years, never to emerge again.

Until recently, the great advantage of the human species was, because it was such a non-specialized competitor in so many different areas over such a broad range, there seemed to be endless room to rock and roll. And nowhere were the horizons and the resources as rich or generous as they were in the "New World." The only barriers to the riches of the New World were the "natives" who had, unfortunately for them, a very different vision of how to live together and how land should be used. Not surprisingly these First Nations were displaced quickly with as much aggression as was needed to push them into isolated, unwanted corners. Is this simplistic? Yes, but in its essentials it's exactly what happened and is still happening. If you have any doubts about the historical record read Dee Brown's *Bury My Heart At Wounded Knee*.[1]

In the 21st century the targets may have changed but not the attitudes which prompted the US Seventh Cavalry to rake a campsite of Sioux tents with grapeshot and kill 300 unarmed men, women and children at Wounded Knee. The newcomer to North America is invited to bring the "right values," i.e., work ethic, good health, an entrepreneurial spirit, loyalty to the new country and best of all, lots of money. Canada allows the very rich to jump the immigrant queue and has been especially successful in attracting rich Hong Kong entrepreneurs and financiers. And if international corporations want to "invest" in oil on lands of the Lubicon Cree in Alberta or harvest trees on lands of the Barrier Lake Cree in Quebec, they get the priority and the First Nations are displaced. Very little has changed.

This carnivorous philosophy can't form the basis for a culture or a general population which creates sustainable communities based on careful husbandry of the commonwealth. This is what the original North American population could never understand in their long, sad meeting with Europeans. For although wars between aboriginal nations were as common as grass, the native nations themselves were organized internally on a cooperative model. Yes, plains Sioux warriors fought woodland Cree people, the Iroquois fought the Algonquin-speaking peoples and so on. But these nations were not internally competitive. A Cree child adopted by the Sioux nation would have to learn a different language, a different culture and a different history from his birth nation, but the cooperative fundamentals on which the two societies were organized were similar. Historically no North American First Nation had any experience with a society that was organized to endlessly compete internally, among its own people down to the last buffalo, down to the last spring of water, down to the last fence line.[2] Even today traditional indigenous people retain these values.

In the aboriginal paradigm of a healthy society, it is impossible to conceive of the new zero tolerance law for welfare fraud that is presently in place in Ontario. This law resulted in a pregnant woman named Kimberly Rogers being placed under house arrest in a tiny apartment in Sudbury, Ontario. Her offence was receiving a student loan as well as home welfare, which she needed to go to school and house herself. The government found out and began to prosecute her for cheating: "zero tolerance." In the heat and exhaustion of an August day, in a tiny apartment, Kimberly Rogers committed suicide.[3]

Incredibly, after 400 years the divide between the First Nations and the European vision of society remains as large as it ever was. Roger Jones, a councilor and elder for the Shawanaga First Nation near Sudbury not far from where the young woman died during the heat of that sweltering August day, says it better than I can. In a few words, he describes the fundamental difference between European-based constitutions and the aboriginal concept of society. This is what he said about Canada's Constitution during the hearings of the Canadian Royal Commission on Aboriginal Peoples:

> You read the Constitution, it doesn't talk about love. It doesn't talk about sharing. It doesn't talk about kindness. It doesn't talk about honesty. It doesn't talk about truth. Where are the values of the people? So really it doesn't have life.[4]

A Cree Elder during the negotiations over lands, lakes and rivers for the James Bay Hydro Project with provincial and federal governments said, "will it take until there are no fish, no animals, no water for the white man to understand that you can't eat money?"[5] The answer is yes, because that's the way the white man has always worked his consumer cycle: the richer the resource, the more violent and persistent the exploitation. The North American landscape is littered with the ghosts of extinct species. Carnivorous capitalism has just moved on from preying on living species like bison to insensate, particulate matter like forests, oil, natural gas, coal, tar sands and diamonds.

Among the First Nations of North America, whether you were a Sioux, a Cree or Mi'kmaq, the land, animals, plants, water and minerals were not consumer commodities that could be bought and sold to whomever had the most money and the best lawyers. At contact, the animating thought among the aboriginal community was that once the white man finally got things arranged to his satisfaction and treaties were duly signed, then the relationship between aboriginal people and the settlers would become something that both peoples could share and be a part of together. Reality never has matched that thought. In the 21st century, legal language may use new concepts like "co-management of resources" to describe appropriation, but the bottom line hasn't changed. For the European colonizers, "it's our way or the highway." In the end, the aboriginal nations remain not just conquered peoples but also a conquered philosophy.

Carnivorous capitalism and the aboriginal paradigm are not compatible and never will be. The fundamentals of the aboriginal paradigm are based on community values and respect for the natural world. The natural world for the white man has the same status as a slave did in ancient Athens: the natural world is here to serve human needs and has no other function. Even Athens' greatest polymath Aristotle could not imagine a world without human slaves. Civilized, comfortable Athenian life required human slaves. The same logic is now applied to the earth. According to the consumer worldview, our planet is not a life system we share with others; it is a vast slave that is required for, and must be exploited ruthlessly to ensure, a comfortable, civilized human existence to be possible. To think any other way is outside the bounds of the "progress box."

The First Nations of North America lived successfully here for thousands of years. They were healthy. The land which sustained them was rich and fruitful. They were confident and had no fear of the future for their peoples. White society in a couple of centuries has managed to turn what was once the very richest, fairest part of the planet into a toxic chemical soup loaded with horror diseases (cancers of all kinds, auto-immune diseases, asthmas, new respiratory illnesses, new animal diseases) while the richest among us build gated communities and buy bottled water to protect themselves from the growing detritus of the trash cycle.

The extraordinary thing is that — in spite of the relentless physical and cultural assault on First Nations from the first contacts on the eastern seaboard with the Mi'kmaq across the continent to the west coast Haida and Salish peoples — so many have continued to resist, to refuse to swallow the western dictum that unremitting competition for wealth must be the dominant motor of society. Roger Jones, Shawanaga First Nations councilor and elder, said to the Canadian Royal Commission on Aboriginal Peoples:

In our teachings there are gifts that we are given. And the gift that we were given was kindness, honesty, truth, wisdom and knowledge, love, caring and sharing. And that's the way our people are. We have always shared with the newcomers. No matter how rough of a time they gave us we would turn around and share some more.[6]

This is the kind of cooperative paradigm for organizing society which must be crushed to sustain the idea that private profit comes first. Or must it? Western science is beginning to catch up with the aboriginal paradigm. The recent emergence of "complexity science" is putting biology and physics behind the notion that successful evolutionary change both in the short and long term is dependent on complex interconnections of which competition is only a very small part and not the determining part.

> The immensely complex network of relationships among organisms involves all imaginable patterns of interaction, and there is absolutely no point in focusing on competitive interactions, singling them out as the driving force of evolution.[7]

In this old conflict between the aboriginal paradigm and the "modern," I belong to the aboriginal side. I don't believe human beings have the right to enforce their stories and their rules on other people's cultures or spiritual lives. I don't believe we have the right to send neighbors to the wall as the price of success. This is a moral issue for me. Carnivorous capitalism has become a cancer that is eating us all up — body and soul. And if we do not learn this lesson, we will one day extinguish not just the aboriginal people but also the modern. In the end, the conquistadors will feel the bite of the bullets that they have fired at others. The bullets will turn on them. This is the logical end of the eternally competitive system on which the Europeans have decided to base their societies and their ideas of progress.

We will devour ourselves in a global swallowing that will leave nothing but the wrecks of communities, peoples and ecosystems, all extinguished in the service of relentless, carnivorous, consumer competition. For we are now destroying the shores on which we are standing, the air we breathe, the water we drink.

Biological and Social Phase Transitions

There must be a great
and natural dissonance
among us humans.
Points where forces,
we can't control collide
and the human spirit cracks
like a rift valley
in the crust of the earth,
leaving mountains on one side
and mountains on the other.

— from Looking for Henry

IN 1945 AFTER THE Second European War had ended, it was assumed the greatest problem facing humanity was the emergence of another dictator in the Mussolini or Hitler mould. The recent international debate and war centered on Saddam Hussein was essentially the same as that which occurred around Hitler in the 1930s and 40s. But the greatest problem facing humanity in the 21st century did not exist in 1945. We're in a different world, and the poor old United Nations has been left to stand on guard against dictators in its grand building like a beached whale on the shores of New York, impressive in its sculpture and ambition but of little consequence.

Unfortunately, the Greeks were wrong about change. Change is not constant. While steady continuums of change certainly do exist, we now know change is not always continuous. Often change occurs in violent, unexpected shifts that is not consistent with the steady behavior of the past. These disjunctures in the graduated change continuum are now being called "phase transitions." Further, they are more frequent and more complex than had been previously understood. Stuart Kauffman, in his book *At Home in the Universe* remarks:

> When one species is driven extinct, the event may trigger a small or a large extinction avalanche (a phase transition) that sweeps through some or all of the ecosystem. Why? When one species goes extinct, it is replaced by an invader. The invader is new to the niche, is typically not at a local peak, and therefore adapts in new ways that change its genotype. These moves change the fitness landscapes of its north, south, east and west neighbours, typically lowering their fitness. As their fitness is lowered, they become more readily subject to successful invasion and extinction. So avalanches of extinction tend to spread outward from any single extinction event.[1]

This notion of an extinction avalanche applies equally to the chemistry of the biosphere. It is entirely possible that a moment can arrive, for example, when changes to the carbon values in the atmosphere have altered the composition of the entire biosphere enough that it suddenly reaches a trigger point and an irrevocable, unexpected reordering of the biosphere chemistry occurs: an atmospheric, biochemical equivalent of a snow avalanche releasing from a mountainside.

Chaos theory is very clear that fundamental changes can occur with little immediate warning. Also there are multiple equilibrium points, and systems do not always return to their original state. It's not always a linear advance and retreat as with a simple mountain avalanche. There is no guarantee that, if a physical phase transition occurs in the biosphere or in the ocean, either medium will return to its former chemistry, even if humans suddenly stop pumping carbons into the environment.

◆ ◆ ◆

Wars could be described as social phase transitions. Like biological phase transitions, they erupt in unexpected ways and have consequences totally out of proportion with the original trigger point.

Who in their wildest imaginations could have predicted that the murder of an archduke in an obscure Balkan city would result in a world war in which 11 million men would die? Or that the peace treaty to end this war would then trigger an even greater war with a death toll between 40 and 50 million?[2] The avalanche of consequences released by the murder of the archduke in Sarajevo continue to this day, for that second war with its death camps would in turn be the inspiration for the state of Israel and much of the instability in the Middle East today.

It seems impossible to credit that such a singular, isolated and rather bizarre act like the murder of an archduke in an open, horse-drawn carriage could light the fuse for such a long trail of human misery; but it did. Trigger points have their roots in all kinds of social and economic conditions. Armies of academics have spent lifetimes analyzing that shot in Sarajevo and its consequences.

Human social conditions are the equivalent of the physical accumulation of snow and temperature conditions on a mountainside. The quality of the snow as it precipitates from the clouds changes over time, yet everything goes on as it has always done. The snow looks much the same, but an invisible point arrives when the temperature and snow conditions are such that the avalanche lets go, taking everything with it.

The same happens with social conditions. Everything seems to be much the same. People go to work. Take holidays. Fall in love. But conditions are always changing, becoming ever more stable or conversely ever more delicately balanced, ever more ready to "let go" like the avalanche, awaiting only the right tipping point. And it's always difficult to figure out exactly what is happening at any particular moment.

Consider how initially emergent, beneficial conditions can suddenly rebound upon themselves to tear cities and nations apart. Great ancient and modern cities have been distinguished by their multi-cultural populations. Sir Peter Hall in his grand opus *Cities in Civilization* documents this again and again over hundreds of pages.[3] From ancient Athens to modern Memphis, cities have always attracted human talent. Ancient Athens pulled talented immigrants from all the other cities around the Aegean basin and as far away as Macedonia and Egypt to "feed" its commercial, artistic and scientific communities. Nothing has changed. Today great cities like London, Paris, Memphis, Seattle, Los Angeles and New York continue to attract large and diverse populations who in turn will create great and diverse things, everything from the music of rock and roll to the magic of computers. Hall is absolutely right about this: the great genius of the city comes from throwing a lot of different people together in a dense and intense situation, and letting creativity happen.

But Hall was instinctively using a linear model for evolutionary change to create his definition of urban success. It's a simple, attractive scenario. Add people and density to the urban mixing bowl, then step back and just let positive progress ensue. There is a comfortable, understandable evolutionary continuum at work here, that everyone can easily comprehend and have confidence in: the quicker the population growth, the greater the accomplishments and the richer the city becomes. It's easy as one, two, three. Don't worry. It's all good.

But unfortunately, there is a flip side. The faster the growth, the finer the line becomes between positive, creative change and chaos. Cities experiencing magnificent, explosive expansion can also quickly, suddenly, unexpectedly flip into brutal disintegration because the cohesive side of the social equation — all the little bits and pieces of connecting social tissue that is needed to keep societies stable — gets thinner and thinner. There are lots of examples. Berlin switching from the effervescence of the Weimar Republic into the dark brutality of the Nazi experience is a mid 20th-century example. Sarajevo is a more recent one: From a multicultural, Olympic jewel into a war zone so savage that shooting unarmed women as they walked to work was considered entirely acceptable.

And now in New York — the richest, most powerful, most connected, most protected city on the planet — suddenly everything is not moving gloriously forward. Thousands of people die. Tens of thousands are suddenly unemployed. Magnificent buildings destroyed. Business evaporates. What happened? Who could have predicted such a disaster?

The answer is that nobody could because the defining characteristics of a phase transition, be it a social or biological one, is that it is unpredictable, not linear, and hair trigger. The scientific metaphor has become "a butterfly raises its wings in Chicago and a tornado occurs in Kansas."

Using a human metaphor for a social phase transition, one could imagine that a man reads an advertisement for a Cadillac SUV. This SUV is described as "Conqueror of the World." The ad states that "the Cadillac SUV has a 345 HP engine, the most powerful in the world, a Bose sound system with 11 speakers and 250 watts of power and the OnStar Premium Services Plan." The advertisement says "it's easy to feel invincible." Can you imagine that somewhere a man is reading this ad? He is a student. Maybe he has the same kind of personality as the young man who shot the archduke. The ad bothers him. "It's easy to feel invincible" echoes in his head. He makes a phone call to a good friend who is studying in Germany, who is also feeling dispossessed. They talk.

Did a man reading this advertisement ever exist? Did he feel these feelings? I have no idea. Did a butterfly raise its wings and trigger a tornado? This is the theory of the tipping point: that an insignificant, trivial action attached to exactly the right conditions at exactly the right moment can ignite a powder train of events that leads to a 9/11 avalanche.

The social phase transition is a modern, scientific metaphor for describing the removal of the last brick in the wall just before it falls down. When the last Roman emperor had General Stilocho and his officer corps murdered in his dining hall at Ravenna by his Praetorian Guards, it was a trivial moment in Roman history. As Roman murders went it should have hardly registered on the Richter scale. Sulla and Marius, two generals from the Roman Republican era, blithely proscribed the lives of thousands of their fellow Roman citizens whom they had decided were their enemies — mostly based on whether they had money and whether or not they were friends. Their proscriptions made General Stilocho's murder by Emperor Honorius look like the smallest of change. Both Sulla and Marius wiped out entire classes of talented people from both the right and left of the political spectrum. Yet the Roman Empire would continue on successfully for centuries thereafter.

Four hundred years later, one isolated and comfortable emperor decides to murder one Roman general and his small officer corps. He invites them to dinner and butchers them successfully. It's a very small deal in the grand sweep of Roman history, but this time it is the avalanche trigger. An ancient civilization crashes down across continents affecting the lives of millions and millions of people for millennia.

I have no idea what the moment was that triggered the series of events that resulted in four planes loaded with high-octane fuel being flown towards four buildings, but I am sure that there was a single moment when it all began. Just as I am sure that such events are flashes from a pan that has long been heating. The Emperor Honorius couldn't sink a vast empire by himself, anymore than George W. Bush can sink the planet. One human being can accomplish very little. The Roman Empire's disintegration had been brewing for centuries. Just as the modern political will to engage in a war for oil has been brewing since the west began its relentless conversion in the 1940s into a society dependent on burning carbon fuels.

The great difference between a social phase transition and a biological phase transition is that the social one is harnessed to a different clock. A generation after the Nazi insanity, Germany was successfully rebuilding. Israel was rocketing into existence. New children were being born, new buildings being built, new train lines and roads constructed. The same thing will occur for Sarajevo and the former Yugoslavia. And life though fundamentally changed went on after the fall of the Roman Empire.

But a biological phase transition is not a social phenomenon. It's a physical one, and life doesn't always continue. This is the terrifying aspect of the moments that we are living right now. For it is clear that we have governments at the national level that are not capable of imagining the possibility of this biological phase transition occurring. There is an instinctive feeling among politicians that we can recover from an environmental crisis just as nations have recovered from the devastation of a war.

"People will suffer; then things will get better. It's a cycle as old as human time." Unfortunately, the evidence for biological phase transitions is that the old equilibrium does not always return. The Aral Sea has never come back.

In retrospect, the warning signs of an impending social phase transition can be identified. It is clear that the West's unwillingness to address Germany's currency inflation and physical starvation arising from the conditions imposed by the Treaty of Versailles had as much to do with the rise of Nazism as Hitler's oratory.

Sarajevo, the multi-cultural, industrial, artistic dynamo chosen by the Olympic Committee to showcase modern Europe, suddenly kicked over into a war so bitter that ethnic cleansing is unleashed. Just as with Germany, the signs — in retrospect — were obvious. By chance, I met a student journalist at a meeting in Ottawa several years before the disintegration of Yugoslavia. She was very pretty and very upset about the ethnic tensions in her city. She predicted unchained violence. But what made her even more angry was there was so little interest in the rest of the world in the difficulties Sarajevo and Yugoslavia were facing. No one cared. Sarajevo and the Olympics were old news. The dictator Tito and Yugoslavia were even older news.

I remember her arguing passionately that the International Monetary Fund's obsession with balanced budgets, reducing wages and public services was forcing the Yugoslavian national government to retreat from its role as re-distributor of wealth and provider of common services. And without the national government acting in a supportive, positive role creating services and connections between people, communities fell back quickly into old ethnic antagonisms of "us" versus "them."

I listened politely, but her story didn't surprise me. We faced a similar situation in Canada. We had ethnic and language rivalries here also. I had lived through the October Crisis at the University of Montreal in 1970, the FLQ bombings in Quebec. Now the Canadian government was also being harassed by the IMF to reduce national expenditures on employment benefits, health and child care. In obedient response, the national government had abandoned universal child support programs, cut back on unemployment benefits (such that only one in four unemployed people now receive them), reduced health care to such levels that people were dying waiting for their cancer treatments. Welcome to the 1980s, I thought. I listened to the young woman from Sarajevo, but sympathy is a cheap commodity. I mentally filed her concerns under "so what?" Things weren't that different in Canada. We were all trying to get by.

Her story remains in my mind because a few years later I saw a picture of her corpse. She was wearing the same green loden coat from Denmark that I had admired when I had met her in Ottawa. It was brand new then, made of very heavy dark green wool. I had never seen a coat like it in Canada. She was very proud of that rich-looking coat. I recognized it before I recognized her when I saw a newspaper picture of her lying twisted on her side as if she had momentarily tried to stand. She was at the foot of some elegant urban stairs. Her hair was fanned out around her head in a kind of aureole that was twin to a bloody stain. There was a man walking by in the photograph; I suppose it was too dangerous to stop. A dark circle of arterial blood bruised the ground under her coat. I looked at that picture for a long time as if by staring at it, I could reach through the interstices of the tiny black and white dots which comprised the image and by force of will, bring that young woman back to life.

When I think of the war in Iraq and all other wars that political leaders begin "to protect democracy" or "to change a regime," I think of that young woman in the green loden coat. She was beautiful. She was young. She was idealistic. She was bright, and with her extinction a unique universe disappeared. That is what happened in Sarajevo over and over again. This is what is happening in Iraq. There are young women in green loden coats dying. We are extinguishing universes.

Out of the sky, two planes swerve towards the twin spires of the World Trade Center, and these great buildings collapse into a pile of smoking debris. Suddenly, we are sending the Canadian soldiers to Afghanistan. There is war in Iraq. Is the world becoming a safer place?

There is something wrong with this picture.

President Bush's response to the World Trade Center disaster is the most dramatic and visible example of the 19th-century nature of national government. It was a response that was utterly inappropriate. From the beginning, responding to the attacks should have been characterized as nothing more than a police action. A well-equipped small group of armed men should have been sent to bring the criminals to justice. It might have taken a couple of years. The time didn't matter. What would matter was that the perpetrators of the crimes be brought to a World Court to be tried for their actions.

A "war on terror" should never have been announced. The vast mobilization of air, marine and land forces should never have occurred. No matter how deep and compelling one's distress was for the innocent victims of the attack, there is something fundamentally repellant in watching the richest nation on the planet spending billions to annihilate men in the poorest nation on the planet.

Cities cannot be protected by armed guards on airplanes or by missile shields in space. No one has ever built a wall around a city that has successfully kept an invader out. It hasn't since the time of Joshua at the walls of Jericho. The Romans tried and couldn't do it. Medieval kings couldn't do it. The Soviets couldn't do it, and the United States will not be able to do it with missile shields.

Nor can signing on for more "good causes" save the day. We don't lack for good causes and wonderful civil society leaders. The problem with "good causes" is that they all treat the symptoms. The fervent opponents of rainforest destruction remind me of the bombardier Yossarian in *Catch-22*,[4] carefully bandaging the leg of his friend who had been wounded by shrapnel as they are flying back to the base. He stops the bleeding, covering the wound with sterile gauze just as he has been trained to do. He reassures his buddy that all is well. But his buddy doesn't cheer up; instead he remains pale and silent, becoming paler and grayer by the moment.

Yossarian finds himself getting a little irritated with his friend. All should be well. He's done what he's been trained to do and put a tourniquet around his friend's leg. The bleeding has stopped, but his buddy is still not cooperating. Then just before the plane lands, he discovers that his friend's intestines have been cut loose of his body via a jagged hole Yossarian hadn't noticed in the back of the flying suit.

The biological phase transition is that hole in the back of the jacket.

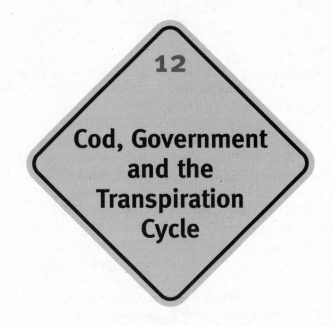

12

Cod, Government and the Transpiration Cycle

There is only lobster and crab left and when these are gone, there will be nothing.

— Fisherman, Cheticamp, Nova Scotia

MY FATHER WAS BORN in a little Cape Breton fishing village as was my grandfather and all the Doucets back to before Canada was Canada. My father was the son of an Acadian farmer and became a Canadian economist specializing in the fish stocks. For me the cod are not some abstract, interesting story in the newspaper. Some of my first memories are of jigging for cod with my cousins. Of all the wonderful dishes in the world to eat, if I could choose one it would be freshly caught cod, pan fried in butter and, after pan fried, cod cakes. To my palate, nothing is tastier. Cod used to be the poor man's dish. Now if you can find cod in a store, they are in tiny little fillets that in my youth we wouldn't have bothered to eat.

Declining cod stocks are not news. Forty years ago, everyone knew the fish stocks were declining. They had always been declining. There have been less cod for every generation. When I was a boy, fishermen still rowed out of the harbor in dories and cast their nets out onto the sea as fishermen had done for millennia. Those who caught fish were never rich, but they caught enough to make an independent living, raise a family and stay out of the clutches of the bank. Then, sometime in the early 1970s, "traditional" fishing stopped. There were just not enough fish close to the shore anymore to make hand casting of the nets worth while. To be successful, you suddenly needed to go "offshore" with nets capable of dragging the ocean floor. Those who could afford the transition began to earn "big money," build big homes on shore and take winter holidays in the south.

Some scientists began to say that the stress on the cod was creating a survival crisis.

Nobody paid much attention. Yes there were less cod, but there had always been less cod. Nothing had changed. Those with big boats still caught their quotas and filled the fish plants. The small fishermen left the village. Nothing much changed. Then to universal surprise — without warning, from one season to the next — the cod winked out, and no one could catch or drag their quotas. After a 1,000 years of commercial fishing beginning with the Basques, the cod fishery was extinct.

The wailing that went up was intercontinental, and the race was on to blame someone, somewhere. Why wasn't there more of a warning?

Some scientists will tell you that they did warn the government, and the government didn't listen. I don't doubt them. There is a whole federal department devoted to reporting on the Continental Shelf fish stocks. My Dad was part of it. But in the boats on the sea where the fishermen passed their lives there was no warning of any great significance. One summer there were enough fish. The next there were not. In the practical daily lives of those who fished, it was as if someone had flipped a switch and turned out the fishing lights.

There are lots of theories. Many of them are reasonable, but nobody really knows for sure. It's much like the disappearance of the dinosaurs. Was it warmer temperatures in the ocean? Less salty water? Was it a precipitous decline in the cod's food chain? The disappearance of feeder stocks like the caplin? Did it have something to do with too many mature fish being pulled out and too many small ones left behind, not yet at the reproductive stage? Did we create an orphan sea? Do cod require a critical population level in order to reproduce? Did the industrial draggers and gill nets scrape the underwater reefs so much that these food-producing areas had their basic biology compromised? Was it just too many people pulling too many fish out of the sea? Or was it all of the above?

If you look to complexity theory for an explanation, what it will tell you is that there is probably no single reason. Ocean warming, over-fishing, disappearance of feeder stocks, dragging the ocean floor: combine these and they add up to a landslide of invisible, underwater changes that reduces the fish in the sea and changes the actual ecosystem which cod needed to exist. But exactly what was the point? What was the exact collection of circumstances that drove the cod over the underwater precipice?

There doesn't appear to be an answer, for once a biological extinction process has been launched, the last seasons or the last collection of moments become irrelevant. Who can stop the melt of Arctic and Antarctic ice shelves from one season to the next? Who can stop the daily spike of UV rays? When it comes down to a single season, it is too late to repair anything. The ship has left the slip.

Blame is a very big feature of the cod stock story. Fishermen blame federal officials for not limiting the catches sufficiently. Federal officials shrug and say the pressure from fishermen's unions was always for more licenses, more fish and never less because it meant more membership and more money for the union. The officials did their best, they say, but the east coast unions controlled the politicians and the politicians controlled the Fisheries Departments. So blame the unions.

Canadian politicians found it politically very advantageous to blame the Spanish, the Portuguese, the Basque, the Greenlanders — the "greedy others" — but they conveniently forgot that many of these "greedy others" had fished the Grand Banks for centuries, for longer than Canada has existed. The "greedy others" had been steadily pushed away from the inshore fishing which had been controlled entirely by Canada for many years. The "others" blamed the Canadians for their constant increases in catches for the inshore fishery.

The Canadian Minister of Fisheries Brian Tobin led a vigorous national and international campaign against the Spaniards who were according to him over-fishing the "tail" of the Grand Banks (the small peninsula of the continental shelf which projected outside of the Canadian 200-mile control). There were some ugly scenes in Spanish and Portuguese fishing towns and a good deal of blustering on the Grand Banks themselves with warships hovering in the background.

Who benefited from the cod war? The principal beneficiary may have been the Canadian Minister of Fisheries. Brian Tobin became very popular. He was nicknamed "Captain Canada." He resigned as federal Minister of Fisheries and Oceans and went back to his home province, Newfoundland, where he was immediately elected premier.

Scientists are still arguing about who or what was to blame and about who didn't listen to whom, but the hard reality is that no one was able to predict that in the spring of 1990 or 1992 or 1989, commercial cod fishing would cease on the Canadian continental shelf. None of the scientists in the Fisheries Department had capacity to say much more than what the old fishermen had always said, year after year: the stocks were declining.

So what else was new?

We learned that the cod had crossed the extinction line when they crossed it and the cod winked out. There wasn't any time to hit the magic policy button, and this happened to the most intensively studied and regulated fishery on the face of the earth. It wasn't off Mozambique in the midst of an endless, mindless civil war. The cod were the basis of a peaceful, billion-dollar annual industry essential to thousands of people and hundreds of communities. The Canadian government knew this and carefully watched over the cod population, measured it, studied it, licensed it and yet was still unable to stop its commercial extinction, a disappearance that has closed coastal communities in Canada, Portugal, Spain, Russia, Poland and the Baltic States.

Ten years later, there is still no sign of the cod re-establishing themselves. This was not supposed to happen either. All that was required was for fishing to stop for a while to allow the cod to re-populate the ocean.

Nor does the size of the environmental resource seem to slow final moments of a decline. In fact it would seem that the larger the ecological shift is, the faster the final moments of phase transition are. For the cod, the decline took place over centuries but the commercial extinction itself occurred in a single, seasonal transition.

◆ ◆ ◆

Shifts in atmospheric chemistry are much larger than fish stocks, but like the cod, as the degradation curve increases in pitch, the changes gather strength and momentum. Like a child descending a playground slide, a point is passed in the descent when the acceleration becomes so swift that the final transformative moments occur with unstoppable finality. In the case of the biosphere, the final transformation is more likely to be exactly this kind of sudden transition, not a predictable, gentle last step down a biological staircase. In other words, it is quite possible as with the cod, that there would be no final warning at all; that it would happen from one season to the next and by definition in a way that no one expected.

If this sounds ridiculously simplistic, consider that the chemistry of the biosphere is planetary. No lab can reproduce the combinations and re-combinations that occur on that scale. The toxic cocktails that pour forth from electrical generating plants, from chemical industries, from the tailpipes of the millions of automobiles outnumber the earth's natural volcanoes many times over. This is an entirely new phenomenon. Until the 20th century it was the natural world that was in the driver's seat. Humanity was a trivial player in the biological life of the planet, but the ancient game has changed. The earth's largest volcano is now fired by human beings.

Some of the consequences are easy enough to see. The ozone decline in the atmosphere means that human skin burns more easily than it did before. As a result sales of protective clothing, sunscreen and sunglasses have boomed. In northern countries like Canada, sunglasses used to be a summertime affectation. Now, they are regarded as a necessity.

Less well-understood consequences include the decline in the insulating effect the thinning of the ozone layer creates. The day's heat no longer remains trapped on the earth's surface as it once did during the nighttime hours. This means that in spite of general global warming, there are larger temperature swings between night and day. The spiking of the daily temperature in the early afternoon is normal and expected, but it is now being followed by a precipitous evening temperature decline, so steep that people are often obliged to wear insulated coats on a July evening. Global warming is also accompanied by erratic weather, torrential rains, very cold months and very hot dry months that arrive out of the traditional order.

In eastern Ontario where I live, in the summer of 2000 there weren't enough heat units generated for corn to ripen in spite of above-average daily sunlight. This year was followed in 2001 by a vicious heat wave and a drought. 2002 was fine in most of eastern Canada, but there was a crippling drought in western Canada forcing the slaughter of millions of animals. In 2003, drought on the Pacific Coast caused raging forest fires, followed by endless rain. As a friend of mine said, "the seasons turn as they always have but each year does not resemble the last."

The increase in the carbon dioxide in the atmosphere and the simultaneous decrease in the ozone layer are combining to squeeze the earth in a vice. The carbon dioxide increases in the biosphere crank the earth's surface temperature up, but the thinning atmosphere lets the increasing heat escape more quickly. Sounds like a nice, balanced arrangement, but it is not a uniform exchange. During the day, the temperature on the earth's surface rockets up and then at night diminishes very quickly; these sharp temperature differentials cause hurricanes and form new deserts because fewer plants can survive to conserve water and create the transpiration cycle that the atmosphere needs to continue a balanced, regenerative behavior.

In Europe right now, it takes years for the vegetation to recover from a severe summer heat wave and drought. The year following a heat wave has less plants, less transpiration, less cooling oxygen, less reduction of carbon dioxide. A destructive, negative feedback loop is created. In the simplest of terms, more heat creates the conditions for more heat. This is what French scientists discovered after they began to investigate the biological consequences of the heat wave of 2002 which killed 12,000 French citizens and 30,000 Europeans.

A great and final transition would occur if hydrogen atoms ever begin flying off into space faster than they can be replenished or contained on the earth's surface. This is entirely possible if the containing layers of the atmosphere continue to degrade and the earth's transpiration cycle continues to weaken. If this planetary imbalance between water molecules produced and lost ever arrives, the atomic structure on which human and more complex life depends will vanish, the earth's surface will return to an earlier evolutionary state and human beings will join the many other species which have enjoyed a flowering, decline and then a sudden disappearance.

These are the dice with which we are playing as casually as a child plays in a sandbox.

◆ ◆ ◆

One thing I've learned from my small career at City Hall is that good governance isn't about polluting the air we breathe and the water we drink. Good governance isn't about allowing tiny groups of people to direct a city's growth or control the earth's vast resources. Good governance is about generating wealth in a way that values the commonwealth as much as individual wealth. But democratic governance must rely on the people. At the end of the day, it is the people who must care about whether or not their city governments and their national governments are protecting them from the more rapacious qualities of human nature. Their governments will not care if they do not care: that is the nature of democracy. So don't look to governments to fix things, look to yourself. If the government isn't working, the reason can be found in the mirror.

13

Care of the Soul/ Care of the City/ Care for the Planet

If you came from the stars
Across aeons of dark and cold
Upon a planet
That was not cold,
That did not burn,
That sparkled
In a great and glorious disk
Of Sea blue and white swirl;
That was bright
Like a great jewel,
You might be forgiven
If, for a moment,
You thought
You'd found heaven.

— from *Canal Seasons*

IF YOU BELIEVE THAT THE SOUL is a shared facility, care of the individual soul also requires care for the collective soul, your city and the planet.[1] Care for the soul must also be anchored in something more than "doing;" it's also got something to do with "being" and the poetry of daily existence which anchors each life. By the poetry of daily existence, I'm thinking about allowing the simple wonder of life to invade the soul: an invasion that soothes, fills it with calm joy and directs it. The poetry of existence comes from as many places as there is life. For me one of those places is when Canada geese come powering over the horizon, then wheel directly above me and descend to land on the lake. The speed, strength and beauty of these aerial creatures always fills me with wonder.

In the summer, the poetry of existence comes from a simple escape into the Gatineau Hills north of Ottawa. Cycling is a sport I very much enjoy. It demands a great deal from the body, but not much from the mind. You can fly along over the earth and let the globe turn on its solemn way as your tires spin merrily over its surface. There is no more beautiful place in the world than the Gatineau Hills to bicycle; trees form a green tunnel around you as you labor up to the crests, only to careen down the other side, the roadway a bar of light ahead. It is the kind of place where a kinship with other living things comes easily.

I have seen bear cubs rocket down a rocky escarpment, traveling with amazing speed, their coats so black they seemed to be dark holes in the landscape. Hawks softly cruise in the sky above like sailboats, their wings broad and aerial. The bicycle makes no sound, and in the spring when I come around a corner I will find a doe grazing quietly at the edges of the road with her fawns. She raises her head delicately, velvet eyes focusing before she springs off into the shelter of the forest.

The Canadian writer Margaret Atwood has moved about the world so much that she can write of human flight divorced from the ground to which it is tethered. This experience along with her great talent has given her work terrific variety. I have had a different experience. There are two landscapes very clearly printed on my soul that resonate like no other and in which I have always been rooted. One is the coastline, mountains and sky of Cape Breton, Nova Scotia. No matter how long I am "away," Cape Breton always feels like home. The instant that I cross the causeway and begin the drive up the Inverness shore towards Cheticamp, there is this great sigh that releases inside me with the message that I am home. For me there is no place else like it in the world, and there is a part of me attached to the sea and sky of Cape Breton in a way that always misses it.

The other is the landscape of the City of Ottawa. Ottawa is a city of the forest, and the best place to see the city is from the Gatineau Hills on a bicycle as you roll down from the heights. The road through the forest suddenly opens up, and there the city is before you laid out in a bend of the river. The other good place to feel the city's place in the universe is from the banks of the river, looking northwest towards the forest and the setting sun. Northwest of the city, the river flows for hundreds of miles cutting through the boreal forests across the surface of the planet up towards the Arctic tree line. Excepting a few villages and farms secluded along the banks of the river, there is very little human habitation. Ottawa is a very different place from Cape Breton. It is as if the forest has never abandoned its rightful claim on the land and will soon march down from the hills to reclaim its place by pushing up through the streets and sidewalks of the city with new growth, so that there is nothing left but birdsong and the creak of forest life.

Ottawa is a city that it is hard to get to know, yet I also feel very comfortable in it. I am used to the arc of the seasons here: the flaming autumns, the cold winters, the short violent springs followed by the long, warm sigh which is summer. Ottawa is not a grand city, but it is home, the place that I can search out the cranky, silent musings of my own soul.

The fit between these two very different landscapes, Cape Breton and Ottawa, is not in any geography but that of the soul and the poetry of my own existence. For me the doorstep of my soul doesn't end at my fingertips. For me, the human soul is not a singular Benedictine flight to heaven, nor is the poetry of existence a solitary affair, but connected like a string of DNA to the community, to the city, to the country and to the planet. And when those connections are broken or damaged, my own soul is diminished and the poetry of existence is reduced for all.

For me, the mundane struggles against school closures, for better public transit, for wider safer sidewalks are all part of something grander. It is part of the struggle for my own soul and the poetry of existence that can be found sitting on my Uncle's Cape Breton stoop, watching the sun sink behind Cheticamp Island. It can equally be found in the ordinary battles of a citizen for a better city and a safer planet.

This is what makes life grand and wonderful: sunsets, friends and purpose informed not by the accumulation of material things but by moments of pure poetry anchored in a life directed towards creating richer possibilities for all. It is what gives life meaning because for me the divine is rooted in the integrity of creation and all those who struggle for that state of mind and state of place which connect us to this ultimate mystery of creation and existence.

Karl Marx observed that people create their own souls through what they do with their work lives. He used the example that if people spend their days manufacturing weapons then this will have consequences for both the character of individuals and nations. Michael Moore has said the same thing using today's language in films like "Bowling for Colombine." In one interview, Moore filmed a well-dressed employee of the military-industrial complex speaking to the camera with an intercontinental ballistic missile in the background. The man muses into the camera in a shocked and quiet way about the children who have been shooting other children in the local school, Colombine High, just down the road. It seems completely irrelevant to him that behind him is an intercontinental missile capable of carrying a nuclear warhead that can extinguish millions of human lives. The problem is the teenagers who have killed other teenagers down the road. The little scene manages to be comic and sad, tragic and righteous, all at the same time.

But for me, the most powerful conveyers of the idea of the soul and its care are not the constipated fury of Marx or the cheery iconoclasm of Moore. It is little known authors like Ilona Flutztejn-Gruda.

When asked what poetry was Sam Johnson replied: "Why Sir, it is much easier to say what it is not. We all know what light is; but it is not easy to tell what it is." You might say the same thing for the soul. You can't explain it, but you can feel its presence when you meet it. It's like feeling the heat of the sunlight on your face. Reading Ilona Flutztejn-Gruda's little book about her childhood, *When Grown-Ups Play at War*, you know immediately that you are in the presence of a wonderful soul.

Ilona Flutztejn-Gruda never preaches about the evils of war, but her small book about her childhood just prior to and during World War II is conveyed with such clarity and honest affirmation that the cruel nonsense adults visit on themselves and the world resonates as ridiculous and ugly on every page without her ever having to cast judgments on anyone. She just tells her story of being a little girl trying to be a little girl as the world disintegrates around her.[2]

Our lives and our souls are given to us through a process that we accept but do not understand. Why is there life on earth but not on Mars? Why do two atoms of hydrogen insist on bonding with one atom of oxygen to create water? Why are trees, trees? And what are we humans supposed to do with our lives besides reproduce? Do we have any purpose in the great chain of life, beyond being in it? These

are some of the questions that are worth spending a lifetime struggling with because they are the elements necessary to form our own
souls and appreciate the poetry of our existence on this planet.

You can't legislate soul, but you can cultivate the conditions under
which the individual and collective poetry of existence are more
likely to prosper — because the soul is both given and created. I
couldn't go cycling in the Gatineau Hills if a French planner named
Jacques Grebner hadn't come up with the idea of setting aside some
land for a wilderness park in the shape of an isosceles triangle outside
of Ottawa. The park is shaped like an isosceles triangle with the
sharp end of this park in the heart of the city, the fat base far away in
the watersheds of the Gatineau Hills. Greber had this insight that if
you shaped the park in this unusual way instead of square or a rectan-
gle, you could make it readily accessible to people in the city on foot,
or skis or bicycles.

Greber may have had the idea but it was Rod Sparks, a descen-
dent of one of the city's first settlers who made it happen. He saw the
value in Greber's idea and more importantly he had land — lots of it
— in the Gatineau Hills. He donated it to the National Capital
Commission on the condition that it become the basis of the new
park that had been proposed by Greber. Initially, the commission
hesitated, fearing the obligation to maintain, but Sparks insisted. Finally they accepted and it did become the nucleus of the new park. I
like this story a lot. It is one that is rarely remembered for there is not
a single plaque or notice of Rod Spark's donation. Yet what a difference his gift made to the soul of our city and the soul of the thousands of people who enjoy the Park each year, winter and summer,
spring and fall.

Gatineau Park is fifteen minutes by bicycle from where I live in
the center of Ottawa. But the second I'm through the gate, I can
wave goodbye to the city. Quelle délice!

We know that our souls are affected by the conditions our lives
are subject to, and as citizens acting in community we create those
conditions. No other living creature on the planet can intentionally
modify the environment so completely to suit themselves. This is
what distinguishes humans from all other creatures. And we know
that communities that are created by inclusive, open, caring democratic assemblies will be different from ones governed by corporate
cliques and slice-and-dice politics.

We know the souls of people will be different if they live in societies where they are confident that their neighbors have good chances

for a decent life, as opposed to one where neighbors are impoverished and hungry. Iron bars fastened across the front of house windows are eloquent testimony to the difference.

Governments that are sustaining and sustainable are about feeding the poetry of existence, and the poetry of existence is about the mundane as well as the magical: about making sure everyone gets a fair chance at education, health and housing. The body and the soul are connected. To be a human being is to be in love with humanity. This humanity is not born but learned like math. We are not born loving the Jupiter Symphony or the way the sun sets behind the sea. We are not born strumming the guitar or reading *Catch-22* or preferring to walk than drive. We learn all this, and in the learning we create our souls. In caring for the one, we also care for the other.

14

1984–2004:
Poets and Visions

Turning and turning in the widening gyre
The falcon cannot hear the falconer;
Things fall apart; the centre cannot hold;
Mere anarchy is loosed upon the world,
The blood-dimmed tide is loosed and everywhere
The ceremony of innocence is drowned;
The best lack all conviction, while the worst
Are full of passionate intensity....

— W.B. Yeats,
"The Second Coming"

YEATS THE REVOLUTIONARY wasn't much, but Yeats the poet had a great and lasting effect. He had a great soul. His poems capture the eternal struggle to create a humane society and what happens when you can feel it slowly, grindingly slipping away. Great poets, great authors, great scientists are distinguished by this incalculable, imponderable quality of "soul." Albert Einstein's reflections on the human condition are as interesting as his reflections on the movement of matter through time and space. Often, great souls are able to plot the future accurately and vividly long before that distant horizon is evident to anyone else.

George Orwell's *1984* enjoyed a great vogue when it was first published in 1949. In 1949, the year 1984 was on a distant horizon, and the dark and dreary world Orwell painted had natural resonance in the ugly, subterranean world of Stalin's Soviet paranoia. In Orwell's grim meditation on the future, Big Brother is watching everywhere just as Stalin was in the Soviet Union. Society in Orwell's book is largely composed of a drifting underclass who lived on the lottery, cheap apartments and staying out of Big Brother's way. Distant wars that never seem to resolve anything rumble on the horizon. Enormous faceless corporations run the planet, which is no longer subdivided by the antique divisions of nations but into vast intercontinental trading blocks. The hero Winston is a minor factotum working at some mindless job for the system in which government and private corporations have become blended. The story is about Winston's attempt to break free without joining the lottery underclass.

1984 created a sensation, partly because it was brilliantly written and partly because readers instinctively recognized it as a modern fable of a possible future for nations released from the traditional, national conflicts which had preoccupied them for so long. You didn't have to believe that Orwell's *1984* would unfold like a Nostradamus prediction to appreciate the raw elements that Orwell had mixed into his tale and the questions it poses. Just how would the modern world evolve? Stalin's Soviet Union was terrifying with its loss of individual rights and massive internal deportations of its own citizens. Would there be more Stalin-type governments?

Then, there was the power of these new inventions — nuclear weapons and the television — where would they take us? What would happen to cities, which were becoming as populous as nations? How big could they become? Would they become like nations? How would it all play out?

The year 1984 has long since come and gone. As the fateful date approached, Orwell's dark tale enjoyed resurgence in interest and then it sank out of sight again. After all, Orwell had gotten so many things wrong. Stalin's evil empire unraveled as harmlessly as a ball of wool. The Berlin Wall fell of its own accord. The television screen has become a friendly internet trader of goods, services and chat groups. Big Brother doesn't gaze out at you as you gaze in at the image. That's all KGB/CIA paranoia.

But look a little harder. In Orwell's *1984*, the planet is divided into vast continental trading blocks. Unaccountable corporations do control the planet's economic, political and social agenda today. Democratic politics and the role of national governments have become servants of these giant corporations. Distant wars are constant, but they never seem to accomplish anything except inspire fear in the underclass and drain off the nation's surplus. The divide between the rich and poor has become continental. The size of the middle class diminishes with each passing year. Are there not similarities with all this and Orwell's vision? Today political leaders seem more like game show hosts than statesmen, and foreign wars are more about corporate wealth and keeping global monopolies in place than anything else.

In Orwell's *1984*, what's left of the middle class is controlled and constantly spied upon. The rich have become invisible and the poor are everywhere. Whole sections of the city are occupied by a vast underclass that lives on low paid, part-time employment, state handouts and lottery tickets. Country life doesn't seem to exist. The rich (one presumes that they are rich, but who knows?) live somewhere nice, but no one seems to know where that is or who exactly they are.

If you ignore the Stalinist, big brother details and focus on the simple lines of Orwell's urban fable, suddenly *1984* doesn't seem so irrelevant. Instead it becomes eerily prescient. When Orwell wrote this book, the world was still largely rural. Cities were blips on the planet's surface. But in the second half of the 20th century, the planet's population urbanized. More than half of Argentina's population is located in one city, Buenos Aires. At the start of the 20th century, Canada was a rural nation, 80 percent of the population lived in a rural or village setting.

At the beginning of the 21st century only four percent of Canadians work in agriculture, and the distribution of the population has reversed itself. Now, 80 percent of the population is urban, and an astonishing 60 percent of the population are in five city-regions. Mexico City contains 25 million human beings, Sao Paulo 17 million and these cities continue to grow. And what isn't urban has morphed into a suburban wallpaper of malls, residential pods, industrial parks, and six lane arterials which is neither rural nor urban.

In 1949 when Orwell wrote *1984*, billion-dollar multinational corporations operating across continents and oceans were a figment of Orwell's imagination, not a reality. They are now the dominant economic force on the planet with financial transactions larger than nations the size of Canada. They control the value of national currencies, national interest rates, social and environmental priorities. And they operate largely beyond the control of any particular government including the United States. Even the smallest check on those corporate powers, like the tiny Tobin tax on international financial transactions, has proved impossible to impose. At the mid-20th century, the United Nations was the symbol of postwar hope and a new world order. It has become an international welfare office, doling out refugee welfare, clean water and wringing its collective hands over genocide — a symbol of international failure.

There is something wrong with the soul of our planet. There is something wrong with the soul of our nations, and there is something wrong with the soul of our cities. Poets like Yeats, writers like Orwell and scientists like Einstein expressed their own soul in the singular, but the soul that they were referring to was a plural construct. Souls are a shared facility. Soul is shared among families, communities, cities, nations and ultimately the entire human race. We exist physically and metaphorically as a series of connections. We change the nature of those connections and we change the nature of each individual life and ultimately the soul of the planet itself.

You cannot legislate soul. Only God can do that, but you can create the conditions in which the souls of humans may prosper. And for the last 50 years, we have built North American cities in ways in which a soul of any depth, of any color, of any resonance is hard to find. The United States and Canada have both become parasitic nations. The quality of the air, even in a non-industrial city like Ottawa, has become so degraded that childhood bronchial conditions that 30 years ago scarcely existed are now so common you can scarcely find a class where there aren't children assisted by "puffers" to help keep their lungs functioning.

It's very clear that the forces of globalization regard local cultures, local environments, local production as nothing more than "products" like the old aboriginal cultures to be consumed by the modern "more competitive" system. The problem is that locals are not products. They are diverse and necessary building elements required for the health of the human and physical environment. Whereas massive, simple systems are immensely powerful, they are also immensely vulnerable; as there is less and less complexity, people are less and less able to feed, clothe and protect their societies as local systems are squeezed out by the global production/consumer conveyor belt. In this way, human society as a whole is becoming more like the dinosaur, immensely powerful and immensely vulnerable to collapse.

◆ ◆ ◆

But a State that has a large middle class…that is neither too rich nor too poor is probably the most fortunate in the long run. They are less easily corrupted and more likely to decide fairly than either the very rich or the very poor.[1]

Democracies require a middle class that is larger than either extreme because the rich can buy whatever they want and don't need any government except a police force to protect their privileges, while the poor are obliged to focus on just getting by. It is the middle class which forms the great backbone of the democratic city and the democratic nation. The middle class both uses the services of the commonwealth and provides them back to the commonwealth. It is the middle class that use the libraries more, the school system longer, the medical and community services more frequently. In turn, it is the middle class who are the nurses, the teachers, the policemen, the firemen, the transit drivers, the paramedics, the community and social workers. And when the middle class retreats into gated communities, malls, distant suburbs, private schools, and wishes only to protect themselves from the demands of the commonwealth, where can a city look to for support? Where can the nation? Yeats had it right. In such a scenario, "Things fall apart; the center cannot hold; Mere anarchy is loosed upon the world."

But what neither Yeats nor Einstein could envisage as they stared into their personal crystal balls for intimations of the future is that a biological breakdown of the entire planet was possible; that was beyond even their imaginations. When contemplating the future, they thought in social and economic terms and of the possibilities of nuclear war, but fundamental changes to the planet's biomass or the biochemistry of the atmosphere just wasn't on their radar.

In the 21st century, you don't need to be a great physicist, poet or novelist to anticipate a different and more profound danger to humanity in your personal crystal ball; being a city councilor will suffice.

15

Cape Breton Beaches and the Gulf of Mexico

I love this old planet.
I love the days
When morning comes to me
On silver wings
And sunrise opens my eyes
With the gentlest of inquiries.
I love this old planet
And if I could,
Would wrap my arms around it ·
And pull it to my chest
To keep it safe.

— from *Canal Seasons*

CAPE BRETON, for all its great scenery, has never had great swimming. Icebergs promenading by in May don't make for warm water in July — or at least that's the way it used to be. I was "home" recently for a couple of weeks in summer and found the village beach busy with locals and visitors. Encouraged, I went swimming myself and found the water to be comfortable, not cold — even though the summer had not been especially warm.

Even more surprising, there were no long lines of salt drying on my skin when I came out. Nor did my skin itch with salt crystals. I felt no urge to run off for a freshwater shower. I wondered if my memory was playing tricks with me and asked a cousin if he could re-member the white lines of salt on his skin when we had been chil-dren. He replied that he did. "But why don't we have them now?" I asked.

He shrugged and said "the ocean is more like Florida now; there's no salt lines on your skin in Florida either." And we left it at that.

But the sensation of something being wrong wouldn't leave me. I went swimming again. Nothing changed. The salt lines didn't ap-pear. The water wasn't cold. Yet I felt chilled. It was one thing to read in a magazine that the oceans were warming and desalinizing, but it never occurred to me that this could be evident in something as ca-sual as a summer swim.

I've been been thinking about that summer swim, about New Or-leans and about how casual people have become about the effects of climate change. In October 2004, National Geographic published an article describing how it was inevitable that a standard force two tropical storm, when it passed over the super-heated waters of the Gulf of Mexico, would quickly ramp up to a three then a four and just before striking New Orleans be at force five.

When such a storm struck New Orleans, the article predicted, the city would be inundated with toxic, foul-smelling polluted sludge, and thousands would be trapped because they wouldn't have the means to get out. Reading the magazine article after Hurricane Katrina, I kept going back to the date of publication to remind my-self when it had been written because the article presented an exact description of what had actually happened.

National Geographic is not a NASA climate change publication. It's not even Scientific American. It's the magazine you read at the dentist's office. It's light. It's got great pictures, and it passes the time. How can it be that the American federal government can invest bil-lions in "Homeland Security", but can't keep up with National Geo-graphic?

For me, the scariest thing about New Orleans and the braggado-cio of pouring $50 billion into re-building the city is the unwilling-ness of people to ask "why?" How can there be such a gap between what most people see, feel and read daily and the priorities of their governments?

So far there is no indication that the political will exists to con-front the consequences of climate change. You can see it in the switch from using the word "refugee" to "evacuee" in the media to de-scribe the former residents of New Orleans. "Evacuee" sounds so much more reassuring; evacuation is a temporary condition. "Refugee," like the older "displaced person," is a permanent designation stemming from an irresolvable political or physical crisis. Nonetheless, the reality on the ground is residents of New Orleans are refugees and that's what people call them in Louisiana.

The reality is even an immensely wealthy nation like the United States cannot afford to rebuild from many disasters like New Orleans. The cost is too great.

The reality is also that New Orleans is not special. Other North American city governments don't govern any differently than the New Orleans city council. We're busy draining the whole south end of the city in Ottawa, and the fruits of this construction are already in: residents in the south end can no longer get insurance for flood damage. Nor will it be long before weather disaster insurance will not be available for anyone.

The reality is city councils, their state, provincial and federal counterparts have created global warming by treating the planet's biosphere like a vast sewer. In the city of Ottawa we've just finished a $1.2 million environmental assessment which is recommending another expressway because it will "improve" the air quality in Ottawa more than electric light rail. This recommendation comes in a city where 70 percent of the air pollution comes out of tailpipes and where recently it was so hot in July that asphalt melted like chocolate on downtown bridges.

In an emergency cities need local food supplies. They need local warehouse capacity. Ottawa, a city of 840,000 people, has no food warehouse capacity, little local farming and is as dependent as most other North American cities on cheap gasoline and 18 wheels. In an emergency, people need nurses, doctors, vaccines, equipment, mechanics, electrical workers, secure electric supply, safe water, public transit, communications. Emergency plans without robust public health capacity don't mean a thing. Ottawa is down with the town of Wawa, Ontario (2001 population 3,668)[1] for per capita public health funding, and this is regarded as a good thing because it keeps taxes down.

The reality is that cities all across North America have spent decades expanding their footprint in the cheapest possible way. None of them are prepared for anything more than business and politics as usual. New Orleans isn't unique. The size and character of the natural disaster and the subsequent meltdown of the urban fabric are all that's different.

Will New Orleans inspire people to demand that their governments do things differently? That's the billion dollar question. Watching my own city council vote down more money for trees and millions to build more roads and at the same time consider bringing back electric light rail, I am holding my breath. It feels like we're balanced on the edge of great change that could go one way or the other.

On one side of the divide is the challenge of creating cities and nations where we can live differently; where humans are just part of God's universe; where we see the animals, trees and the great bounty that used to populate our hemispheres return, not to be dominated by human beings but to be partners in sustaining our planet; where we are able to create new more democratic politics and new more sustainable economies; where the litmus test is always "does this make human society and the planet more just, more enduring?" This is what must happen if we are to survive.

In 2006, we are either living at the end of something or in the confusion of a new beginning.

PART III

Trying to Create a New Order of Things

We spent all our wealth acquired in the 20th century building an infrastructure of daily life which will not work very long into the 21st century...suburbia is best understood as the greatest misallocation of resources in the history of the world...somewhere up in the tens of trillions of dollars...

— James Howard Kunstler,
The Long Emergency

IF YOU ARE FINDING Urban Meltdown tough going, you don't want to read *The Long Emergency* by James Kunstler.[1] Kunstler is much less optimistic than I am that any government will be able to react with enough dispatch to mitigate the coming consequences of oil price rises and absolute declines in resource supplies. Not only does he think national governments will soon be irrelevant to people's daily lives as they are proving in the Gulf states right now, but he expects that large city governments will also crumble, the larger the city the faster the decay. His prediction is that we will have to return to low-cost, low-energy, small scale urban and rural environments. The best way this can be done is reinventing the small cities and rural landscapes that prospered in the mid-19th century when farming was based on horse-powered machinery (as the Mennonite communities remain today) and cities were basically walking environments.

I recommend his book to you and do not disagree with many of his conclusions. But I am not ready to abandon hope for large cities or some role for national governments. Right now, each year China is building coal-fired electrical generating stations equivalent to bringing on-line the entire electrical capacity of Switzerland. We need to have an international dialogue around that with a view to stopping this manner of creating electricity. It is simply too environmentally damaging, and national governments have a role to play here as does a reformed version of the United Nations.

Simply throwing up your hands and saying "well, it's going to happen" is not in my nature, nor is it in most people's. Nonetheless Kunstler's scenario is certainly possible. Rome declined from a population of a million people in 400 A.D. to a town of 15,000 after the dissolution of its empire. A similar fate may await our large cities if land values collapse and there are no jobs to support what is left.

Oil and natural gas supplies will continue to be available for some time to come even if the prices are much higher. There is a window of opportunity here and now to make changes which will ease the transition back to urban and rural landscapes which are less fuel dependent. But part of the trick of getting that window open is understanding the political and social journey that got us where we are today.

How we did we get into this merry, massive misallocation of resources? How did the success of cities result in a dangerous decline of the planet's biological integrity? Part III is about exploring how many people have tried hard to take a different road from the one that was followed, and what we can learn from those experiences to start succeeding.

16

The Rise of Cities and the Decline of the Planet

The word government derives from the Greek
word meaning row. An antique relation
until one recalls the Greeks conquered the world
and began to invent the west
with the idea of democracy,
citizenship,
mathematics, philosophy,
medicine, poetry, theatre,
architecture, sculpture,
and ships like the great triremes
powered by free men
choosing a destination,
then rowing towards it.

— from *Canal Seasons*

EDWARD GIBBON SPENT his life researching, thinking and writing about the decline and fall of the Roman Empire[1], a subject which fascinated him ever since the moment he saw a flock of sheep grazing in the ruins of the once mighty Forum of Rome where Cicero had thundered his great speeches against Marc Antony and where Julius Caesar was murdered. When Gibbon saw it, the city of Rome was a country town of about 15,000 people. Once it had been a city of a million people, alive with commerce, political and cultural life, embellished with majestic buildings and public places so grand and harmonious in design that just the few broken shards that remain delight the eye. Who could not be impressed with the departure of such an astonishing human accomplishment?

Modern libraries are filled with books, essays and speculations about why something so vast as the Roman Empire could have crumbled so completely. But what interests me more is how did it come to be so durable, to prosper for so long? Even after Alaric sacked Rome in A.D. 408, Roman cities continued to flourish in North Africa, in the Middle East and Europe for centuries under different guises and different rulers. It would take repeated murderous attacks by thousands of nomads who had absolutely no interest in anything but acquiring the moveable goods of the residents before the Roman civilization of connected cities finally lurched forever into stone skeletons.[2]

The first reason for the Roman empire's durability is well known and well studied: the success of the Roman military. The Roman armies and navies were the world's first professional military organizations and evolved over many centuries. They were not just forces of order, but great integrative organizations capable of providing careers to Roman citizens and non-citizens alike, building cities, harbors and great public works. They were Rome's public service staffed with administrators, mail carriers, doctors, engineers, architects, craftsmen as well as soldiers. These military organizations were above all durable, surviving republican democracy, good and bad emperors, foreign and domestic disasters. Rome was not possible without her legions and navies.

But at the end of the Roman Empire in what is now Tunisia, there was only a single legion at about half strength, about 3,000 men, to keep order for a vast territory. In Britain, there was none. They had all been withdrawn. While Gibbon describes the gradual erosion of the legions' manpower as the principal reason the Empire could no longer defend itself, what is extraordinary is what so few men were able to accomplish for so long.

The legions contained all the skills necessary to build, maintain and populate a small city, and this is exactly what they did. When a Roman legion was retired (which happened every 20 years) it was "settled" on land acquired through its military successes. Once this happened, the legionnaires simply built a permanent version of their campaign winter camps, using the same skills, technology and town plans.

The Legate's or General Officer's Quarters at the center of the camp became the forum, (the place of government and business), with all the streets, public baths, sewers and waterworks servicing the town much as they would in a winter camp — except built from permanent materials. A retired legion could throw up an impressive town like Orange in France — complete with a municipal theater, public baths, sewer and water systems — in just a few years. To the native populations, it must have seemed close to magic. The legions built these small, robust cities all over Europe, North Africa and the Middle East and in this way created the world's first civilization of cities.

What isn't so well appreciated is that the urban form they created had extremely low maintenance and energy costs. It was astonishingly sustainable such that even when the empire as a global federation was collapsing, these small cities continued to function until they were extirpated by literally smashing the buildings physically and hauling off the stone for other purposes.

Roman cities worked with a kind of public and private efficiency that is difficult for modern city residents to imagine. They had no police force or jails. Roman cities were able to dispense with these enormous expenses (somewhere between ¼ and ⅙th of every modern city's budget) largely because of the urban forum they created. They were fractal. Just as the human body is constructed from one basic biological cell that serves as the building blocks for all the body's tissues, the Roman city had one basic building form, the insula or "island."

The largest expression of the insula form was the forum at the center of the city, which was a great square with the "capitol" or federal buildings along one side, municipal offices, commodity exchanges and financial businesses along another, and shops in the leftover spaces. In the open square in the center, there was often a market place. Around three sides, the federal temples excluded, the larger forums had a two-story canopied walkway under which people could stroll about their daily business shaded from the hot sun in summer and from intemperate weather in winter.

It is hot work today walking across the open fields of ruined buildings among the first-floor remains of a Roman city, but when these cities existed as functioning entities, they required no air conditioning in the summer and little heat in the winter beyond a kitchen stove. The buildings were covered with thick red tile roofs, and what wasn't roofed with tile had awnings so that almost everywhere you walked you were protected from the direct force of the elements. It was a remarkably "snug" environment.

Police could be dispensed with because the exterior walls of the forum and all the housing was windowless and thus presented a blank, impenetrable wall to any intruders. At the close of the business day at the forum, security was as simple as people locking the front doors on their stores and the watchman locking the forum's main gate. A thief could always enter, but he would be obliged to scale a smooth, vertical face three or four stories high, crawl across extensive roofs and then lower himself down carefully via ropes on the far side. It would be difficult to do this unobserved and even more difficult to exit with anything of value if you could.

Private homes were sealed squares built in the same basic urban form: blank exteriors shielding interior walkways, gardens and living spaces. It was a neat, secure, low cost, low energy, comfortable environment, and it was replicated over and over again from the meanest rented rooms to the richest villa. The city landscape was formed from private insulae built in a square or rectangular shape; several insulae would make up a city block. The poorer the quarter, the more insulae (housing) were jammed into the block, the richer the fewer.

Each private insula was an efficient combination of domesticity, business and urban agriculture. At the back of the house were baking ovens, a cooking area and a small garden open to the sky, which managed to produce a substantial portion of the household food. At the front of the house just off the street were business offices, and often on commercial streets, small stores were rented along the outside walls. Sleeping chambers were off the central area, which was a private version of the grand square of the forum. Like the forum it was open to the sky, but unlike the forum it was entirely private and had an impluvium (water basin) in the center to catch rainwater and often a household cistern underneath. These provided both a decorous centerpiece to the house and fresh water from the cistern.

All that really varied between the insulae was the size and opulence of the residence. Some were magnificent with ceremonial main rooms decorated with gorgeous mosaics and spacious, ornamental rather than functional gardens at the back of the house. Rich homes were also often graced with a library and reading rooms. Rich and cultured men like Marcus Tullius Cicero owned city houses and country villas worth millions that were considered works of art. At the other end of the scale, some insulae were more like a human stable with tiny rooms, little furniture and nothing but the roughest, barest necessities.

Together the private insulae and the grid of streets separating them (on which our modern city blocks are still based), the many public buildings, the baths, theater, fountains, aqueducts, bridges and government forum formed the city. Once it was up and operating, the Roman city whether it was in Roman Gaul, Spain, Africa, Greece or the East provided the residents with a secure, clean and comfortable environment to go about their lives. Millions of people from different cultures found the Roman city an attractive, comfortable way to live and adopted this global lifestyle with enthusiasm.

Roman water systems were all designed to function using only gravity for propulsion. There were no turbines required to pump waste across miles of underground tunnels. The Roman storm sewers were so well designed that even today, you can go to a little Roman town like Dougga in Tunisia and see that the town's drainage system still functions, keeping the streets dry. The Roman system of aqueducts, cisterns and piping which provided fresh water had to be physically destroyed by the various invaders before they stopped working.

The great public baths, which were very large buildings by any standard modern or ancient, required remarkably few people to operate. Wood, charcoal or coal had to be transported to the baths to build the fires in the hypocausts (a raised, heated floor) to heat the hot water pools of the public baths, but this was no more difficult than stoking a 20th-century steam engine's boiler with coal.

Fresh water in the baths was constantly arriving and old water constantly draining off; in this way the bathing water always remained clean without any chemicals or treatment. Compare this kind of operation to the high-energy maintenance required for a modern indoor swimming pool, which needs a battery of chemicals, tradespeople and annual closures for maintenance to ensure the health and security of the pool users.

Much is made of the Roman slave population (which was extensive), but these were private slaves owned for private homes and private businesses. There were very few public slaves. In short, the Romans created cities that had minimal maintenance costs but provided attractive, successful commercial opportunities. People in the highlands of North Africa, Portugal and Britain were connected to cities and towns thousands of miles away in Italy and France. The urban civic and economic environments were constantly renewing.

Pompeii endured a terrible earthquake, but ten years later was on the way to being entirely rebuilt when the volcano erupted and ended the life of that city forever.

When Roman emperors were rising and falling like tenpins in Rome, Roman citizens were getting on with their lives in interesting ways thousands of miles away with little reference to or care for the machinations of the central government. The Roman empire disintegrated not because the cities didn't work. Quite the reverse: the cities remained vibrant politically and economically long after the Senate and Emperor's court had disintegrated into a presumptive mess.

The cities worked. The roads were communication marvels, the ports and industrial enterprises active and successful. Barbarian armies rarely defeated Roman generals. Most of the time, they were nothing but distant bad weather. The idea of a barbarian chief penetrating Italy proper and crashing through one of the 12 giant gates of Rome was ludicrous to consider. It hadn't happened since the days of the Republic, more than 500 years before. The Roman Senate did not take Alaric seriously even when his army parked under its walls. They refused to negotiate with him and treated him as if they had the genius of Julius Caesar and his veteran legions at their back.

In Rome, the population murdered General Stilocho's widow on the scapegoat assumption that the Emperor's murder of her husband had saved the Emperor from Alaric's army and thought the same would result when they murdered his widow. The citizenry were confused when her murder accomplished nothing but her death. It wasn't just the Roman government that has lost touch with reality; so had the citizens of Rome. It was all pathetic and ridiculous. The Senate had nothing much but the memory of Roman arms and their own vanities. They were entirely blind to the grim reality before them.

The city of Rome required imported grain from its colonies to assure its security. This was the federal government's only social service to the people of Rome, but it was essential. Without it a million people could not exist in Rome. Alaric realized this, and he made no attempt to breach the vast walls of the ancient city. Instead he cut off the grain supply by blockading the port of Ostia. Rome wilted like a flower.

The smaller cities of the Roman Empire did not require massive injections of distant food supplies to remain viable, but they needed Rome's central administrative capacity and military safety net to keep the system as a whole functioning. Thus when Rome suddenly collapsed — in the same way the collapse of great centers like New York, London, Paris, Berlin or Tokyo would today — the consequences ricocheted across nations and oceans creating a cascade of local business and municipal failures.

Today North American cities large or small are not self-sufficient. Like ancient Rome they depend on the transcontinental shipment of food and just about everything that can't be produced super-cheaply locally. Most of the food on the kitchen table has traveled about 1,100 miles to get there. If the day ever comes when this kind of transportation extravaganza becomes too costly or too difficult to undertake, modern cities will shrink back to the size that can be supported on local resources.

It was in the cities that the idea of the modern nation and the modern age was born. Two thousand five hundred years ago Pericles said, "all good things flow to the city." In short, without cities there is no nation. Venice and Florence invented modernity with the Italian cultural, business and democratic Renaissance. Paris invented the French Republic with liberty, equality and fraternity. When Alexis de Toqueville reported on American democracy, he was talking about the democracy as expressed in the town halls of New England. It was these little urban places and a couple of greater cities like New York and Philadelphia that set the entire, democratic skeleton in place for what would become the United States.

The irony is that although the magnificent success of cities has made nations possible, the largest cities have become the servants of the nations they created. The relationship is symbiotic. Nations need great cities, and cities need a national structure. For without a supportive hinterland and some peaceful co-existence between nations, cities are the first to crumble; that was why Troy fell to the Greek federation and Athens in its turn fell to the Romans. Sarajevo was disemboweled by ethnic hatred from beyond its valley, and New York has seen its golden towers crumble. Cities, no matter how powerful, when left to their own devices soon fall prey to the wider human geography. Pericles failed utterly to understand that Athenian democracy to remain successful needed to find a way to live in harmony — not in competition — with its rival Sparta. Thus Pericles saw his city crumble because of that failure to realize his city's limitations.

◆ ◆ ◆

Pericles's famous line "all good things flow to the city" is not correct. All good things cannot flow to the city. There must be a rough equilibrium between the creation of money and services in the city and flow of raw materials from the countryside. The city can't be allowed to suck the countryside dry, but nor can the reverse happen.

There must be an environmental balance. Industrial practices in city X can't be allowed to destroy the water quality of downstream city Y. A specific example would be Israeli cities using Palestinian underground aquifers to service Israeli populations without reference to the needs of Palestinian cities. This is a genuine causus belli and a one-way ticket to environmental and social instability. So national governments must ensure there are environmental mechanisms in place to ensure urban and rural environments cohabit in a way that each strengthens the other, not exploits one in favor of another.

Second: trade has always been the principal source of wealth for cities, and trade requires the safe, secure transport of goods and people. Otherwise commerce is impossible and cities shrivel. National governments need to assure trade routes remain fast, efficient and secure.

Third: cities require some rough redistribution of wealth such that disparities between cities and regions are not extreme.

These three objectives are not easy to guarantee. We have been failing for a long time on the question of environmental balance and redistributive fairness. We have been going in exactly the opposite direction of the Periclian maxim — all good things flow to the city. The Greater Toronto Area generates 42 percent of the entire Canadian federal tax revenue. Some nine billion in tax revenue is created each year that does not return to that urban area. The same inequity is occurring with New York City and every other North American urban area. In the city of Ottawa economic activity creates about $1.5 billion more in taxes than returns to it. The larger the city becomes the less sustainable the situation becomes. It is the reverse of the Pericles maxim. Presently, the American and Canadian federal governments simply get too much tax money and the cities too little.

In Toronto each year, the city provides less public health services, less affordable housing, fewer libraries, fewer community services and builds less public transit than are required for a healthy environment, yet must still find some way to integrate 100,000 new people a year. The city alone can't do it. In the last twenty years Toronto has sunk from one of the cleanest, most desirable places on the planet to one where rock stars need to throw benefit concerts in order to convince people that the city is healthy enough to visit. Just ten years ago, this would have been laughable.

There are now so many smog advisory days (signalling serious air quality degradation) in Toronto during the summer months that the city now generates smog refugees who migrate north, east and west to escape the poor air. But unfortunately the bad air is following them. Remote wilderness areas like Algonquin Park are now registering poor air quality days as the plume of noxious city air drifts relentlessly north. SARS, a new and deadly virus, was fought to a standstill by the city's health professionals while the provincial and federal governments stood around watching and making rather odd public announcements which served only to illustrate how disconnected they were from what was going on in the viral ground war being waged in the city.

No, things are not going well for Canadian nor American cities.

"Pax Romana" worked for a thousand years because at rock bottom its low-energy, low-cost urban environments needed only a modicum of international security to assure the flow of commerce. Everything else the cities were able to manage themselves. The word civilization comes from Latin and means "of the civic." Thus from the beginning the city, civil society and civilizations were inextricably intertwined. Civilization didn't arise from a shepherd's field. It arose from a town square.

I have trouble imagining living in the filthy alleys of medieval Europe be it London, Paris or Rome. From the distance of four centuries, Elizabethan London looks romantic, but it was filthy and disease-ridden. Plague seasons aside, thousands of people died each year from waterborne diseases that were unknown to the Romans simply because the Romans understood the concept of public health. Even today, I find a stroll through the medieval streets of a European town leaves me feeling claustrophobic. It's easy to imagine how narrow, cobblestone paths served as open sewers running with human feces and urine, and how abutting these surface sewers, people lived in lice-ridden dark rooms much less attractive than a hillside cave. Urinating behind stairwells was standard practice in Versailles. The royal court was obliged to promenade from chateau to chateau every two or three months so that servants could flush the royal buildings out like stables.

On the other hand, I don't have much trouble imagining living in a Roman city — whether it was a large and comfortable one like Pompeii appointed with a theater district, grand public forums, gymnasia and a diverse population, or a frontier town like Volubilis in the Atlas mountains of Morocco.

Volubilis is a peanut compared to Pompeii; the whole town could be set down in one of Pompeii's neighborhoods. Volubilis would be comparable today to a Midwestern American town or a sleepy Ontario one like Brockville. Coming upon its ruins in a pleasant highland valley uncluttered by modern development, it was easy to imagine that people had once lived in this town in a safe and civil way. Walking the streets I could feel the friendly presence of these ancient citizens everywhere: men discussing corn and oil prices and distant politics in the forum, children playing in the streets, women shopping. The courts, temples and cafes would be busy with gossip and conversation.

The main boulevard of Volubilis is wide and spacious with a shaded, colonnaded walkway to protect pedestrians from the summer heat. Everywhere in the town the residents had a pleasant vista of their gentle, rolling mountain valley. The town was not huddled behind walls on the top of a hill, but spread about comfortably on a broad rise in the land, which gave it a vista and a defensive position without turning the place into a bunker.

In the museum on the site I found a toilet kit. It looked exactly like a modern toilet kit: tweezers, nail scissors, razor and so on. These little instruments looked fragile and so utterly human. There were bits and pieces of derivative statuary art collected from houses in the town and displayed in the museum's garden. The statues must have been imported from the ateliers of Arles or another more important Roman center. Perhaps because I come from a provincial place myself, I found this ancient provincialism endearing.

Walking over the paving stones of the broad main boulevard still lined with broken stumps of columns, in this remote place buried in the Atlas mountains of Morocco, I was overcome with the vivid image of thousands of provincial towns like Volubilis spread over the many nations we now know in Europe, North Africa and the Middle East.

It is only in the last century that we have matched the Romans, and in some dimensions we are still behind them. North Africa, for example, has reached no political accommodation with Europe and enjoys little of the vast agricultural wealth it did during the Roman era. Most of the lands that was once graced with vineyards, olive groves and wheat fields have become desert and are wracked with violent religious and internecine conflicts.

When I look back on the last 2,000 years, I see no inevitable march to some human nirvana. Although Roman society prospered for 800 years, it had many bloody reverses and tightrope passages when it tilted on the edge of chaos. When the Roman civilization of cities finally did irrevocably implode, it would take more than a thousand years before humans were able to start to rebuild the culture of cities, science, engineering, public health, arts and democratic civil society again.

Today cities have risen again and are pre-eminent in a way the ancient Romans could not imagine. Cities have become not just a Mediterranean phenomenon but a truly global one. Human habitation is moving towards 80 percent of the population living in cities. This is where Canada is now. Everywhere the countryside is depopulating in favor of cities. There are 20 modern cities with populations larger than the entire citizenry of the Roman Empire which has been calculated to be about 20 million. Human life has again become city life.

◆ ◆ ◆

Will the modern incarnation of the urban endure for 500 years as the cities of the Roman Empire did, or will they crash again like the phoenix?

There are two general constellation of reasons which makes long life for modern cities more problematic than it was for the ancient ones. There are more urban people today, both in absolute and relative terms, unable to obtain the basics of life (clean water and clean air) than there were in Roman times, and that number is growing, not shrinking. Roman cities for all the territory that they covered and their intense urban character were at base very simply and efficiently organized. The modern city is not. It depends on complicated electronics, complicated computers, complicated institutional arrangements and vast global resource-delivery systems. If any of these systems of organization are seriously impaired (which because they are large and complex is more probable than not) our modern cities are in trouble.

A good example is the attack on the World Trade Center. As the history of world catastrophes go this was a peanut: a couple of large buildings and a few thousand people were directly affected. Think of the London blitz during the Second War; at its height 500 people died every night. Yet the city continued to function. Life went on. The electrical system continued to work. The underground and the buses ran. City life went on. But in New York two office towers came down, and an entire nation ground to a halt, thousands become unemployed and people living thousands of miles away from the incident were affected. This says to me that the modern urban system is not very robust. There isn't much redundancy or flexibility in the modern city as there was even a short a time ago in war-time London, where if one part of the electrical system went down the whole did not.

No modern city can operate without electricity. We now need electricity to run everything from water filtration plants to food storage to police forces. Without electricity, modern cities are unmanageable. Yet it's clear from recent brownouts that the electrical supply is becoming more vulnerable, not less. It's now possible to have a brownout that can affect half a continent. This has been made possible by the desire of the "energy industry" to move electricity around the continent like a commodity in order to be able to sell to the highest bidder. By creating this continent-wide delivery system, we have created the possibility of continent-wide failure. There is no redundancy in the system, no flexibility, no independence. It all works or nothing works.

Secondly and more seriously, the energy consumption of cities is literally burning up the planet. Greenhouse gases, 80 percent of which are produced by cities, are creating unstable climate conditions of calamitous proportions everywhere. Modern federal governments treat the greatest danger to modernity — climate change — as if it didn't exist. Like the Roman Senate which refused to admit that the arrival of Alaric at the gates of Rome was anything more serious than an annoying gnat, modern federal leaders of the earth's most populous nations (China, India, Europe and the United States) treat climate change in the same way, like an annoying gnat that persists when it has been asked frequently to leave.

Mr. Bush is burning up trillions of dollars chasing "terrorists," destroying the carrying capacity of entire nations and creating "space shields" while the first urban casualty of climate change has already arrived in his own backyard. New Orleans literally washes back and forth in surge of the Gulf of Mexico with little succor while Mr. Bush fights terrorists everywhere.

To the north Mr. Harper the current Prime Minister of Canada behaves much the same way as he pours Canadian national resources and political capital into "troops" in Afghanistan. At home the nation he leads remains one of the most polluting on the planet, and he refuses to admit that the Kyoto carbon emission reduction targets are attainable. His approach is "Sorry. No can do. We'll just have to learn to live with climate change."

If there is one thing the collapse of the Roman empire teaches us, it is that continent-wide complex societies are not defeated by "terrorists" (an external enemy). They simply lose their own ability to continue. Alaric never defeated Roman arms. The last Roman general to fight Alaric, Stilocho defeated him twice using the same cautious defensive techniques that Julius Caesar had used more than four centuries earlier.

But just as the Berlin Wall came down without a shot being fired, so did the great walls of Rome. The one thing that Gibbon got perfectly right and upon which his fame will always rest, is that in the end Rome simply faded away. There was no military defeat. The planet's first civilization of cities came apart like rotten stitching coming out of an old baseball.

When the frontier walls were breached by Alaric, Stilocho and his officer corps were invited to dine with the Emperor at his castle in Ravenna. They were told not to bring weapons. They did as requested. The general and his entire officer corps were slaughtered by the Emperor's house guards while they sat defenseless waiting to be served dinner. These things happened. Roman history is filled with outrageous acts and poisonous moments as well as achievement.

Stilocho was a bright, energetic general. His fatal, but entirely understandable, mistake was assuming that he and the Emperor were both citizens of Rome and both playing from the same page at a time of national crisis. He was about as wrong as a person could be, and his mistake cost him his life. The Emperor's house guard washed the blood off their swords, scrubbed down the hall, and continued to live comfortably along with the boss while the empire went up in flames around them.

What made the murder of Stilocho and his officer corps different from other cruel and unusual Roman acts was that Emperor Honorius had no Plan B. He had no intention of defending Rome himself or had anyone else in mind to do it. Emperor Honorius became the first feudal king of Europe. In this personal ambition, he was entirely successful and lived to a ripe old age in Ravenna surrounded by the delights of that charming little city, his little army and the subservience of his retainers.

Honorius survived Alaric's invasion because he had marginalized himself to such an extent that he was of no consequence. In just the same way George Bush may comfortably survive the coming climate crisis in his Texas eco-bunker. Honorius's importance had shrunk to the gates of his castle walls. Alaric didn't bother attacking Ravenna. What was the point? Without the Roman legions or a government to organize the defence of the empire, there were thousands of square miles of rich countryside, undefended villas, villages, towns and cities over which his warriors could graze for years at their leisure like locusts slowly moving through fields of ripe grain. Life would be good.

Rome was left to defend itself, a task that in the Republican era the citizens of Rome could have done capably enough installed behind their immense city walls. But it had been centuries since Roman society had been organized around the idea of citizen-soldiers. The citizens of Rome were civilians. The professional armies of Rome were supposed to defend them. When Stilocho was murdered, the citizens were left with nothing but misplaced pride, confusion, fear and suspicion. Eventually, someone opened the gates of the city and just let the barbarians in.

The old men of the Senate dressed in their finest togas sat at the entrance ways of their houses silent, awaiting Alaric, defended only by the pride and courage that had made Rome mistress of the world. They did not carry swords or make any aggressive move. At first Alaric's men were not sure if they were statues or animate, and pushed cautiously at them with the tips of their swords. When they realized that they were just old men they butchered the senators in the casual, cheery way a lawn pot is smashed by a drunken teenager.

At the end of the day, the collapse of Rome was not a military one nor an economic one: it was political. Rome no longer had a political system capable of addressing the problems of the day. The Emperor and the Senate were so divorced from the real problems of their age that they had become nothing more than barnacles on the ship's hull. The Empire as a political entity had sunk into a phantom state. It existed but real life went on disconnected from it. Business was still conducted. City councilors were still elected. Cities like Arles, towns like Volubilis still functioned. Games and theater festivals were still held. Public baths still had hot water. Artists still painted frescoes and carved statues. Doctors, engineers and architects still practiced their professions. The commodity exchanges still traded goods. The temples still had priests. The sea lanes were still useable. As the kids like to say today, it was "all good."

At the beginning of the 5th century, Pax Romana was like a vast ocean liner, so massive that it was impossible to imagine it ever doing anything but moving slowly and majestically across the sea. But no ship, no matter how large, can continue sailing when there is a fundamental disconnection between those on the bridge and the those in the engine room.

The beginning of the 21st century has the same potential as the 5th for social breakdown. I look at the federal leaders in Ottawa and Washington, and no matter what their party they have no priorities that are my priorities. Mr. Harper's five priorities are all about containment and restraint; increasing the size of the military; making more rules for bureaucrats, tougher laws for criminals and so on. These are not the priorities of a city councilor. A city councilor is primarily concerned with improving public capacity.

I imagine a 5th-century decurion (city councilor) in Massila, Gaul must have felt about the Roman Senate and Emperor in Italy much as I do today about federal politicians in Washington and Ottawa. They are irrelevant to my concerns, and this is confirmed by how city residents vote. They vote against the government. The present Canadian government did not get a single seat in the largest Canadian cities and very few in the rest. The same voting pattern has unfolded in the United States, demonstrating the same disconnections between the urban centers and the national administrations.

◆ ◆ ◆

The importance of Edward Gibbon's *History of the Decline and Fall of the Roman Empire* may be difficult to understand today because so many of his ideas and points of view have been incorporated into society's vision of how society functions and doesn't function. He was writing in the age of enlightenment for the age of revolution. Without ever intending to, he became the Tom Paine of the English middle and upper classes.

But he was as unlike Paine as you could imagine. He wasn't a brilliant, human rights pamphleteer with nothing more than a few years of schooling. Gibbon wasn't a revolutionary in any way. He was a man of inherited wealth and privilege. Tom Paine would have regarded him as a member of the oppressing classes, but ironically Gibbon released mind-changing ideas into society just as Paine did and with as great effect.

Prime ministers and philosophers like David Hume read his books. The first volume appeared in 1776 and immediately went through three editions. With those volumes the revolutionary idea began to circulate that society wasn't something handed down on a

plate to an inherited and inheriting gentry. *The Decline and Fall* was
a new kind of history, one that was more than an assembly of person-
ages, events and dates.

It was an account of the past that kept asking the question "why?"
Why did things happen the way they did? The question led Gibbon
down some unexpected roads. Contemporary British clerics de-
nounced Gibbon as a pagan, demanding he withdraw his comments
about the Christian church being "defeatist" and "parasitic" on the
Roman state by preaching this world was just a way station en route
to heaven.

Gibbon fought back because he was an authentic scholar, and
authentic scholarship always ends up offending because it holds
nothing sacred. It took an eccentric genius to write the six volumes of
The History of the Decline and Fall of the Roman Empire, but it doesn't
take a genius to draw contemporary parallels with the British Empire or the American one. Three hundred years later, we are still com-
paring.

Will the decline of the American empire and the western idea of
progress be linked to 9/11 and the invasion of Iraq? Or will it be the
melting of the polar ice caps? Or will we figure out a way to defeat
these modern demons? Time will tell, but the concept that great empires precipitate their own demise will always remain Gibbon's.

As yet, there has been no modern equivalent to the Roman experience. Even after the conflagration of the Second World War, the
nightmares of the death camps, the nuclear bombing of Hiroshima
and Nagasaki, civilization has been able to pick itself up and continue remarkably quickly even in the most devastated nations. But
after Rome fell, there was no quick recovery; the very fabric of civilization unwound like a ball of wool. The most basic concepts —
the rule of law, citizenship, literacy, public and personal hygiene,
medicine, the plastic and literary arts, the sciences, engineering and
architecture, visual perspective, pluralism, agnosticism, the theater
— disappeared.

The fundamental lessons for us today from reading *The Decline
and Fall* are simple enough. The actors and specifics of the situation
have changed, but the 21st-century urban crisis shares many connections with the ancient. Cities can survive a great deal, but they
cannot survive the abandonment of responsibility for the commonwealth. When enough people lose interest in civic and public life,
neither great cities nor great nations can endure.

Mr. Bush's concept of what constitutes the nation called the United States and the many territories it controls like that of the Emperor Honorious is essentially a private one. He is a "saved" Christian. He "doesn't get poverty." He's not interested in environmental issues nor world governance. His focus is on protecting the walls of his castle. Hence he would create a missile shield around the United States and foreign policies based on protecting oil supplies. He talks incessantly about "protecting Americans" from the terrorist threat as if they lived in a planetary fortress all by themselves, divorced from other peoples. There is no interest in a world order of government like the World Court, the Geneva Convention or Kyoto.

The extent of the retreat from the optimism of the past is astonishing. Do we remember that it was the American humanitarian Clara Barton on the world stage who convinced the United States Congress to sign the Geneva Agreement on the treatment of the sick, wounded and dead in battle, and the treatment of prisoners of war? Clara Barton did this in 1882. How is it that such a noble and important impulse could be quashed so easily in the secret prisons of Guantanamo Bay? The treatment of defeated armies with magnanimity has made ending wars with dignity possible. Without it, wars are reduced to tribal vengeance to which there is no end.

Ordinary people are retreating into "family values" and religious simplicities. We are beginning the 21st century with citizens who can't read as well as previous generations; who can't quote a single verse of any poet; who can't concentrate as well as previous generations; whose idea of historical context is what happened on CNN last week; who are fearful of "terrorists" and ready to exchange basic democratic freedoms for special laws which create, in effect, two orders of humanity. This is stuff right out of the Middle Ages. It is not a recipe for moving calmly and confidently forward. It's a recipe for a sudden rupture with the past.

Citizens are no longer rowing together towards a common end because they no longer have an idea of what that common end might be. If our modern civilization collapses, people some day will surely ask what happened? Was it terrorists? Was it the oil wars? Was it climate change? Was it the differences in wealth that emerged both inside nations and between nations? Was it governments that paid more attention to corporate profits than the environment? But the precise answer will be as difficult to describe as it has been for the Roman Empire, because in the final days it will be not the last bricks that cause the walls to crumble; it will be the accumulation of removals.

Nothing is constant in either the physical world or the human. Individuals grow smarter or stupider. Collectively, nations grow wiser and happier, or stupider and crueler. Citizenship expands or shrinks. The biosphere grows more malignant or more benign. "The only thing constant is change."

If western citizens continue to retreat into gated communities and make protecting those communities their principal priority; if national governments continue to behave like client states that serve the industrial/military complex instead of reforming their own democracies to genuinely share both the planet's governance and its wealth, the urban empire of the 20th and 21st centuries will also fade. The end will come just as the Roman Empire's did — with no one really believing it could happen.

But until the final meltdown arrives, there will be people and key moments when the necessary changes can be made for societies and civilization to successfully continue. General Stilocho saw what needed to be done and could have done it, if he had enjoyed the confidence of the Emperor and Senate. Vanity Fair's Special Green Issue of May 2006 is chock full of national and local heros who know what needs to be done. On the cover page they have the Stilochos of our age: Robert Kennedy Jr., Al Gore, George Clooney, Julia Roberts. There's no shortage of heroes, but that doesn't mean the end won't come anyway and won't surprise everyone when it does. At bottom, we believe ourselves to be eternal and that the only social life we have known will continue, even if individuals don't.

Not even Alaric expected the Roman Empire to fall away in front of his army. He was ready to withdraw from Rome if the Senate would have guaranteed him title to one small Roman province, Noricum, which Gibbon described as impoverished. But the Roman Senate was not about to demean itself by negotiating with a barbarian and so the end arrived — to their great surprise. The end for the great cities of our age will also come if we cannot focus on the real problems that beset humanity.

The 21st century future like the 5th will be defined by our political capacity to react positively to environmental and social challenges.

The enormity of the challenge that is approaching is impossible to grasp, because no one has the slightest idea of what specific climate calamity will change our civilization forever. But what I am absolutely sure of is that, when it arrives, it will be a total surprise. Like

Hurricane Katrina breaking the massive Mississippi levees, no one will really believe it until it actually happens. This is not pessimism. It is simply how ends are defined. Ends become ends by being final and they always astonish. This is the way it was for Roman society, and this is the way it will be for ours.

17

689 Spadina and Coming of Age in Toronto

*The fault lines in rock
are invisible to the rock
like the heart scars in humans.
Dividing universes
into before and after,
into different shapes,
and different feelings
crashed on one side of the scar
the thin white line
separating one world
from the other.*

— from *Soul Stones*,
an unpublished manuscript

I GREW UP IN what people now refer to as the "old Canada" as opposed to what my children refer to as the "new Canada." In this
way, they distinguish between their reference points and mine. It is
useful because these two Canadas are different places. The old Canada was a country of small cities, small towns and small farms. There
were no globalized businesses and only a few national ones. Many of
the most important businesses were crown corporations like Trans
Canada Airlines (TCA) and Canadian National Railways (CN).
The old Canada was a thoroughly conservative, provincial place. It

had a few large ethnic groups — the English, the Scots and Irish, the French and the aboriginal people — on the distant margins. There were of course some immigrants, but they were mostly white and mostly you would not have noticed them unless you were one.

My hometown was an Ottawa valley timber town with a big pulp mill in the center of the city, rafts of wood floating down the river from the upper valley in the summer and old streetcars rumbling back and forth along the main streets. Except for the Parliament Buildings sitting on a bluff, it wasn't a whole lot different from any other town in the valley. From kindergarten to graduation, I can remember only one person of color in the city schools I attended.

There were some differences. There was the French side of town and the English, but these differences had been around for so long that we hardly noticed them. Many families, my own among them, had these differences integrated in our own homes with one parent being French and the other English, and both languages echoed back and forth. I attended first year at a local university without a thought that it was worth the money to leave for another place. But after only a year the fever of those years caught up with me, and suddenly I decided that I wanted out. I had had enough of playing the same sports, hanging out with the same friends; I wanted to leave the city for another place.

I was a football player, and as a football player you weren't allowed to transfer from one university to another and still expect to play without an academic reason. The rule was set up to prevent coaches poaching players from one university to the next. So I picked a course of study that my hometown university didn't offer: anthropology. It worked like a charm, and I was off to the biggest city in Canada to play football there.

That first bus ride towards Toronto is etched in my memory. After hours of rolling by the forests, lakes and the small farms that I had grown up with, we came out onto the broad ribbon of the 401 highway. There, we were soon into the suburban outskirts of Toronto. As far as the eye could see there was nothing but miles of TV aerials sticking up like tiny steel umbrellas from flat bungalow roofs. I couldn't get over the view. The bungalows drifted along towards a horizon as spacious as the ocean. I tried imagine how many streets there were and couldn't, and what were all those people doing to earn a living?

Then finally beyond the bungalow horizon, the city began to appear: the tall buildings distant needle points spiking along the lakefront. It all seemed monstrous, enormous — as if no adventure was too big for this place. My first ride on the subway was euphoric: the rattle and roll of the ride, the shriek of the brakes, the glowing commercials, the mysterious station stops with escalators rising steeply to the surface. I felt I was discovering the city as Stanley and Livingstone had discovered Africa, as if it and the natives had been created especially for me. Toronto was a place that was strange and possibly dangerous. When I emerged from the subway at the university stop, the first image to greet me was a large billboard filling the entire end of the street with the words: "Varsity Stadium, Home of the Varsity Blues."

The thrill of seeing the team I had arrived to play for advertised in such a bold way jolted through me like an electric shock. Awed, I picked up my bags and walked slowly off towards a fraternity on Madison Avenue where I was to stay. It was situated in a large friendly house not far from the stadium. Here I was given a large room to share with a member of the fraternity. It had two bay windows and a gas fireplace that worked. There were bookcases and comfortable desks. It was the kind of elegant, academic setting young men at college are supposed to have but I never dreamed I would.

There was a sorority conveniently located on each side of the fraternity. These houses had lace curtains, and someone called a den mother to preside. The notion of so many young women being so close was invigorating, but unfortunately I had no chance to consider this advantage in anything more than a glancing way. Football practices were twice a day, and I soon discovered that the practice field was filled with enormous young men of intimidating disposition. At six feet two and 200 pounds, I had become used to dominating high school football playing fields without thinking much about it, but the arena had changed.

The Varsity Blues had a team composed almost entirely of returning veterans, a team that in three months would win the prestigious Yates Cup. As we lumbered through the heat and long hours of rookie training camp and I glanced across at the veteran side of the camp it seemed clear enough that the veterans didn't need any help. It seemed equally clear not many of us were going to survive; by the time rookie camp closed, there were only four of us chosen to move on. I can't say I had a great camp and was a little surprised to have been chosen. The only reason I could think of was that I was versatile. I could play a number of positions.

Ylo Korgemanni was the first veteran I lined up against in block-ing drill. He did not look that intimidating. He was shorter than I and on the rotund side. I congratulated myself on getting someone of reasonable dimensions to pair off against. We went into a three point stance. The whistle went. I launched myself at him, confident, my back in a straight line to absorb the shock, legs churning, head slightly raised to catch his chest with the tip of my helmet to force his body up and back. I had done it a thousand times and expected him to bend to my will. It was like hitting a cement wall. Ylo did not budge one inch. I bounced off him like a child hitting the edge of a playpen. Then he began to inexorably, embarrassingly grind me back. The whistle went.

As we walked back to the ends of our respective blocking lines, I asked Ylo, in a hushed tone, how much did he weigh? He grinned and said 240 pounds.

Alex Squires was the tallest man on the team. He was about six feet five inches with a build along the lines of Michelangelo's David. Nonetheless, I lined up against him with considerable confidence. He was no bigger than Mike Lapp, my buddy at home, and I had learned that tall men no matter how strong are often handicapped in blocking drills by their height. You could connect with your helmet just slightly lower on their torso than they did against you, and a tall man could tip over like a pine tree going down. The whistle went and I launched myself at Alex determined to prove that I belonged on this team. Our helmets connected with the solid crack of two young bulls loose in the barnyard. But Alex had played against the tractor gravity of Ylo Korgemanni for too long to be fooled by a low charge.

My next move was automatic, I brought my forearms up against his ribs hard in an effort to straighten him up. There was a solid thud as they connected but to no visible effect. I took a step back to get my balance and we cracked against each other again, the shock of the blow cannonading down my neck and back, but this time I was not moved. We growled back and forth to a seesaw. The whistle went signifying the drill was over. Alex smiled at me in a friendly way and tapped me on the shoulder as you would a friendly puppy.

◆ ◆ ◆

Looking back, I realize now that my initial reaction to Toronto was absolutely correct. It was strange and a little dangerous. I had naively headed towards the heart of one of the great conflicts of the 20th century: the struggle to create a different kind of world. My friends would become refugees and deserters. My long hair and my ideas about what was important would be transformed forever.

It came in fractured bits and pieces, not so much as news but by the creak of electronic and continental tectonics. News from the barricades on Paris streets in 1968, news of the thousands of Mexican students marching in their city streets towards their eventual brutal repression, news of the amazing Stonewall Inn riots over gay rights in New York would come stealing towards us. The Port Huron statement of the SDS (Students for Democratic Society) circulated. These distant events flared on the horizon as foreign reflections of our own very local passions and preoccupations.

I would be reinventing the past to say that I understood the importance of this grand canvas. At the time its significance largely eluded me. Woodstock was a bunch of friends in a loaded car. Did I want to go or not? I flipped a coin to decide. Most of the great events of that time were governed by not much more than a flip of a coin. Somebody said, "we're marching on City Hall against the Spadina Expressway." A mental flip of the coin, and "I'm in. Where do we start?"

Looking back, I find it astonishing and mildly embarrassing to read histories of the 1960s and wonder how I could have been there. Done it. Wore many T-shirts but paradoxically have missed so much of what was at stake. Yet the decade changed me, but there was no great moment which set the changes in progress, it all happened with nothing grand at all, in nothing more than the accretion of little moments. The first was deciding to quit the football team.

◆ ◆ ◆

We have two childhoods — the one that we actually live and the one that we decide to remember. They rarely coincide. Part of the one that I remember was the sensible decision to quit the Varsity Blues. There was more to life than football. It was time to grow up and move on; time to sever the umbilical cord which had tied me to a game that bestowed prestige and position without thought. It was time to learn what life was about without the game to shape my days. This is the version I prefer.

The one that I actually lived was a little different. I had no intention of quitting football. I had come to Toronto to go to university — yes — but also to play football, and I had come to the right place. The Varsity Blues had a winning team. You could sense it from the first moment that you stepped on the practice field with them. There was that heady mixture of talent, poise and chemistry which announced an exceptional team. It was clear before we played a single game that this was a team that was going to be hard to beat. Any college player would have given his eye teeth to step on the field with this group of athletes and wait for the kickoff to come whirling. But unless either Alex or Ylo fell down on their safety razors and slashed a tendon, I was going to sit on the bench while they played football. And the bench is not an easy place to be. You are part of the team, but you are not part of the team. It is as if you have contracted some mild but debilitating disease which no one wishes to mention but is present constantly. At best, your teammates treat you with charity. At worst, there are slighting remarks because at the end of the day, they know you are waiting for someone to get hurt or play badly. It is like sitting through a self-inflicted social disease.

I did it suddenly. Like diving off a high board, there was no point in hesitating at the edge. A few days away from the first game, I walked up to Coach Murphy and told him I was quitting. He nodded briefly, and it was done. I walked out of Varsity Stadium, never again to return to a football field. It felt like a substantial section of the stadium had just caved in on my heart.

◆ ◆ ◆

Looking back on a lifetime, it is disconcerting to realize how much is decided by happenstance. I was no longer a football player, and my privileged residence disappeared with that status. I no longer felt comfortable staying in a fraternity. I found a tiny dirty room in a broken-down house on Spadina Avenue. Spadina was a broad, busy downtown street. For people passing by in their cars, Spadina was nothing more than an inconvenience — too much traffic, too many streetcars, too much coming and going. But that place would quickly become my home. Its bookstores, laundries, cafés and taverns would fold me into their lives.

The room I rented would have made a better broom closet, but it only cost fifteen dollars a week. For this I received one narrow bed, one window with a clear view of a brick wall, one stand-up closet and one telephone table called a desk. In a neigborhood distinguished by many decrepit buildings, 689 Spadina was a star. Every room was occupied by a student, with mouse holes in the kitchen floor, windows that shook in their frames and dirt by the barrelful. Not the kind of place that you would think would make the news, but the broad avenue that 689 fronted on would soon become the center of the largest urban protest ever mounted against a city freeway. It was here that I began to grow up.

◈ ◈ ◈

Chief was the star of 689. Besides his exotic name and pedigree (his father was a tribal chief in Tanzania) Chief also had a deep, compelling voice that immediately inspired affection from the opposite sex. His complexion was a soft clear Belafonte brown, and he had a way of squaring his shoulders and throwing his head back to laugh that simply delighted anyone within hearing. Going to a party with Chief was terrifically discouraging because inevitably the best-looking woman in the place would sidle up to me and begin to ask discrete questions about Chief with the object of getting an introduction. I would console myself with the thought that I was not the ugly friend but simply the youngest in the house and therefore regarded as more approachable.

Before he had come to Canada, Chief had never seen a white man clean a car windshield or do any other menial chore. In his modest opinion, this alone had been worth the price of admission. Chief would definitively declaim this in a calm, devastatingly courteous tenor — usually in front of some susceptible female humanitarian anxious to try out her universal principles. It seemed to us hardened cynics at 689 Spadina that the more repressive a regime the girl hailed from, the more interested they were in Chief. One absolutely stunning, athletic, blonde girl from Georgia practically climbed over me to get at Chief when I accidentally positioned myself between her and her desired objective. "Don't you think he's attractive?" she asked as she pushed past.

Our landlord was a recently graduated student in engineering, appropriately named Bill. He lived in the largest room in the house overlooking Spadina Avenue. He rented the entire house from the university and then sublet to students. At the ripe old age of 26, Bill was busy renting two other houses, working at his day job, investing in the stock market and otherwise beavering away at making his first million.

I was the only undergraduate in the house. Bill was not that keen on "letting the barbarians in," but for some reason he made an exception for me. The other men in the house were either in law or graduate school. On weekends the house as a whole turned into a kind of human cattery. On Saturday night it was surprising the entire structure did not shake rhythmically up and down. The first time that I heard a young woman wailing in the throes of desire on the other side of a bedroom door, I was so innocent I thought someone was in pain. This is the kind of mistake you make only once.

Paulo who had recently arrived from Italy had the room down the hall on the left, and Peter Dubchek from Smooth Rock Falls was on the right. Paulo was of middling height with glossy, curly hair and a ruddy complexion. He dressed stylishly and thought the Canadians in the house entertaining but primitive. Peter deliberately played up to Paulo's concept of the Canadian as primitive. His father was a miner, and the instant that he got home from his articling job he would strip out of his shirt and tie into jeans and an old, plaid shirt. On his door he had a sign which said Smooth Rock Falls, South. Peter played the balalaika quite beautifully, and after I had pestered him long enough he would bring it out and play for us. He was distinguished in all things by a sardonic sense of humor and a firm grip on the concept of "hoser" long before Bob and Doug Mackenzie got around to inventing a name for it. He and Bill were often at odds on the stock market, which they were both trying to bilk at the same time. Cries of "you shorted me, you bastard" were familiar in the house.

The sex was not free at 689, but it certainly came close. Young women tended to stay at our house for one purpose only, and when they had accomplished this, no matter how long it took, they left directly for healthier climes. The kitchen cockroaches never saw a human female. The women would disappear into a room and emerge only to leave sometime Sunday without touching down elsewhere. For 689 Spadina was the kind of house where only those young and fearless of contagious disease would be content to live.

The kitchen floor sloped and there were mouse holes everywhere. The paint on the walls had once been white but was now a grubby grey. The only public furniture was a beat-up gas stove, two rickety refrigerators, four chairs and a table that had been cheap and old in 1942.

We had another African student at 689. He had a room on the third floor and was studying journalism at Ryerson. His name was also Bill, and we took to calling him Bill Two and the landlord Bill One. Although you could not imagine two more dissimilar men. Bill One was Nordic with a very pale complexion and straight blonde hair. Bill Two was from Cameroon, dark complexioned with black curly hair.

They were also completely different in personality. Bill One was a man whom I presume is now living in the Bahamas where he has been enjoying retirement since the age of thirty. Bill Two bubbled with great insouciance, could cook, was studying to be a journalist and cared more about a bon mot than the stock market. I imagine him back in Cameroon now running a newspaper to the great entertainment of all.

The quietest man in the house lived in the room next to Chief's. He was a graduate student from Vietnam studying biology and chemistry. He worked so hard that we saw little of him. Even his name was mentioned in hushed tones; as anyone who studied that hard must have been sent as a caution to the rest of us.

Leo, the third and last articling student in the house had ground through Osgoode with Peter Dubchek. Like Peter, he had grown up in the country. His father was a one-legged farmer in Essex county, but Leo eschewed Peter's "hoser" pretensions; instead he conducted himself with a quiet simplicity that was impossible not to admire. His room was also on the third floor and filled with books and light. I learned to watch for Leo's reaction to the bullshit that tended to fly around an all-male household because in the end it was his opinion which frequently prevailed.

In short 689 Spadina had within its grungy walls exactly what I had come to Toronto for: friends the likes of which I had never imagined but to whom I immediately took a great liking. Friday evenings Peter, Leo and I would adjourn to the Black Diamond tavern which was big brawling place at the corner of Spadina and College. Here Leo would walk me through the city newspapers explaining what was "really" happening at City Hall. It had never occurred to me before that there might be a difference between what the newspapers said was happening and what was actually taking place around things as mundane as who got what contract "to study" something. Peter considered himself an expert on bar room brawling and thought given my size that I had potential. His advice in these matters came down to "it's all in the first punch. Get the first punch in and you're golden." He was an equable man, though, and I don't think he had ever hit anything more than a fly. I was most delighted by the strippers, some of whom could be persuaded to share a beer at our table and tell us Toulouse Lautrec stories.

Things were not always sweetness and light. Around the tension of midterm papers, things could get shirty. One time I called Chief a "son of a bitch" because he would never answer the front door although his room was the closest to it. My room was on the second floor, and I would find myself running downstairs, often to answer the door for one of Chief's many admirers. Chief overheard me and came storming out of his room trembling with anger: "You don't call an African that word." Chief's deep voice had descended by several octaves to leonine level as he roared into the kitchen with murder on his mind.

"And you never answer the door," I replied calmly, certain of my facts.

The reply was unwise. Chief advance towards me fists raised, but I didn't much feel like backing down and didn't.

"In case you haven't noticed, Chief, this isn't Africa. And maybe if you ever bothered to answer the door, I wouldn't call you a 'son of a bitch'."

To my surprise, the usually calm and measured Chief wasn't faking his anger. He was trembling with rage and took a hefty swing at me. I blocked the blow and then we fell wrestling to the floor, Chief determined to murder me and me determined he wouldn't.

A girl appeared at the doorway of the kitchen.

"What's up with you two? Stop! Stop!" She began pulling us apart. My shirt was ripped, and neither of us were in a mood to stop anything. I remember bellowing, "you answer the door, I'm not your servant," and Chief bellowing back, "you don't call me that word." All this bellowing and wrestling began to settle us down. And eventually, like two little boys who have been caught playing in the dirt, we stood up and began dusting off our clothes, muttering.

The girl was tall, lithe and quite beautiful.

"You sure it was Chief you were looking for?" I asked.

The girl who did not know me from Adam looked puzzled. Chief began to laugh.

◆ ◆ ◆

Besides requiring a certain formality of address, the Africans at 689 had another great advantage over the natives: they could cook. Peter, Leo and I had achieved nothing more than the basic "hoser" cuisine: if you can't fry it or toast it, eat it raw. This works well for breakfast but begins to wear thin as the day goes on. Paulo's Italian approach to the kitchen stove was that he didn't; your mother or your girlfriend cooked, and if they weren't available you went to a restaurant. He regarded anything else as uncivilized and hence didn't eat at home much.

Bill Two was the house's great chef. Each Sunday, he would cook an afternoon meal for several of his friends, and the heady aroma of bubbling spices, chicken and vegetables would begin to permeate the house. The centerpiece of Bill's Sunday meals were always mounds of starchy stuff. I never found out what this was except it looked like very thick cream of wheat. It was eaten with the fingers and used as we would bread. In other bowls, there would be chicken, vegetables and tasty sauces. When the Africans were sitting down for Sunday dinner, the rest of us would prowl around the edges of the dining room table like stray dogs after a hungry bone.

Relations between Chief and I remained a little on the frosty side for some time — Chief feeling his dignity had been compromised, myself sure of the justice of my position and unprepared to be repentant. Until the night of the black cocks. At least that was how it was remembered. It started innocently enough. The girls in the house next to us who also rented rooms from Bill One decided to throw a party. We were all invited. Peter brought his balalaika. Chief brought his deep voice, and we all brought Saturday night fever.

The music popped around the little room. Chief played his favorite role as the "simple handsome native" who is also a humble but brilliant student at law, unexpectedly surrounded by admirers. Peter had his own circle of admirers, and I as usual was struggling to keep up with my older more accomplished housemates. I began to get a little drunk. At some point in the evening I began to circulate the idea that the some of the white guys in our house had black cocks and some of the black guys had white cocks, hence what you saw was not necessarily what you got.

This created something of a stir, especially with Chief who could not stop laughing. Then Bill Two stepped into the fray and said he thought there was something in the water at 689 because he had noticed that his own cock was getting paler with each day.

I nodded and said equally seriously. "Same for me. It's getting blacker with each day. It must be the water." For once the crowd around our house stars, Chief and Peter Dubchek, thinned a little, and for a few moments Bill Two and I hustled to the center stage.

Fortunately, one ridiculous thing led to another.

◇ ◇ ◇

When I think back on the 60s, it isn't the protests that I recall. I have to work hard to dredge up memories of demonstrations against Dow Chemical, the fabricators of Agent Orange and other such war delights, or against the bombing of Cambodia. The same goes for campus daycare, the organization of a food co-op and this new idea that we should buy foods that were "organic," not factory farmed. But the memories of 689 Spadina come roaring back at me and had the most lasting effect on me. At 689 I began to live differently and understand the world differently.

I knew next to nothing about the black experience in North America. Reading books about young black men made me understand immediately that they were no different than me, but they had had a very different life with much uglier pressures to overcome. I can still remember turning the pages of *The Autobiography of Malcolm X* [1] entranced and admiring of the gentle sensibility of soul that I discovered there.

I liked my African roommates, and so when I read *Black like Me,* [2] it took no great leap of imagination to see Bill or Chief being treated badly because of their color. The evidence wasn't just in little paperbacks that cluttered around my bed but in the newspapers and on the news with stories coming up from Selma, Alabama. It was all very real, and this imprinted on me the notion that discrimination was evil.

I missed football and looked for a sport to fill its place. Someone invited me to come out and try out for the university rowing team. It was such an absurd idea — getting up at 5:30 in the morning to be on the water at six — that I thought I would try it just to see what it was all about. It was an entirely different sport from anything that I had done before. Rowing was quiet, reflective, exhausting. It had no spectators. Most of it was endless hours of practice. If you can fall in love with a sport, I did. I loved it from the first moment I saw the sun rise on the water and felt the boat jump, then glide delicately over the water like a racehorse flexing its muscles.

I love to row to this day and am still enraptured by early morning on the water. Without realizing it, the great tracks that would direct my life were being laid down at 689 Spadina.

◆ ◆ ◆

Toronto was awash in draft dodgers, and the city felt like what it was: a neutral zone on the edge of an ugly war. Neutral zones are always strange and charged places, and Toronto was both in the Sixties. It was charged with the detritus of a distant war: draft dodgers, deserters and protests of every size and description. At night, I avidly read cheap paperbacks which became the avatars of the time. These books were not just about the black experience but by authors that had begun to sound the alarm bell about the environment: *Small is Beautiful* by E.F. Schumacher[3] and *Silent Spring* by Rachel Carson.[4]

I began to understand that society wasn't something that existed in some independent way like a tree; it was simply an invention of people, and like any invention it could change in any number of ways depending on what the people who formed it decided. A society could be violent and exploitative as easily as it could be trusting and confident. Likewise cities could be dirty or clean, safe or dangerous, depending how they were organized and funded. These thoughts both exhilarated and unnerved me because I began to see how fragile it all was, how easily things could go well or badly.

My hair grew long and my cherished football jacket disappeared into the closet. I was "against" the war in Vietnam, but there was always a faux feeling to the war protests in Canada because it wasn't really "our war." Prime Minister Pearson had had the sense to keep Canada clear of it. Perhaps that was one of the reasons the "made in Canada" protests attracted so much support, as we students looked for our own radical territory to occupy. Yet those protests got little attention in the press. It was always the "anti-American" protests that were reported. For example, I remember that protests against Dow Chemical recruiting on campus were reported on the national television news, and we all thought we had done something of great importance. In fact it was a demonstration of little consequence and had no lasting effect. The corporations we picketed are richer than ever creating new generations of weapons for new wars. Nothing much changed then or now.

But marching in support of the co-op nonprofit housing movement had a great and lasting impact. This housing kept downtown Toronto populated and lively with a diversity of population and incomes. It changed the face of Toronto by ensuring that the city didn't become simply a place for the very rich or the very poor. It gave the middle class a place. Similarly, the low-key campaign to increase city funding for the arts to a dollar per capita (at a time when other cities were still investing pennies in their arts) had a galvanizing and permanent effect on the entire city and later the country as other cities tried to catch up with Toronto. When Toronto theater exploded with new plays, playwrights, actors and directors, and the visual arts followed with new galleries and artists, ultimately a film industry evolved, and Toronto became Hollywood North.

The struggles to get the federal and provincial governments to invest in daycares and community healthcare centers also succeeded in cities across Canada and made the country a more humane and more livable place. There's nothing like the happy cries of children at a local daycare to cheer a neighborhood up or the security that a community healthcare center brings by treating those who are in need. These little social movements all had great and lasting effects on Canadian cities.

But the crown jewel of the 1960s protests in Toronto was the long struggle to "Stop Spadina." The protests against the construction of this expressway was one of the very few in all of North America where a people's movement successfully beat back the cement, asphalt and automotive lobbies. Everywhere else — in Ottawa, Brooklyn, LA, Pittsburgh, Montreal — in the sixties and seventies city councils built urban freeways, flyways and "parkways" like Toronto's Don Valley. These huge roads — six, eight and ten lanes wide — cut neighborhoods and river valleys like cement knives, reducing the quality of life everywhere to serve the needs of the automobile.

In Toronto the resistance was started by a couple of young mothers in the Annex, one of the neighborhoods adjacent to the proposed Spadina freeway. The opposition quickly spread across the city jumping like wildfire from community association to community association, to student groups, to thinkers like Jane Jacobs, to young city councilors like John Sewell. A film was made about the Stop Spadina movement. Visitors came from around the world to check into what was happening. The interest and the movement was intense, but nothing seemed to be able to stop the determination of the city and the province to turn Spadina Avenue from a city street into another traffic sewer.

Stop Spadina was my first introduction to civic activism. Like other students, I sold buttons on Bloor Street, gave out pamphlets and, knees trembling, made a speech on the campus opposing it. It felt terrifically important to do these things, but looking back at all our efforts they all seem hopelessly ineffectual. How could selling buttons on Bloor Street to passersby stop a multi-gazillion dollar road lobby?

Demolition and construction began at the north end.

◆ ◆ ◆

The importance of stopping Spadina was never clearer than when I moved to Montreal and saw what the Bonaventure and Decarie expressways had done to that beautiful city of treed boulevards and graceful Victorian town houses. These expressways had ripped apart the city's oldest and most vibrant neighborhoods from one end of the island to the other with dozens of high-speed traffic lanes.

The Bonaventure Expressway divided Old Montreal from the newer part of the downtown. It destroyed some of the oldest streetscapes in North America by gouging a gaping cement trench between the harbor, Le Vieux Port, and St. Catherine's Street, the city's modern and principal commercial avenue. Neither St. Catherine Street nor Le Vieux Port ever really recovered. Forty years later, the city is still trying to patch together some kind of "renovation" that will reanimate this part of the city. The renewal of the downtown area would have occurred naturally and easily if the historic district of connecting streets between the old and newer town had not been torn down and replaced with eight lanes of high-speed traffic, trench walls and access ramps.

The wretched thing about urban expressways is that they create a landscape that never heals. Ribbons of poverty form along their edges; anyone who can picks up and moves away from the noise, pollution and social dislocation urban expressways bring. In the sixties I had only a slender grasp of the philosophy of Herbert Marcuse's *One-Dimensional Man*[5] which our professors obliged us to read, but living on Spadina Avenue my imagination needed no maturing to appreciate the immediate toxic effect of converting a lively and wonderful street into a north-south traffic sewer.

But nothing seemed capable of stopping it. By 1970 many of us had become so frustrated and angry that there was talk of violent action to stop the bulldozers that had begun cutting an enormous trench in north end of the city which was aimed straight for the university, Kensington Market, the old warehouse district, the heart of the city.

Civilian struggles are distinguished by their volunteer character and also limited by it. I hadn't signed on for any war, wore no uniform, received no pay and hence it was relatively easy for me to move on. When I was accepted at the University of Montreal for graduate school, it was with a sense of guilt that I left town. Part of me felt like I was running away, but it was also relatively easy to stifle any concerns and abandon my own small role and drive towards other adventures. I had intimations of it at the time, but would not understand until much later that this lack of focus (the Stop Spadina movement was just one of many activist concerns) combined with the ease with which activists could do as I did — simply drive away from their engagement — was at the heart of the failure of the 1960s to reform the North American paradigm into a less carnivorous one.

◆ ◆ ◆

In Montreal, I was looking forward to reacquainting myself with the French language and thinking about what kind of thesis I might try my pen at. I arrived at the University in September. Montreal was shining under an autumn sky. Patty and I got settled in our first apartment. I registered at the university, bent my mind towards re-learning French, and then all hell broke loose.

First a British diplomat named James Cross and then Pierre Laporte, a provincial cabinet minister, were kidnapped by cells of something called the FLQ, the Front de Liberation du Québec. Within a few days, Pierre Laporte was found in the trunk of a car murdered. Suddenly there were combat troops in the streets, "white nights" and "poèmes de la resistance." John Lennon arrived at the Queen Elizabeth Hotel with Yoko for their "sleep-in" for peace. Jacques Rose, one of the kidnappers, was hiding out just around the corner from our apartment. Patty and I had front row seats on a roller coaster that was moving a hundred times faster than anything we had been involved with in Toronto.

I think that my own feelings were shared by others in that I was starting to have trouble seeing the connections between anything. Where we going with all these protests? What did food co-ops or Stop Spadina have to do with Pierre Laporte's murder? Or Woodstock with the Hell's Angels beating a kid to death with pool cues at a rock concert in California? What exactly was the point of it all? Where were we going?

I don't think I was alone with these confused thoughts. Even a long, reflective book like Paul Berman's *A Tale of Two Utopias: the Political Journey of the Generation of 1968*[6] manages to miss great chunks of the 1960s. He revisits the gay rebellions in New York, student protests in France, Mexico, Italy and Germany. There's lots about the student and labor politics around the Port Huron Statement, but the country to the north of him doesn't warrant a paragraph. There's not a word, not a sentence on anything that transpired in Canada during the sixties and early seventies. Yet in the argot of the time, there was "a lotta' shit goin' down."

To live through the October Crisis in Montreal was to live through something far scarier than anything that happened south of the border including the Chicago and Watts riots. When Trudeau abrogated civil liberties and called the troops in, it was as if the entire city went into suspended animation. Montreal streets went eerily quiet for weeks, but it wasn't the quiet of tranquility. Those October days took on a deathly pallor that had nothing to do with the autumn season. The city descended into a tense half light, as if the Gods had turned the weather Shakespearian and decided pathetic fallacy was the only possible condition.

At the University of Quebec, students decided to strike in protest of suspension of civil liberties and the imposition of the War Measures Act. Under the Act this was considered treasonous. Professors and student leaders began to disappear into Montreal city jails. As a radicalizing experience, it's difficult to beat jail time. It's the gold standard. At the University of Montreal, we assembled in the largest hall on the campus and also voted on a strike. We stood up by row to record our vote, so there could be absolutely no mistake on the count. It was a very public declaration of where you stood. The first rows were completely dominated by separatists and they voted unanimously to strike, but as the vote moved up the rows, more and more students voted "no" until it was clear the balance was very fine between those who were willing to strike and those who were not.

When the vote came to our row, the uncertainty on how to vote was so high and the balance so delicate that the entire row waited before standing. A strike in support of kidnappers was not something I was keen on. Murder is murder, no matter what your motivation. On the other hand, I didn't favor the idea of sending a message to Trudeau that we thought the suspension of civil rights and throwing a lot of innocent people in jail was a great idea either — which was how a "no strike" vote would be interpreted. There was no positive way to vote and yet we were obliged to vote.

What to do?

I voted not to strike and so did most of my row. In the end, the "no strike" vote at the Université de Montréal carried the day but only by a few dozen votes out of 500. It wasn't a vote of confidence in the government. Our "no" vote was part of the suspended animation of the streets — the quiet of a city with its breath held. All it would have taken was one 19-year-old soldier to have shot someone in a nervous moment, and the city would have exploded. Trudeau took a tremendous risk in suspending civil liberties. It was a risk that he won and lost: won in the short term because the kidnappers were duly caught and punished, but lost because the suspension of civil liberties alienated and radicalized an entire generation in Quebec. The suspension of civil liberties invigorated the moribund Quebec independence movement which had been mired at less than 20 percent of public support. It grew very quickly to within one percentage point of voting to leave the Canadian federation.

That autumn almost unnoticed in Montreal, Bill Davis, the Premier of Ontario, signed a document stopping the construction of the Spadina Expressway. I remember hearing about it in a few lines during an evening radio newscast with a sense of both shock and relief. Somewhere, somehow, good sense had prevailed — although I was completely ignorant of exactly how this had been achieved.

In the spring of 1971, I left Montreal buoyed by the thought that Spadina had been stopped; unsure of my own future or the future of the country; but my own course had been set. Where I would live, what I would value and what I would do with my life had all been decided. I would spend my life in city cafés, in conversation and on city streets. I would devote my life to trying to create more sustainable urban environments. While this narrow objective was clear enough at the time, it would be many years before I would be able to piece together what exactly had been at stake in the many distempers of the 1960s and the grave consequences of the losing side, losing.

The 1960s:
A global paradigm shift that didn't happen and how the same pattern is repeating itself

There is nothing more difficult to take in hand,
more perilous to conduct or more uncertain of success,
than to take the lead in the introduction of a new order of things.

— Nicollo Machiavelli 1469–1525

I T IS ALWAYS IN THE INTERESTS of the winning side to trivial-ize the losing side, and the campaign to marginalize the 1960s into a folk opera has been largely successful. The image of the Sixties even for those who actually lived during that decade has been turned into a cartoon series of songs, pop images, flower power, bell bottoms, long hair, marijuana and make-love-not-war slogans. What was ac-tually at stake has been successfully buried in these caricatures along with most of its heroes.

What was at stake was a global, axial moment. For six giddy years a vast, popular sentiment surged between nations and continents, and some extraordinary leaders emerged with the desire and the ca-pacity to re-orient the governments of the west with new values and new goals.

It failed, and what arose is what we have now: private empires which control the world's resources to feed vast corporate profits and a world financial system that has colonized and crippled the govern-ments of all nations. But in the 1960s, none of this had happened. The globalization of capital and corporations had not occurred. The public sector was dominant, attracting the best and the brightest of the young generation. But the times, as the old song said, were "a-changin'." Beyond the pop songs and postcard images which now dominate the collective memory of the 1960s this decade had two faces, inter-related but separate.

The first face was simply that of a post-World War II generation coming of age in a rich and confident decade when many futures seemed entirely and simultaneously possible. It was a decade when it appeared reasonable to "return to the land" with a garden hoe in one hand and a guitar in the other and by that simple act to change the world. And in the city it was possible to write manifestos, demonstrate, poster telephone poles, smoke dope and by these simple acts change the world. It was as naive and fun as the institutional cartoon memory of today wants us to believe.

But the second face of the Sixties was an undeclared civil war; this face of society was infinitely more complex and infinitely less comic. The first shots were the ones that ripped through the back of President Kennedy's head in 1963. The end came six years later when President Nixon was elected and President Johnson's "War on Poverty" was immediately turned into the "war on drugs" — nothing more than a "war on the poor." And this transformation was just the opening salvo from a succession of American corporate administrations that would rule the richest nation on the planet and decide the fate of the poorest.

The ugly truth is that since the 1960s millions have died needlessly of poverty, of polluted water and in corporate wars. All the studies show that, with some small exceptions, the gap beween rich and poor continues to grow everywhere. The winning side thinks of social justice as a luxury; that's the reality of 2006 because the Sixties civil war — excepting a few minor, unexpected blips like Watergate — ended in a complete triumph for the Kissinger-Nixon-Corporate side. No, the other face of the Sixties was not a cartoon. It was not funny at all.

◆ ◆ ◆

As a Canadian, it always seems a little strange that Canadians should be so well-informed about our neighbors, yet our neigbors should know so little about us. We are the United States' largest trading partner, larger than Japan, larger than France or Germany. Yet our complicated political and cultural history remains invisible to Americans. For the USA nothing much happens north of the 49th parallel except snow, hockey players and maple syrup. End of story.

But it isn't the end of the story. The closer you get to the Canadian experience, the more intricate and complicated the differences between the two nations become. From the outside, the French-English Canadian divide seems simple enough. It isn't. I speak French. My family's history begins in what is now Canada in 1632, but I'm not a Québécois. I'm Acadian, although I think of both Acadians and Québécois as being Canadians. This kind of multi-layered national identity has endured for centuries in Canada and is not something familiar to Americans.

To be American generally means to have no hyphens. John Updike has written that the thing he would mind most about death was no longer being an American. It makes me smile just to think of a writer from Canada composing something similar; it's just not a line that would occur to a Canadian to write.

These differences between nations are expressed in both subtle and obvious ways that effect the broad strokes of civic and national life. Anyone familiar with Canada could prepare a laundry list pages long. At the top of mine would be "gated communities." In Canada there is a strong and important sense that communities should be inclusive, that it is a serious civic failure to be obliged to lock your streets up against your neighbors — whereas 40 percent of the new homes in the US are in gated communities. Another at the top of my list would be that Canadians have also always been more willing to value public enterprise as a public good, not a public imposition. Eighty per cent of electrical power in Canada is generated by public corporations. In the United States, it's not quite 25 percent. We used to have public corporations like Air Canada, Petro Canada and Canadian National, although all of these have been sold off or are in the process of being sold. ·

These Canadian characteristics are not aberrations to be "corrected" so that we can become more competitive on the global markets. These are choices that reflect how Canadians choose to define the concepts of progress and express our identity among the nations of the world. We choose different values. We choose to provide ourselves with electricity, not to depend on someone else. We choose to provide ourselves with healthcare, not depend on the power of the individual's wallet.

But perhaps the greatest difference between us is that it is not possible for Canadians to be unaware of our neighbors; that's just the way life is north of the border. It doesn't make us less Canadian; it is just one of the ways we are. As Pierre Trudeau once said, sharing the North American continent with the Americans is like "sleeping with an elephant," and it behooves us to always know what the elephant is doing.

And the elephant was on a rampage in the Sixties. Although the movement was worldwide — Paris in May of 1968, the Mexico City student protests, the scary Italian and German armed cells — it was only in the United States where national leaders emerged to capture the attention of the entire world. Jack Kennedy was one of them. From the moment of his inaugural address in 1960, Kennedy sensed the ground was shifting in America. He was unsure of its exact direction, yet nonetheless managed to begin harnessing the seismic tremors in ways that also began to shift the nation.

The exploration of space became something he called "the new frontier," and remarkably quickly this notion of a new frontier beyond the earth's own skies evolved into the more complicated notion of a new frontier on earth. The blue and white pictures from space sent from Apollo 8 quickly became more about how we saw ourselves than how the planet appeared from space. For the first time in human history, the scales began to tip towards humanity instead of nationality. Some people began to think that our home was the spaceship earth, not a piece of ground where national flags fluttered. And leaders emerged who were able to catch the essence of this complex unwieldy shift in consciousness and consequences, and nurture it into a transformative political one.

Bobby Kennedy was saying in his run up to the Presidency:

We will find neither national purpose nor personal satisfaction in mere continuation of economic progress, in endless amassing of worldly goods. We cannot measure national spirit by Dow Jones Average, nor national achievement by the Gross National Product. For the Gross National Product includes air pollution and ambulances to clear our highways from carnage. It counts special locks for our doors and jails for the people who break them. The Gross National Product grows with production of napalm and missiles and nuclear warheads…it includes the broadcasting of television programs which glorify violence to sell goods to our children…it does not allow for the health of our families, the quality of their education or the joy of their play. It is indifferent to the decency of our factories and the safety of our streets alike.[1]

The Kennedy brothers were maverick members of the American establishment. Jack Kennedy's basic instincts were not profoundly anchored in the status quo. He was too quirky, too independent and charismatic to allow any ideology to capture him. He was, for example, perfectly capable of going into a nail-biting showdown with the Soviets over missiles in Cuba and at the same time arriving at a "détente" with Fidel Castro.

Forty years after his death, it is clear that he was regarded as a threat to the forces of the status quo, no matter what domain they occupied. He was a threat to the Miami Mafia, to the Texas oil barons and California real estate czars because he had something any great leader has that can't be bought or controlled: enough individuality to absorb a new idea instead of defending an old one, combined with a personal charisma able to rally public opinion to the new idea. Was he assassinated via a conspiracy using an isolated gunman set up to take the fall? Or was his killer just another gun-toting American flying solo?

What remains astonishing is how every person who was close to the murder moment or able to say something directly about the murder quickly was also quickly murdered, disappeared or expired. The case Louisiana lawyer Jim Garrison built for a conspiracy collapsed not on the logic of it, but because all of his key witnesses died before they could testify. The same pattern of witness disappearances would happen all over again after the Sirhan Sirhan murder of Robert Kennedy.

But for 1,000 days, Jack Kennedy blew along with a new wind across America and the world. The grief at his death was expressed as vividly in Moscow and Ottawa as it was in Washington.

"Ask not what your country can do for you, ask what you can do for your country." To this day that small sentence remains a stirring call to the arms of principle instead of the arms of war. After years of national leadership preoccupied with defining America in terms of what it wasn't (e.g. "Americans are not Communists") Jack Kennedy and Martin Luther King both started to talk about what it meant to be American and not just by raising the flag, but rather in a new sense of self at home. Together, they represented more than just another changing of the presidential guard. They represented the possibility of the United States becoming a different kind of nation, of finally moving away from the "in God we trust" mode of thinking to "the government is us." It was nothing less than a fundamental paradigm shift in how Americans were to define being both American and citizens of the world.

Central to that paradigm shift was the idea that the principal role of government was not about administering greed and controlling compassion but about controlling greed and administering compassion. Kennedy and King were not alone. It was a paradigm shift that was coming from many different directions and had many different voices, but they were its greatest voices.

In 1967 a year before he was murdered, Martin Luther King said:

> We must rapidly shift from a "thing oriented" society to a "person oriented" society. When machines and computers and profit motives and property rights are considered more important than people, the giant triplets of racism, materialism, and militarism are incapable of being conquered.[2]

Reading these words today is like reading something from a different age, not from my lifetime. These are not words that lead us to climate change and a war over access to oil. They are the words of someone who had a different idea of how society should be ordered and what priorities should count.

At the beginning of the 21st century I find it impossible to imagine any major national leader in the United States or Canada ever stating that people come before profits. It is impossible to imagine a major national leader saying that the US was on "the wrong side of a world revolution" as King did. The paradigm has flipped back to administering greed and controlling compassion. In the 2004 Kerry vs. Bush campaign both candidates sounded as if they were singing from the same songbook. Kerry and Bush sounded like two kids in the school yard each shouting, "I'm more brave than you are!"

"No, I am."

"No I am."

"No I am"....and so on.

I have no idea who is braver, but I do know the guts have been sucked right out of politics for people. No one wants to risk anything because when they do, like Howard Dean, they get crushed.

In an unscripted moment in 2001 the then Canadian Minister of Finance Paul Martin uttered the mild thought that maybe rich countries should think about transfer payments to poorer parts of the planet in the same way that richer Canadian provinces transferred some of their wealth to poorer Canadian provinces. The reaction in the national (corporate) press was scornful, and the suggestion was described as "bizarre." Paul Martin never made the mistake of mentioning this possibility again.

But in 1967 there was still the hope held out that government could be about something more than administering greed and controlling compassion. In 1967 Martin Luther King had already moved on past black enfranchisement. He realized that the fundamental issue facing the west was a combination of physical poverty and poverty of political vision; it was not a black versus white issue. The majority of Americans below the poverty line were white.

King died in the midst of organizing a multi-racial poor people's campaign. His vision was flowing in the opposite direction from feeding the military and the associated corporate agendas. King's vision was driven by a smaller scale, less rapacious form of capitalism characterized by smaller corporations, smaller farms, a smaller military and a national income profile that spread wealth more evenly across the population. But his earliest message was very simple, and it is one that applies as powerfully today as it did then: Every person had a vote and in this way the poorest person is the equal of the richest, but if you do not vote, you are not equal. When I was a young man King was not just a great hero on university campuses around the world; he had emerged as an unelected world leader, and there were few places he could not go and find an enthusiastic welcome. Winning the Nobel Peace Prize in 1964 was a coronation.

It is the disintegration of the worldwide movement of which King's voice was a central part that preoccupies me more today than the years of its ascendancy. The losing side had all the good songs, all the shiny new ideas and all the great orators, but it lost all the same. It lost because the forces aligned against it were immensely powerful. Powerful state agencies like the FBI and the CIA, no matter what your feelings may be about them, are not institutions of change. Their job is to protect the status quo. They wanted leaders like King to disappear, and the reality of the raw institutional power of the status quo was always underestimated by everyone including presidents like Kennedy. These organizations are not benign.

And new visions lost because the successful prosecution of any new national direction whether it be civil or military requires more than shiny ideas. There is a saying in the high-tech industry that "ideas are sexy but genius is in the implementation." The losing side in the 1960s was never able to articulate clearly enough what its implementation plan was, except the idea of a "better world" or as has been said in French newspapers "un monde plus décent." In his book Paul Berman captures this confusion of implementation brutally and comprehensively.

Ironically, in spite of the superficial confusions, at bottom the ideas of the losing side were all inter-related. Civil rights were related to environmental rights to voter registration to ghetto soup kitchens and the creation of new economic opportunity; and all these ideas were connected to stopping the Vietnam War. But these different objectives were never successfully brought under one political or visionary roof.

The 1960s opponents of the status quo could be compared to the North American First Nations trying to resist the arrival of the Europeans. They had fine leaders, great rhetoric, brave troops, long standing rights and useful visions for society, but absolutely no common organization, no common direction or consensus between the many different groups about where they were going or how to get there. Like the Mi'kmaq nation in the east fighting the British army in the 17th century and the Sioux warriors in the west hurling themselves against the 7th cavalry in the 19th century, tribe by tribe the First Nations went down to defeat.

The entire leadership of the Black Panthers was murdered, jailed or exiled — some 27 young men — without that self-advertised violent group ever responding with much more than bold photographic images of resistance: black berets, leather jackets and guns. The Panthers were harried into exile, jailed and shot in their beds without ever giving up on their rhetoric of oppression and resistance; without ever figuring out how to take their battle beyond words and provocative photographs; without going beyond the image of change. No new successful politics came out of anyone's camp.

The Black Panthers' many deaths and total marginalization as a political force were so successful that in the end, the Panthers weren't even pitied. They seemed more like harmless cartoon characters. The FBI's involvement was a complete success.

At Wounded Knee, the drama of the previous century when the 7th Cavalry raked an undefended Sioux campsite with grapeshot played out again on a smaller scale, but it was just as ugly. The young Indian national leadership were killed or jailed or exiled for daring to appear threatening just as the Black Panthers had been. But unlike the confrontations with the Panthers when it was only the young black leaders who were killed, this time along with young Indian leaders, two FBI agents were killed in a confused shootout between Indian leaders in a cabin and agents in cars. It was a scene reminiscent of "Gunfight at the OK Corral." Everyone was shooting, and no one quite knew exactly what the hell was going on.

Thirty years later, Leonard Pelletier is still rotting in jail serving concurrent life sentences for shooting the two FBI agents even though it has been proven he was using a different caliber rifle than the one that killed the agents. He rots in jail as a great beacon to remind others what happens when struggle gets violent. The relentless power of the status quo has not changed since the days of Sitting Bull when the "good old boys" of the Royal Canadian Mounted Police turned Sitting Bull and his harried, hungry people back to the tender care of the 7th Cavalry. A hundred years later the RCMP did exactly the same thing: this time it was turning the young Leonard Pelletier over to the American authorities. Plus ça change, plus c'est la même chose.

Stopping the Vietnam conflict was one of the few victories in the 1960s civil war, for the idea did have a clear focus and it did eventually take hold that Vietnam was just a brutal military adventure. As a military joke at the time went, "it ain't much of a war, but it's the only one we've got." Ironically the very success in stopping the war derailed the student resistance even further. For once the war was over, the Student Non-Violent Co-ordinating Committee and the many complicated factions of the student movement both in the US and Canada disintegrated organizationally and rhetorically.

The young soldiers came home and were absorbed by the same forces that sent them over. Many of them joined the police or became bitter reactionaries to what they saw as betrayal. There was little effort made to integrate the war veterans into a new way of thinking about what really counted; instead they were made to feel like losers, and many became devoted to suppressing the people and democratic conversation that they had left home to defend.

After Vietnam the status quo had to make do with smaller wars: Central America, Chile, Guatemala, East Timor, the Middle East. And in the euphoria of the Vietnam war ending, it would take a very long time for students to realize that although stopping that war had been a fine thing, little had changed in the mentality of the nation's political elites. The CIA and the FBI changed their foreign targets, but the desirability of seeking world dominance and securing the world as a safe place to provision corporations was never questioned. Until the Iraq invasion, they were just more cautious about choosing their targets.

◆ ◆ ◆

There has never been a casualty list compiled for the Sixties civil war. In Mexico, no one has ever been able to document how many students were killed in the Mexican version of Tiananmen Square. The scene was so chaotic, the defeat so complete. In the United States — from Medgar Evers in Mississippi being shot in front of his home, to Martin Luther King, to the students killed at the Kent and Jackson State campuses — I've never seen any accounting of the heroes. And just whom do you count a hero? Outside of King getting a national holiday, there were no medals given out. Do you count the thousands of young Americans who were exiled for refusing to participate in the draft? There are now half a million Americans in Canada.

As civil wars generally go the 1960s casualty list is hardly worth mentioning, but the casualties, prison terms and exiles were very effective because they were focused on the key leaders of the movement. Those in power never let up. The repression endures to this day. Even after serving prison time, changing his religion and name, H. Rap Brown has discovered that the police are still at his door.

The devastation of the 1960s civil war defeat has never been catalogued or even understood. The clever sanctifying of King's memory is one of the examples of the success of the rout. King was murdered because he was a menace to the old paradigm, not because he was black. He had the capacity to be not just a voice of dissent, but a vehicle for change. He was a threat because of his capacity to mobilize people in the service of a new vision, one that didn't include corporate oil and General Colin Powell playing fourth fiddle.

It's all been very subtle and very effective. The winning side in awarding King a national holiday has declawed his message by reducing him to a noble fellow who led the battle for racial integration and voter registration. Happily he was able to fulfill his life's work before he was assassinated by one of life's losers. Sad end to his story, but let's celebrate his achievements with a national holiday in his memory.

The reality is otherwise. The reality is that as King was getting "recognized" with a national holiday, the new transformative paradigm that he died fighting for was being chopped away at a dizzying pace. In Florida even voter registration has been trashed through the ruthless expunging of black names from the voter registration lists and the use of cheap outdated election machinery. Police, prisons and the war on drugs have been cranked up so that now one in five black men in America are in prison or on their way to or from those institutions.

These were just some of the consequences for the losing side.

The completeness of the defeat can also be gauged in other, even more subtle ways. Note how Clinton's sexual assignations were treated versus Kennedy's. Kennedy's were more frequent and flagrant than Clinton's. Yet they never compromised his ability to be a presidential leader. Clinton's presidency was derailed by an intern's blow job.

Why?

The reasons are political, not moral. The political horizon changes with each generation. Kennedy's presidency was not far from the great democratic memory of Franklin Delano Roosevelt. John Kennedy was riding on the crest of a young, engaged electorate who frankly didn't care about his sex life, but cared a lot about what he thought about nuclear weapons, the legalization of marijuana, funding of social programs, racial integration and environmental policies. These were the things that counted, and Kennedy had begun to move on them. His sex life was never on the radar screen.

The corporate sector did their best but could not contain Roosevelt during his lifetime. He simply went over their heads and drove "the new deal" for people forward with weekly radio fireside chats and with Eleanor Roosevelt's syndicated "My Day'"column in newspapers. The best the corporate sector could manage was to make sure another FDR was never possible again by limiting presidential terms to eight years.

Clinton was charismatic and troublesome but bringing him to heel compared to FDR or a JFK was a piece of cake. He served up a blow-job, and the Justice Department moved in to prosecute him with the devotion of a jihad. One of Clinton's supporters served two years in a maximum security penitentiary with child murderers for refusing to testify against Clinton; that is a vivid testimony of the change in the political landscape. Can you imagine one of Kennedy's staff serving a two-year jail sentence for refusing to describe one of his late night pool swims with a woman other than his wife?

The assassinations of the great religious and political leaders worked to crush the movement, but there were many other ways the losing side was dispersed and defeated. Some of the most devoted joined the churches or spiritual movements seeing in them the only way that they could find a platform for social activism and some soul peace. Others just gave up and joined the "get rich now" crowd — trading bonds, selling real estate, running franchises — and some just tried to make do with the remnants of what was left.

Civilian struggles over ideas and the destiny of nations finish the same way that military wars over territory do. The defeated side first loses its leaders and with them the possibility of focus. Then, it disintegrates into individuals wandering across a landscape controlled by the winning side until one can scarcely remember that there once was an organized, successful opposition to the side that controls the political, economic and social landscape.

It's a long ago war now. The foot soldiers are grey headed and the generals are dead, but it is worth remembering that there once was a movement and a generation who believed human rights came before property rights, drugs were your own business and not a reason for years in prison, and that getting somewhere did not necessarily mean getting richer.

It's worth remembering the losing side now because we didn't get to this ugly invasion of Iraq by accident. We got to this point not just because of what happened but because of what didn't happen, and what didn't happen is the hardest thing of all to recall, because it's not something that the status quo has an interest in anyone remembering. Thus the Sixties story has been trivialized, sanitized and manipulated to serve the myths of the winners.

People have been persuaded that if it's cheaper for the consumer, it's good for society. "Cheap" prices justify kicking small farmers off the land because it's more "efficient" to factory farm with chemicals and enormous machines. Low prices justify advantaging warehouse stores like Walmart and disadvantaging small stores.

People have been persuaded that
- a fair day's work doesn't require a fair day's pay because low wages mean you can lower prices and increase profits.
- Muhammad Ali was a great athlete and not a great opponent of an unjustified war.
- Martin Luther King was shot because of his color, not because of his ideas.
- The Kennedy brothers were shot because they were unlucky.
- Death row makes the world a safer place.
- The war on drugs makes the world safer.
- Using unverifiable computer accounting systems to count votes is fine.

After traversing the richest decades of the twentieth century — perhaps the richest period of human history ever — access to affordable housing, health, education and public transit has diminished because there's "not enough to go around," but there have been trillions to invest in oil wars and weapons of "protective" mass destruction. Welcome to some of the consequences of losing the 60s civil war.

When Martin Luther King said we're "on the wrong side of the revolution," it's difficult to believe he could have imagined just how long we would be on the wrong side. It's hard to see 1968 from the hillock of 2006, but what was lost can be imagined by anyone who takes the time to look beyond the cartoons and caricatures. Eleanor Roosevelt captured that great spirit of hope for a better world that the Sixties triggered when she wrote at the end of her autobiography:

> As the campaign advanced and I followed Mr. Kennedy's speeches, I came more and more to believe that he has the power to engender the sense of identification with him which is so important. If a man has this quality he can call out the best that is in people. Today, the United States needs to be reminded of its greatness, and the greatness of a nation can never be more than the greatness of its people.[3]

It didn't turn out the way she had hoped. The defeat of the 1960s civil struggle is evident in the way the Russian "glasnost" revolution was allowed to sink into the ugliest of carnivorous, capitalist carnage. The right side lost, but the wrong side won.

The values and vision of the old frontier have been in charge for so long now that it's easy to forget how many amazing individuals sustained the great national voices for change. They weren't alone.

Ralph Abernathy was the anchor of the extraordinary circle of supporters that surrounded Martin Luther King. He was the down home preacher who reminded everyone that, at the end of the day, ideas had to be about people. He was King's best friend and with him at all the pivotal moments.

Dr. Spock was an icon for upper class white liberals. With Spock on board the freedom train, it had to be the right train. Spock carried a different kind of moral authority, one anchored in liberal philosophy and exceptional individual achievement. He was an Olympic gold medalist, a best-selling author, a pediatrician and a physically imposing man who was unafraid to oppose the governing paradigm. When Dr. Spock spoke on the care of infants or the importance of saying "no" to the Vietnam War people tended to listen.

The Berrigan brothers were courageous Roman Catholic priests from Irish Boston. They were at the barricades with students against the war and continued after the war against corporate and social injustice. They went to jail frequently, triumphantly, confidently.

Jane Jacobs turned the entire urban development model on its head by arguing persuasively in her book *The Death and Life of Great American Cities*[4] that the old way of building cities in pedestrian-oriented blocks adjacent to main streets, instead of in pedestrian pods around malls and freeways was a safer, cheaper and more lively way to build. She never quit. Her last book *Dark Age Ahead*[5] continues to make the argument that we've chosen the wrong path.

Noam Chomsky never quit either. He emerged from MIT's academic halls to become not just a great critic of the Vietnam War but of American foreign policy and has remained so. His courage and energy is phenomenal. In his seventies, he still has the courage to remind his fellow citizens that the US is the only western democracy convicted by the World Court for terrorist acts and was only saved by United Nations condemnation by its own veto. He is unafraid to remind his compatriots that the US is the only nation state to have used nuclear weapons against a civilian population. He's the most quoted American outside of the United States and the least known of all the major figures within it.

Martin Luther King died in 1968 four years after he received the Nobel Peace Prize. He was 39. His public life had scarcely started. When Ralph Abernathy beheld his dying friend and said brokenly, "it's over, it's over," he immediately understood the length and breadth of that ending. For in the deaths of great men and women, a little bit of all of us dies. With both King and Kennedy it was not just present hopes that were expiring, it was the possibility of a different kind of future.

Imagine the many people who would have become central to the governance of the United States and ultimately the world instead of marginalized by it if these men had not been murdered? I recall the image of John Kenneth Galbraith coming home from being Ambassador to India for the funeral of Kennedy, his public service career effectively ended.

Imagine the possibilities of Martin Luther King as the first black US president. I am certain he would have developed the same stature as Franklin Delano Roosevelt, whose "new deal" policies successfully carved a path out of the Great Depression. Kennedy and King together could have charted a new more humane, more sustainable course not just for the United States but for the entire planet towards the 21st century. Instead we've seen the clock rolled backwards to old ideas and old paradigms that have steadily impoverished the public culture and physical environment which we all share.

In a curious twist of fate the old Soviet Gulag has now shifted to the "land of the free." The US has more folks in prison than any other nation on the planet, and its culture of zero tolerance for aggressive behavior in schools has become a recipe for repressing youthful dissent. Zero tolerance has become a new tool for inspiring fear and conformity.

The paradigm of the "new frontier" anchored in humanist values that was attached to the first photographs of the planet taken from space — that incredible big blue and white marble hanging like a Christmas tree ornament in the darkness of space — was not just defeated. It was obliterated.

Henry Kissinger took the winning side on the road. President Nixon kicked off his presidency with instructions to "make the economy [of Chile] scream." This campaign finished with President Allende's murder followed by the murder of thousands of his supporters. Political genocides are not without purpose. They drown the opposition in a sea of pain, fear and refugees.

The Kissinger-Nixon offensive then broadened out to support military dictatorships throughout the Southern Hemisphere and around the world. In Central and South America, Iran, Iraq, Cyprus, Bangladesh, East Timor, Africa and South East Asia, the legitimate aspirations of ordinary people expressed through democratic voices were suppressed in favor of supporting military dictators favorable to the corporate west. The invasion of East Timor by the Indonesian military killed somewhere between 50,000 and 80,000 Timorese within the first 18 months of Indonesian military's war on the island.

The essential elements of the new paradigm foundered one after another.

The small scale, organic farm movement without any national policies to limit the size of farms or the food processing industries was drowned in industrial hog, dairy and chicken farming. In New Brunswick, a picture book Canadian province with a landscape ideally suited for small scale farming, "43 per cent of the rural population farmed in 1951, less than 2 per cent did so two generations later. Farm operations fell from 26,431 census farms in 1951 to 3,252 in 1991."[6]

Much of the rural environment both north and south of the border has become a chemical cocktail of a bewildering complexity that has realized Rachel Carson's dire warning of a Silent Spring. Carson was the Jane Jacobs of biology. She took a very practical look at what was happening in the physical world and came up with some revolutionary conclusions. She was a small, unassuming woman blessed with extraordinary courage. Her research at the Marine Biology Labs in Woods Hole and most of all the eloquence of her pen in *Under the Sea Wind, The Sea Around Us* and finally *Silent Spring* started the environmental movement. It gained strength and public attention so quickly that Interior Secretary Morris Udall and President Kennedy formed a commission to study chemical applications which ultimately led to the banning of DDT.

The pesticide industry spent more than $250,000 to discredit Rachel Carson. Monsanto, one of the largest producers of DDT, said her books were not written as a "scientist but rather a fanatic defender of the cult of the balance of nature." While her work did result in some of the most obvious toxic pesticides like DDT being banned, it was only after there was unassailable proof that there was a direct link between DDT and the declining raptor population. Once there was incontrovertible scientific evidence and the support of the general public that there something in the environment which was softening egg shells and that this was destroying the capacity of many birds to reproduce, DDT was banned.

Unfortunately this kind of direct, simple one-to-one link is very difficult to establish in the complex interactions of the natural world. The effects of pesticides and genetic modifications tend to be diverse and obscure. The blanketing of rural areas with pesticides has continued. The new genetically modified crops are designed to have all the properties of plastic, i.e., they have no interactive possibilities with the environment therefore are impervious to any "natural" infestation. They are the biological world's equivalent of "category killers."

◆ ◆ ◆

President Reagan, the winning side's most popular US president liked to use the game of football as a metaphor for national and corporate success. There is a hard fought battle on the national field, and at the end of the game, after a struggle, the best team wins. "This one's for the 'Gipper.'" The charm of a sports season is that no matter how many games are lost or won, at the end of the season the slate is wiped clean and next year a new competitive season begins. Everyone gets another chance at winning the national championship. There's something wonderfully benign and eternal in the sports cycle. But in real life, the losses don't conveniently disappear at the end of the playing season. In real life, the losses of flora and fauna, underground aquifers, oxygen, the growing gap between rich and poor, all keep on adding up. The slate isn't wiped clean for environmental and social degradation every 12 months.

Success beyond the football field is composed of many things. Most of them have nothing to do with winning. A successful philosophical life is about inventing purpose and meaning for existence. A successful social life is about sustaining friends, neighbors and family. A successful economic life is about adding value where before there was less value. Upon these simple precepts, complex successful individuals, cities and great nations are created. None of these successes have anything to do with the old frontier paradigm of dividing life into winners and losers.

◆ ◆ ◆

It is a melancholy thing to watch Odetta sing the traditional, joyful songs of justice and fraternal love that made her famous during the 1960s. Her voice is still strong and beautiful, but her heart isn't in the songs and her demeanor is that of someone who is going through the motions for her fee. "This little light of mine I'm going to make it shine. This little light of mine I'm going to make it shine." It's a simple song, but infused with joy and belief in one's capacity to live fully and usefully, the words can ring out with grand gospel confidence. When Odetta sings today, she clearly no longer believes her voice is connected to the world in the way it once was. The song is no longer a wild yearning for a better world that must be answered. It's just an old song.

It is a melancholy thing to hear people of my generation talk about the hopes and dreams of their youth as if they had belonged to some foreign country which they once inhabited but has now disappeared. I hear this wistful voice when a nurse now in her fifties says, "the Peace Corps seemed important, that's why I went" before she goes on to explain how she came home to become "successful" doing something entirely different. It is as if looking back on the Sixties, people can no longer really quite understand what in the world possessed them to be a nurse in Africa or a small farmer in some rural state. They had meant well but it seems a bit odd now; they are a little embarrassed by it all.

In 2006, the power and consequences of that 1960s civil conflict are worth recalling because we are going down a different version of that same protest road all over again, and it wasn't a success the first time.

Paul Berman reminds us about this failure with a clarifying eye in his *Tale of Two Utopias*. On the student and worker movement in Mexico he writes: "At the end the Mexican government was as despotic as ever and the oppressed were no less poor and oppressed. But the guerrilla groups had succeeded all too well at stamping out whatever democratic sentiments lingered on from the original radical impulse."[7] On the west, he writes: "For all over the western world, the uprisings proved amazingly unproductive in regard to conventional political and economic change. Several years of radical agitation came and went, the Atlantic Alliance was still in place, capitalism was not transformed, the poor were no less poor…"[8]

The same thing is happening today. It is clear that even a vast, popular intercontinental movement for progressive change has little chance of success unless the objectives of the movement are clearly defined. The goals weren't well defined in the 1960s, and they aren't today. We are repeating exactly the same errors. The anti-globalization movement is an incomprehensible smorgasbord of environmental, social and political chaos. The possibility for change today is suffocating in a confusion of protests just as it did in the 1960s.

Let's count some of the current crop. There's third world debt; IMF and World Bank Structural Adjustment Programs; resisting the imposition of monocultures and agri-businesses; saving endangered species everywhere; protecting public education and promoting public healthcare; resisting privatization of common goods such as water; preserving local democracy and local cultures; world poverty and the growing divide between rich and poor states; rich and poor classes within rich states; the invasion of Iraq; the genocide in the great lake states of Africa and southern Sudan.

You could write a book on any one of these issues, and many have been written. What does enhancing local democracy have to do with factory farming or third world poverty? There are, in fact, links just as there were links between causes of the 1960s. But as in the 1960s, the links are not immediately obvious. No one has devised an easy way to make the links among the many protests clear. So, what gets the attention of the press? In a repeat of the 1960s, it's violence that gets top billing.

A hooded youth broke a McDonald's window in Ottawa during the G-8 conference. This television visual of the dramatic shattering of a great pane of glass by a dangerously shrouded youth with a stick was repeated over and over again on worldwide, prime time news. It was the only act of civilian violence during three tense days when thousands of people gathered to peacefully protest a meeting of the world leaders behind closed doors. Yet this image of the youth smashing the window is the primary memory people all over the world carried to bed with them and to work the next day.

The breaking of one window was such a trivial part of the three days of protests that if you had been there, you would be confident that it wasn't worth recording. The protest was a true world gathering. I heard speakers from Nigeria, Nicaragua, Indonesia, South and North America and Europe, but you would never know it from the news coverage. I never saw any news cameras at the events I attended, mostly in churches and community halls.

The Nigerian speaker from the Niger River Delta spoke passionately about the need to stop the oil exploration which was killing traditional fisheries and traditional ways of life. He concluded with these words:

> We don't need your sympathy. We don't need your aid. We need you to create a more just society here. In the south, we need northern nations that will stop exploiting their own people and their own environment, because when you stop doing that, your corporations will stop exploiting Africa.[9]

His message wasn't about the poor underdeveloped south. It was "fix thyself." How could it be otherwise when six percent of the world's population is consuming 40 percent of the world's resources? When for every dollar in aid that goes to the Third World, three dollars comes back in interest payments on debt. There were many other equally compelling speakers on everything from neo-natal care in Nicaragua to the new human slaveries in cross-border trade. But for the 99 percent of those who watched the protests on television in two-minute sound bytes, their principal conclusion had to be that these protestors are all violent and the protests ill-considered.

This image does not move us forward. It does the reverse. It fractures both the window and the possibility for change just as those ridiculous little mini-revolutionary cells did in the 1960s. Does anyone remember the Symbionese Liberation Army? Or the Weathermen? Adjectives like pathetic, sad and stupid apply to these little violent movements. Nobody could even figure out what they were really about, but they existed and did immense harm — not to the tidal forces of the status quo that they had declared war on, but to the possibility of developing a new political consensus around new priorities. The same thing is happening today in the great popular protests.

Successful campaigns for change need an ABC approach; that's the way corporations create great change. Corporations use the KISS principle (Keep It Simple, Stupid). They have a few simple messages and they keep pumping them out over and over again until enough of the public are convinced the product or the subsidy they are pushing for is needed and achieved.

The first principle in forming a campaign for successful change has to be a simple, clear statement of objectives that everyone can understand. A learned opus like the Port Huron statement is not helpful. A one-page press release "to do" list will do just fine. Some of the A list objectives should be:

1) Politics: Democratic governments must represent a majority of the electorate, not a plurality, and be elected with public electoral funding, not private donations.
2) Money: City and national governments should decide their priorities via "participative budgets" using the Porto Algerian community decision-making model. (No more back room deals between elites)
3) Trade: World trade deals are desirable but only when the terms of trade are the result of the widest public debate, not the result of secret negotiations between a few powerful individuals.
4) International: The United Nations must be empowered with elected representatives, not appointed party hacks. A source of funding must be provided for the UN mandate which is independent of any single nation so that the UN can independently prosecute nations for grave environmental and human rights violations which threaten humanity.

None of this is rocket science. It's all immediately achievable and would change politics, the economies of nations and the world immediately for the better by making nations and cities more responsive to the commonwealth instead of individual profits.

The A list objectives need to be backed up by implementation strategies which should include: activists must cease demonizing the police. Sixties activists were complicit in the murder and isolation of activists by the police. They were complicit because they made it easy for the police to be manipulated by old, mean, paranoid white men like J. Edgar Hoover. Calling the police "pigs" (a popular epithet at the time) played right into the hands of all those who wanted to focus the police on suppressing dissent instead of thinking about why it was taking place.

Progressive change happens when the police become part of it; that's been the modern reality in Brazil, Bolivia and Czechoslovakia. Where change is successful, the police decide that they will be part of it by staying in their barracks and refusing to shoot their fellow citizens. Demonizing the police is tactically wrong — and it's morally wrong because there is no more important identity than that of citizenship. Citizenship should always trump the identity of police officers because it is our most fundamental connection to society. We are citizens before we are police officers, nurses, doctors, lawyers and construction workers. Demonizing trivializes the police officer's citizenship. It's just another ugly "ism."

For those who don't much care for principles as long as the end is admirable, it is tactically stupid to demonize police because modern police forces are excellent at suppressing dissent and they just keep getting better. Prior to the large demonstrations in Ottawa around the G-8 and World Bank Meetings, the combined police forces covering it were tracking activists that they regarded as possibly dangerous from the moment they left their homes to the moment they showed up at the barricades. To put the police resources in perspective, in Ottawa policing costs us about $170 million annually or about 20 percent of our disposable income. Toronto's police budget is $440 million. Across the border, the CIA has an annual budgetary allocation of $40 billion. The American military's total annual allocation is reported at somewhere around $500 billion. I cannot comprehend $500 billion. It is beyond my imagination. But I can imagine that real change is happening when the police themselves decide that to serve the broader currents of social and environmental justice is more important than protecting a glass window.

Finally an implementation strategy must not only have objectives clearly stated. They must be ranked in priority. What comes first? What is second? What is third? Unfortunately the world can't be saved in every direction simultaneously. I would urge that the first priority for the new century should be political reform. New politics now will give us new solutions now.

For me, correcting the democratic deficit is the number one priority because without true democracy, it's business as usual no matter who is elected. Single parties can control governments with a minority of the popular vote, and millions of voters are disenfranchised.

A vivid Canadian example is the last election in British Columbia where 12 percent of the voters voted for the Green Party, and not one member was elected. Presently, we have a national government that two out of three Canadians didn't vote for. This government has pronounced the secret prisons of Guantanomo Bay are a good idea. This is not responsible government. Responsible government must reflect the wishes of a majority of voters, not a minority.

The general public remains to be convinced of the importance of political reform, but the corporate world understands the necessity of not changing. For if you control the election process through funding, you control the creation of the legislative agenda. That's real politik. Somehow all those engaged citizens protesting in favor of their many worthy causes (there are 4,000 charities in my city alone) never seem to grasp this simple, fundamental truth. Perhaps it just isn't sexy enough. Images of orphans and dying whales are powerful, vivid images whereas proportional representation and elections paid for by the public instead of the corporate world have no bleeding images. Political reform seems desiccated and academic instead of vital to the innards of a nation.

Tobacco companies did not want a connection established between lung cancer and cigarettes and successfully fought it off for 50 years. Corporate globalization doesn't want city, national or international government to become more genuinely democratic because once these governments do, the rules of economic engagement will also change. Then the wealth generated in cities and in the country by rural life will be more equally shared and profits thus less concentrated in the largest corporations.

What would happen, for example, if governments which represented the majority of the people, not a majority of the corporate wealth passed a law which said, "no one can transport animals more than a hundred miles for slaughter because longer distances are inhumane?" This very small law would transform our countryside immediately. Suddenly, small farms would have a great advantage over industrial farms. Suddenly small community slaughterhouses would be possible, and the day of two international companies controlling the slaughtering of animals would be over. Suddenly, the local would be invested with a whole new meaning. This very small law would not be good news for agribusinesses — just as urban streetcars are not good news for the asphalt, cement, banking, land speculation and automotive industries which now control so much of how our cities grow. But it would be good news for the rest of us.

19

The World Social Forum II and Trying to Change Things

Why are there no city politicians from the United States here?

— Participant, World Social Forum

I AM WRITING THIS IN Porto Alegre, a city in the south of Brazil not far from the border with Uruguay. I am attending the section of the World Social Forum for mayors and city councilors interested in creating more humane, inclusive cities.

The World Social Forum is a gathering of the human family, people from every corner of the planet, and it is so enormous that it overwhelms. The organizers were expecting 20,000 and 50,000 came, and it is only the second year that it has been held. It is clear people are tired of protesting at doors of hotels while meetings are held in secret inside by aging politicians. The finance ministers in Davos may have the money, but the World Social Forum has the people.

The Forum has this enormous ambition to define and then build a planetary consensus about a new way of running the world. The animating thought of the Social Forum is "another world is possible."

The focus of the Mayors and City Councilors Forum for Social Inclusion is less grand. As the name implies the focus is much more precise; it's all about ways to increase social inclusion in cities. How do we battle homelessness and urban poverty? How do we keep common goods like water in the public domain? How do we create communities within our cities where residents are not segregated by income and status? How do we cope with too many responsibilities and too small a share of the national tax revenues? The speeches about debt and the distribution of taxes especially resonated with me. In my district, a resident who earns $50,000 pays about $20,000 in federal and state taxes, and $2,000 in city taxes. We, city councilors, are obliged to run the entire city on about $2,000 per taxpayer. That just isn't enough, so the city gets poorer with each passing year.

At the national level, the financial scene is grim for different reasons. In the last 20 years, Canada has gone from a nation whose debt was held exclusively by its citizens via national savings bonds (just as city residents used to own their own schools with school bonds) to a nation that has a large foreign-owned debt. Canada now receives annual "report cards" from the World Bank and the International Monetary Fund just as poor African countries do telling Canadian politicians how much we should be spending on healthcare, social security, culture and so on. Our great national services — healthcare, public education, Air Canada, Canadian National, the CBC once the pride of the nation — have all been steadily reduced or privatized. Where does the World Bank get the authority to write these "report cards?" Neither I nor any other Canadian elected these World Bank directors, yet they behave as if the Canadian government reports to them.

I often wonder what would happen if one day we elected a national government which insisted on repatriating our foreign debt? I can't imagine that international business interests would permit this to happen, because if citizens own their own debt they also own their country. They don't have to listen to "report cards." If it happened, I am sure immense banking and business pressure would force the Canadian government to "open" the Canadian economy to international debt so that Canada could "modernize" just as Egypt and other countries have been forced to do in the interests of "trade liberalization."

The internationalization of debt has been a great corporate success. The global capital market has pushed every nation of the planet to carry a maximum debt load and put a maximum stress load on its physical resources. Slower growth and less intense consumption of the planet's physical resources is not on the corporate agenda, nor is it on the national agenda in Canada. The Alberta tar sands exploitation has become the poster child for physically ripping the planet apart to serve the corporate financial model.

Under the North American Free Trade Agreement (NAFTA) it's no longer possible for Canada, in the interests of resource conservation and domestic sustainable environmental practices, to set limits on the amounts of oil and gas exported. How can you create another kind of world when so much of the daily economic and social life of every nation has been proscribed by unelected international financial organizations and rapacious trade agreements?

A nation's destiny, even a powerful one like Brazil, becomes speculative rather than directed. For example, the value of a nation's currency is a fundamental aspect of its independence. If its currency has little value relative to the most powerful nations, in a globalized economy the country's resources can be bought and sold as cheaply as people once traded slaves. A low-value Canadian dollar makes Canadian businesses, products, oil and natural gas cheap for global corporations to buy and very difficult for Canadians to hang on to. This resource loss is exactly what has happened to the city of Ottawa's dynamic high tech industry. It enjoyed a brief flowering, but once the centers of capital realized how much money was being made it was bought up and the most productive parts moved south to become "integrated" into more powerful conglomerates.

Economists love to argue through the details of capital flows, but the fundamentals are simple enough. Creativity increases productivity which creates wealth. Wealth is desired and unless there are strong impediments, the creativity and production associated with it will always migrate to the largest centers of capital accumulation and currency strength. Without impediments the best and most productive resources including biological "products" and people's skills will be bought up and centralized by the largest and most powerful corporations where the profits can be more easily controlled and accessed.

You don't need any complicated regression analysis to track this movement of resources towards capital and currency power; anyone can see it. It's one of the principal reasons resource-rich nations remain poor. They hang on to such a small share of the final profits that they remain constantly subservient to the larger more powerful system; their currency values are too low to retain their most valuable products and their most valuable labor. Further poor nations have had governments (usually military dictatorships or elite cartels) that have assumed debts for mega-projects which require interest payments that send more public resources out of the country than return to it.

There is no escape because the international economic system is designed to work this way. It's not designed to share the wealth of the richest countries. It's designed to ensure that they stay the richest. Coffee beans are bought cheaply in Sri Lanka, oil and diamonds cheaply in Nigeria, dates cheaply in Morocco — then these products cycle into the high-value-currency economies (the American dollar or the Euro). Result? The country with the low-value currency retains very little of the international value added to the original purchase because the principal "mark up" or profit points occur well after the product has left the low-value or penny-currency economy.

Countries with low currency values protect and stablilize the American dollar because the higher valued dollars become refuge currencies for international investors and currency speculators. No one saves money in Tunisian dinars. Low-value currencies are just traded up and down for short-term profits. Hence, the lowest value currency's economic relationship to the highest value currency is one of perpetual servitude.

For African countries, low value currencies combined with fluctuating interest rates on their debts create a waterwheel of borrow-and-repay debt slavery. If a very rich nation like Canada must slash and burn its greatest national services to the bone and still take ten years to simply reduce its debt load, how can a poor nation ever get out of the clutches of these international financial obligations? In a word, they can't. Their national agendas are controlled by the International Monetary Fund's (IMF) "structural adjustment programs," not by the needs of ordinary people. The rate of neonatal deaths was higher in Nicaragua after ten years of "structural adjustment" than it was during the civil war.

I expected passion from the delegates from Africa, Indonesia and Latin America who came to the World Social Forum II to protest World Bank policies. For these delegates the World Social Forum II was their Boston Tea Party, and the violence of their slogan "don't owe! won't pay!" rocked the amphitheatre where they were gathered. The stories from Africa especially had me riveted, but it was the emotional pitch of the mayors in a very expensive downtown hotel that took me completely by surprise. It was as if each one had been waiting for this moment to speak, and like starving hounds released from a tether they one after another leaned into the microphones and bellowed out their frustrations and anger.

It didn't matter if the mayor was from a rich city like Geneva or from a small, poor Brazilian city. Each, in their own way, was saying, "we need to change things."

The Mayor of Geneva Manuel Tornare had the temerity to phone up President W. Bush at the height of the World Trade terrorist crisis and inform him that he had to change. Tornare told Bush that it was no longer "my country right or wrong"; it was now "my planet right or wrong." I was astonished at his boldness. I had never heard any elected official in Canada speak like this.

I listened to the French Minister of Housing Marie Lienemann, who also happens to sit on a suburban city council. (In France you can hold a city and a federal political position simultaneously.) She spoke about the importance of bringing in a Tobin tax (a one or two percent tax on all international financial transactions) that can start funneling some of the wealth generated by international financial speculation back to the poorest countries. Presently, fifty percent of all international financial transaction profits are tax free. And she spoke passionately about the absolute centrality of creating a chain of citizenship and elected responsibility that stretches from each city through each nation to a planetary level of government. She concluded with a story taken from a very violent French film called "La Haine" (Hate).

In the film, two black adolescent boys are staring up at the night sky in a bombed out concrete building. They live in an environment of drugs, violence and concrete ugliness. One says to the other, trying to comfort him with the thought that the futility of their own existence is a natural, universal thing, "we are just specks of dust in the universe, that's all." Lieneman's last words in her speech were a battle cry that still resonates with me. "They are wrong. We are not specks of dust in the universe. We are citizens!"

I am not a professional politician. I haven't been elected for 25 years as Minister Lienemann has been. I am mostly a poet who contrary to everyone's expectations was elected to my city council. In the last election, I was hesitatingly endorsed in the local press with the caveat, "you wouldn't want more than one Doucet on city council." Yet here in Porto Alegre I discovered that the thoughts I have been thinking and the words I have been saying are the same thoughts and words which mayors and city councilors in many cities and many other parts of the world have also been saying.

They also are emotional about the dangers to human life biosphere degradation is creating and the blight homelessness and urban poverty bring to their cities. The mayors of European cities (to my surprise because you hear about racism in both France and Italy) understood also that there has to be immigration from the south to the north because the North has most of the planet's capital locked up; hence the jobs are in the North. And until the South gets fair terms of trade, immigrants must journey north. What choice do they have?

To my astonishment, the mayors also believed that the American war on drugs was just another war on the poor. They hold the same opinion that I have always had: that the war on drugs has no effect except to push profits into criminal hands and incarcerate people who need medical help. On and on my colleagues went, for two days from dawn to dusk. Mayors and city councilors from Africa to Europe to Latin America, all of them convinced that "another world was possible" — if we are open to reforming the way we govern ourselves. All of them sure that the governance that we have now is not working.

I spent most of my time in a kind of emotional and intellectual shock with my headset pressed to my ears trying to make sure that I was really understanding what the translator was saying. At one of the coffee breaks, I was standing at a table laid out with publications from various cities and picked up a little booklet containing a letter signed by the Mayors of Coastal Cities in support of the Kyoto Protocol requesting that President Bush sign the Protocol. All the great cities of the planet were represented from Asia to Africa, Europe to the New World.[1] Nowhere will you find a better example of the disconnection between the world view of cities compared to the fierce and parochial desire of nations to protect their largest most polluting industries. As I quickly flipped through this booklet tears surprised me and began to run down my cheeks. I wiped them away as discretely as I could but was embarrassed to notice the lady behind the counter looking at me curiously. They were neither tears of happiness or sadness. They were just tears, for I — suddenly — did not feel so alone.

20

World Social Forum III and Failing to Change Things

Politics is certainly not always good, but its devaluation or its discredit is invariably a worse symptom.

— Fernando Savater, *Chosir Liberte*

THERE IS AN ADVERTISEMENT on Brazilian television. Two women are walking gracefully across a dry, wind blown field. They are carrying something on their heads. Three boys are playing in the field. A car appears. Its metallic sides glow in the heat. It has tinted windows everywhere so you cannot see who is driving or indeed if anyone is inside. For no apparent reason, it stops. The three boys run towards it. The women watch.

The boys clamber all over it, peering in the sun roof, polishing the headlights with the sleeves of their thin shirts, then like young monkeys losing interest with a new toy they climb down. The car moves slowly away, leaving the boys and the women to continue on their way. We never see who is in the car. There is no dialogue. It could be an ad for a particularly expensive car. Then an advertising band appears at the bottom of the screen. It says: "Another World is Possible, the World Social Forum III, Porto Alegre, January 23 to 28."

There has emerged in the south of Brazil a city and a civic culture which is effervescent and transformative. You feel the difference between Porto Alegre and North American cities from the first moment that you step off the plane. It's in the banners which hang boldly from the airport rafters, "Porto Alegre embraces the world." It's in the sense of openness and confidence which you discover in the public parks and on the streets and in the cafés.

People walk everywhere. Even the airport is easily accessible by foot. The light rail line drops people off from the downtown, and broad comfortable sidewalks sweep people right to the front door of the terminal. The city of Porto Alegre has changed itself through a participative budget process which changed how it invests in itself. The new President of Brazil, Luiz Inácio "Lula" da Silva is a former metal worker who ran for president four times before winning. His final success came out of the civil society movement that the unions were part of but did not control, a movement which has spread from Porto Alegre to over 200 Brazilian municipalities including the largest, Sao Paulo.

I came home from the World Social Forum in 2002 exhilarated by the possibilities of the Porto Alegran model and did my best to advance the idea of a participative budget in Canadian cities. A year later finds me in a different, more cautious frame of mind. It is not because I regard less the participative budget and the civic engagement success of Porto Alegre; my caution comes from a realizing how impermeable North America seems to be to new governance ideas of any kind. A bunker mentality has settled over North America. You can feel it from the moment you walk up the ramp towards the door of a North American airport. A soldier wearing flak gear and carrying automatic weapons waits for you. Air travelers don't speak to each other. There is an eerie silence that descends on people from the moment they approach the security check point. People are afraid to talk for fear of saying something that might be misinterpreted. I wonder what it must be like to be a security guard working all day long amidst this silent, shuffling, compliant, anxious crowd?

"Take your shoes off, please. Take your coat off. Do you have any change, any metal in your pocket? Reverse your belt, please." Travelers are now left with only their trousers and shirts on, and these are pushed and prodded with electronic scanners.

The war with Iraq has pushed North America even further back into itself than it was after the attacks on the World Trade Center. It is a curious thing to observe the richest, most powerful nation that has ever existed on the planet spending more than $440 billion on military and armaments per year, hunkered down behind psychological, social and military walls that grow higher with each passing day.

I see it in the triple lines of defense — concrete barriers, steel bollards and steel fencing — bunkering the concrete walls of the American Embassy in Ottawa. This building looks like something out of Star Wars and remains a constant reminder to everyone who passes by that the folks inside are frightened. They are building their own defensive perimeters everywhere to protect themselves from "bad guys."

The World Social Forum III couldn't be more different. It was twice the size of the previous year. 100,000 people participated. It was the largest conference on the planet, and it hardly penetrated the North American news outlets of any kind. I rarely saw a police officer or a security vehicle anywhere in spite of street parades with 50,000 people walking. In Canada, there was one newspaper article in the entire country about the Forum. The disconnect between the English-speaking part of the world and the rest of the planet is truly extraordinary.

Nonetheless it was exhilarating just watching German, Spanish, Italian, Portuguese, French, Brazilian, Argentinian and Venezuelan city councilors talking of building better cities and a better world. I was welcomed warmly everywhere, but this time I was the lone city councilor from North America. It would have made such a difference if we had had many Canadian and American delegations that could have participated, learned and come back to their own cities invigorated with new ideas and new friendships.

The only world politician to attend both the Social Forum at Porto Alegre and the corporate forum at Davos, Switzerland, the new President of Brazil Luiz Inácio da Silva said that, "the only war politicians should be engaged with is against poverty and social exclusion," but he was alone. It is a message which distinguished him not just by its content but by its singularity. Other politicians aren't hearing it.

I had come to the Forum in 2002 to find out about Porto Alegre's participative budget, which has transformed the city and is being adopted throughout Brazil. Critics say only about ten percent of every city's annual budget is uncommitted, but ten percent is not an insignificant number. In my city, ten percent translates into about $200 million per year. Two hundred million can bring a lot of change if you decide to spend it, for example, on daycares, community health centers, the arts and parks instead of roads. The effect on the city of Porto Alegre has certainly been galvanizing.

Is another world possible? I don't know. On the yes side, there is an amazing planetary discourse which is underway about the future.

This discourse is taking place completely out of sight of the English-speaking media and has the potential to change the world the way it has never been changed before — peacefully — by changing enough people to think that priorities other than the military and private wealth counts.

On the no side, the global corporations don't want to see society change. They want more of the same: less government, more tax cuts, less democratic participation, more consumers, fewer environmental controls. That is exactly what they are getting. Consumerism has become a civic and national virtue.

On the no side, the Reagans, Bushes, Thatchers, Blairs and many other political administrations want to go back to the "security" of the 1950s. But it is not the 1950s; it is not even close. Unlike the fifties, the median income has stopped growing. The rising economic tide which lifted all boats back in the 50s and 60s now lifts only the yachts. By 1995, the top one percent of American households owned almost 39 percent of the total household wealth. If you exclude home ownership, it was 47 percent and the top fifth owned 93 percent. In Canada, the top ten percent have never been richer and are getting richer each year. The poor are increasing and the middle class decreasing.

This decline of the median income and the collapse of corporate taxation in the wake of the global trade deals has led directly to the impoverishment of all the great public services — health, education, transit, libraries, daycare, parks, air and water standards — on which so much of the modal quality of life depends. It's a vicious circle. Declining income makes people insecure, and insecurity feeds the status quo. When people feel threatened, they are much less willing to risk change. So the corporations feed the fear beacons because fearful people are compliant, anxious only to get "value" for their shrinking amount of money.

Yes, another world is possible. We can build our cities and our nations in more democratic and less exploitive ways. Anything is possible, but it certainly won't happen because of the World Social Forum. The conversation here is simply too diffuse. It has too many threads to it with too little willingness to move towards anything that might smack of creating a political agenda that can actually lead somewhere. As marvelous as the politicians, artists, authors, speeches and panels are, it's not enough to just talk and feel good about the talk.

At the bottom, there's a daffiness about the World Social Forum that doesn't recognize how change happens. The G-8 conferences in Davos, Switzerland are the reverse. There's no show and little spark, but the institutional levers, the "structural adjustment programs" and everything else that are needed to maintain the status quo are reinforced. The taxes that need to be imposed to create a greater sharing of wealth are not imposed. It's all very quiet and all very effective.

Politics is where change happens. Martin Luther King understood that when he was organizing at the grass-roots level. The ultimate goal has to be about changing the political system. King worked for political change by persuading the politically excluded to register and vote, and this began to change the system. The organizers behind Fair Vote Canada understand this and are slowly grinding a new electoral system onto the national agenda. But no one at the World Social Forum seems capable of understanding that outrage is only the starting line. The finish line can only be reached if there is a concrete action plan that can be integrated into every national and local election. Otherwise, it's all just words in the wind. People need to go home from the World Social Forum with a common "to do" list that they can mobilize elections around. This is the hardest thing in the world to. Even presidents like Lula cannot do it. It takes a paradigm shift among the general population which is broad and powerful enough to insist on political and institutional change.

It is something that happens only rarely. The natural and reflexive reaction of all governments to social and economic stress is to reinforce the status quo. This is what is happening in the United States today and throughout the west. It's what has happening in the past. Feudal cities built massive walls against the "barbarians." The Roman and Chinese Empires expanded their city walls into walls that crossed continents. In 2006, President Bush is building a wall — his space missile shield — around North America, and talks constantly about the need "to protect America." But in the global world the only frontier that means anything is the biosphere, and that frontier cannot be divided into the American, Chinese or African sectors. It is not possible to put up a wall around your portion of the biosphere.

The crisis today is not one of terrorism. It's a crisis of imagination and governance. We have federal, state and provincial governments harnessed to horse and buggy constitutions written in the time that men rode horses and waged war with single-shot rifles. It's a world that no longer exists. If I want to talk to a colleague in New York or Austin or Paris, I sit at my computer and write an electronic letter. With a few keystrokes, I can learn how the city of Austin has organized its public service and about the success of St. Louis's new metro link.

Cities have been globalized. Ottawa city council governs looking at Calgary, Quebec, Portland, Denver, Toulouse. The federal government — whether it's American or Canadian — is largely irrelevant to its citizens, both as a provider of public services or as a regulator of the private sector. We have come through two of the richest decades the planet has ever seen and where is the federal public infrastructure? Where are the new national rail lines? Where are the public airports? Airports are now owned by parking authorities.

The kind of global capitalism that has evolved in the last thirty years is a unique phase in human history. We have never seen anything like it before, and it is not a conserving or conservative phenomenon. The Roman Empire, which lasted a millennium, was both conserving and conservative. Global capitalism is neither.

Global capitalism has no values and no frontiers. It operates like an opportunistic virus, jumping from cell to cell wherever an advantage appears. If greed had a gene it would be called the globalization gene. If a nation or a city or a class of people stops producing the best possible profits, global capital moves on. Not surprisingly, the greed gene is capable of producing vast transcontinental "profits" and at the same time equally vast transcontinental "collateral damage." Isn't this essentially how cancer cells propagate in human organs? The principal difference is scale. The host for global capitalism is not a single, living organism; it is the planet.

Politics is never perfect and has been the vehicle for great evil as often as it has for great good, but flawed as it is, it is the principal tool we have for change. Unfortunately, the World Social Forum does not seem capable of creating an international political agenda based on the overwhelming need to reform our governments so that they can start to meet the new global realities. In Porto Alegre, I saw the flip side of President Bush government's policies in a civil society experience that paralleled my experiences of the 1960s; rhetoric and an immense diversity of objectives are marginalizing the movement. Like the political theater of demonstrations, it pleases the participants, but achieves little but the occasional headline. Porto Alegre, January, 2003.

21

Saving the World with Stephen Lewis?

*When I give food to the poor, they call me a Saint. When I
ask why the poor have no food, they call me a Communist.*

— Dom Heider Camara,
Retired Archbishop of Recife and Olinda, Brazil

A FEW NIGHTS AGO, I went to a packed church hall to listen to a
speech given by Stephen Lewis, the United Nations Envoy to
Africa on behalf of the victims of HIV infections and AIDS. The
hall was sold out and had been for many weeks. I think of this man as
simply "Stephen" because he has been such an intimate figure in the
Canadian political scene for so many years: as leader of the Ontario
New Democratic Party, Canadian UN ambassador and so on. Lis-
tening to him speak is much like watching Jean Beliveau play hockey.
Beliveau played so elegantly, it was wonderful just to watch him carry
the puck up the ice. Stephen Lewis speaks with the same controlled
passion that Beliveau played hockey. His sentences, scenes and stories flow out elegantly, compelling the listener to pay attention to
every word. He's one of those charmed individuals who never needs
to say, "I will try to be brief."

Fifty minutes flow by like five minutes and he scores his points
with devastating regularity. At the end of the evening, you have a
feeling for just how awful AIDS is in Africa. You have lived with him
for a few minutes in an African hut with nothing but children; all the
adults are dead, the average age of the "head of the household" is

eight years old and children must help their mother die because she cannot help herself. Her children must try and clean her up when she is incontinent. Where a family is lucky enough to have a grandmother alive, it is she who must find the energy to prepare the next generation with the love and knowledge they will need to survive.

The UN has given Stephen Lewis very little except a fancy title and a travel allowance, so he organized a Foundation and raised $11 million for drugs that can convey AIDS into remission, that can give parents a chance to be parents, that can build latrines and drill for clean water; that can make life not just better but possible in places where people live on a dollar a day. Needless to say, I admire his work and all the good people who came out to listen and donate to the cause of AIDS relief. It is necessary wonderful work that Stephen is doing, but it is treating the symptom. Canadians have been treating the symptoms in Africa for a long time. Twenty years ago, they supported David MacDonald to fight famine in the horn of Africa and raised $50 million to do so.

When someone is starving, you must find the food to feed them. When someone is suffering from a terrible disease you must find the necessary medicines, but I have come to believe that these are all band-aids which obscure the fundamental problem as much as help. Like the food banks do in my city. Why should it be necessary to donate money for food banks in a rich city? Why should it be necessary to raise money for medicines to stop AIDS in Africa when there are trillions of dollars to wage a war which accomplished nothing but spread terror-based violence from Israel to Iraq, to Pakistan, to Madrid, to London?

More charities and more preachers are not the answer.

Everyone is looking in the wrong place to find a solution. The AIDS disaster in Africa is not about "losing our moral anchor" as Stephen Lewis would have us believe. It's not about racism. It's about a carnivorous capitalist system that treats both the human race and the environment like gas to be put in a car's tank. Whether the "resource" is cheap Asian labor in Dubai, cheap Mexican workers in Los Angeles, mineral deposits in the Canadian Shield, an aquifer in the Black Hills or oil in the Arabian desert, it's all just grist for the mill of carnivorous capitalism. This is why there have been no life-saving drugs in Africa. The Africans can't pay for them, and the capitalist system is very clear about people who can't pay whether they're infected with a virus or just hungry. They must find a charity soup kitchen or they die.

Combine carnivorous capitalism with a political system where the principal responsibility is to feed it and we have the present recipe for social and environmental disaster. It's not just Africans dying of AIDS. It's Russians who can't get medical care or community services while a few individuals scoop billions out of this energy-rich nation's soil. It's millions of Americans who live in Third World conditions. George W. Bush has said "he doesn't get poverty." It's easy to understand why. At the same time as fundamental environmental breakdown is occurring, millions of people appended to the great financial centers of London, New York, Tokyo, Toronto and Paris have been getting ever richer. So it is entirely possible to become confused as to what is actually happening.

What is happening on the planet is that we are seeing the beginning of a massive contraction of the human population. One out of six couples in Canada is now infertile. In Russia, people are not only not reproducing at population replacement levels, but the life span for those living is retreating; the population is shrinking from both ends. In two decades the Russian population is predicted to decline from 143 million to 90. The only folks who are escaping this for the moment are those so locked into faith systems that they are reproducing according to their "beliefs," not what their experience should tell them to do. This is exactly what is happening in North America. While the birth rate in the fundamentalist Christian part of both Canada and the US is expanding, everywhere else it is retreating.

George W. Bush is not a sociopath, but he might as well be because he is pushing humanity away from what he says that he wants to achieve — a safer world. And he's doing it quickly. He appears to have no idea how the world has changed since he was a boy. The Second World War world was sold as good guys lined up on one side of the line and bad guys on the other. Whether or not it was true doesn't matter. What matters is that that world no longer exists.

Globalization has compressed time and space. This is its singular accomplishment, and from this compression everything else has flowed: the separation of management from production and wealth from taxes; the conversion of national currencies into commodities; the surge and sway of commodities themselves from Chilean blueberries coming to Canada and Canadian oil moving across the planet; the travel of people across continents and oceans.

It's also compressed and simplified religious visions into two points of view. Religion, no matter what the brand, is now divided between those who believe God to be an "a priori" external creator and those who regard God as an internal creative force for good. The Islamic world is divided this way and so is the Christian.

And politics is now divided into two similar views. There are those who regard human nature as essentially positive and thus think human institutions should be principally directed to helping that "positive" or "good" nature flower and those who view human nature as so malign that human institutions should be devoted to constraint. The latter vision is the one of the current governments of Canada and the United States.

If you examine the Canadian Conservative party's five national priorities, four out of five are devoted to constraint.

- Crime: mandatory sentencing, hiring more police, mandatory DNA data bank for sex offenders, arm border guards, canceling the gun registry, a new national Security Commissioner, new measures against the use of drugs.
- Accountability: Accountability Act for government (more rules).
- Child Care: no national daycare.
- Tax Relief: will cut taxes.
- Healthcare: will legislate mandatory wait time rules

Prime Minister Harper is bending the resources of a powerful G-8 nation towards making the world "safer" by spending more on jails, police, defence and various constraints on public servants to make sure these people conform to rules. The rule of constraint is the rule of suspicion, distrust and fear.

Prime Minister Harper's priorities that aren't devoted directly to constraint are focused on serving a limited part of the population. Mothers who stay home with children will get some financial assistance, but the ⅔ who take their children to daycare will go without. The question that is before Canadians during Mr. Harper's government is not whether or not Stephen Harper is a good or honorable guy. My guess is, he is. He works hard, has nice kids, a spunky wife, goes to church and controls his temper. But the question should not be whether or not the Prime Minister is an honorable man; the question should be "will his vision of a world based on more and better 'constraints' lead Canada towards a more secure and happy future?"

In Canada, the immediate answer from the electorate was clearly no. It was only through a deficient electoral system rather than popular will that Mr. Harper became the Prime Minister. A clear majority — two out of three Canadians — voted for parties that do not belong to the model of human society that Thomas Hobbes first described as "solitary, nasty, brutish and short" — without the constraints of government regulation.

In Canada the Liberals, the New Democratic Party, the Bloc Québécois all inhabit the other side of the divide — the side that views humanity as basically positive with government intervention and regulation focused primarily on institutions that are of an "assisting" nature rather than a "constraining" nature.

It was no accident that residents of Canada's largest cities did not vote a single representative of Mr. Harper's party in. It was no accident because cities are at the heart of globalization. Canada's cities produce 80 percent of the greenhouse gases, contain 80 percent of the Canadian population and suffer more from climate change and will suffer more in the future. Not surprisingly, city dwellers tend to be sensitive to the present realities of globalization as population growth compresses people together, and it is clear in this environment public services count for more, not less. City dwellers also understand instinctively that security and quality of life depend on strong, inclusive public services such as adequate daycare, public transit, more libraries not less, more community centers not less, more public health nurses not less, and so on. People need these things to be better people and for their cities to be more secure places.

Mayors and city councils are closest to most of the problems facing residents of cities and understand them best. But unfortunately because of national constitutions written for a rural age, municipal government doesn't have either the power or the right to act on behalf of their constituents as they would wish.

Most of the time, municipal governments are working in opposition to their national governments instead of in cooperation. We see the Mayor of Seattle putting together a national coalition of cities to enact Kyoto regardless of what Mr. Bush does. We see the Mayor of Hiroshima putting together an international coalition of mayors to ban the production and stockpiling of nuclear weapons.

And in Canada we see mayors starting to suffer from collective apoplexy as they begin to calculate the social costs of the constraint model: city daycares unable to grow with the population; the cost of more jails from "tougher sentencing"; the human cost of the loss of the gun registry (violent crime with weapons was down, not up); the environmental cost of transit lines that won't get built and greenhouse gas-producing roads that will, and so on.

What to do? That is the question. Shall we donate to a great cause like AIDS in Africa? Yes, of course. But as worthy as this cause and many others are, they won't solve the fundamental problems before us: a carnivorous economic system designed to treat the planet and all its species like a great, fat turkey needing only to be plucked; and political systems unable to deal with the crippling negative consequences of globalization.

This failure is so deeply rooted and runs in so many directions that even when you have a book to write about it, it is hard to get one's mind around all the tentacles because there are so many of them and they run in so many different directions. They start with questions so fundamental to our common existence: ideas of what progress is and such entrenched ideas of how government should operate and economies should function that changing them approaches the difficulty of changing your skin color. For example I don't talk about it in this book, but how does government pay for the costs of running a city or a nation when the largest, richest corporations export their profits to tax-free islands? This has been standard operating procedure for large corporations for decades. Thus corporations profit from all the benefits a country like Canada provides — stability, an educated and healthy population, well run cities — but they don't return their share of their company's profits for the provision of those services. These are quietly sent off shore to banks in places like the Bahamas and Bermuda. Globalization has made this extraordinarily easy to do. Computers can move trillions and do every day. Thus the nations of the world are bled white with a smaller and smaller portion of the population carrying a larger and larger financial burden to run the country.

Many corporations now have larger bottom lines than all but the largest nations. They grow more powerful each day while the health of the planet declines — largely through the inability of all governments to govern for the well being of the Commons.

Another complex tentacle is that production can now be separated from management because management depends on information. Information can be transmitted from Mumbai to Los Angeles as fast as it can be from Orange County. So the folks running industrial enterprises can be anywhere. Coca-Cola, a little company that began in Atlanta and then became a great symbol of America, now belongs to no nation. A management computer terminal has no loyalty to anything but its information source.

The globalized compression of time and space also means corporations can now be globally "efficient." In practice, this means they can cherry pick only the most profitable operation or resource from a nation and leave the rest to rot (or as the IMF likes to say "structurally adjust"). This applies to oil in the Gulf of Mexico, oil of the Niger River Delta, the Canadian Tar Sands, carnations from Peru, coffee from Sri Lanka and so on. All these countries have been sucked into a global economic model, which creates vast wealth for some people but also vast distributive inequalities for a larger number. This generates social instability because the largest single predictor of violence is income inequality. It's not how much you have; it's how it's distributed.

I'm beginning to feel like Cassandra at the walls of Troy. Recently in northern Canada, the temperature was up an average of an incredible nine degrees Fahrenheit. Yet when I turn towards the national political scene and look for some comfort in the new government's national priorities I realize with a sinking heart that there is worse than nothing. The new government is following the Bush model and has slashed the nation's environmental services by 40 percent; it is cranking billions into the military and handing out tax cuts. These policies are a perfectly proven recipe for urban and environmental impoverishment — exactly what has happened in the United States.

Taking refuge in the simple objectives and clear achievements of Stephen Lewis feels like a good way to be useful and escape the difficulties that surround us. Unfortunately, saving the world cannot be done by charity. Saving the world is about changing the relationship the human species has with planet Earth. We humans have a relationship that is fundamentally different from any other species with which we share the planet. Unlike the polar bear or the buffalo or the birds of the earth, we modify the planet to suit our needs. We burn down forests for grasslands. We replace grasslands with wheat. We divert rivers, drown shorelines, create deserts where there were none. We change the molecular balance of the biosphere.

Saving the world is about taking responsibility collectively for our relationship with Mother Earth and with each other. This means feeling kinship with and doing everything we can for those attacked by the HIV virus, but it is also about a lot more. It's about our common heritage, our common home, our shared relationship with the Earth in all its various places and manifestations. We cannot do that within our present political and economic systems. We cannot do this when some people are permitted to "own" the Commons and sell it to the highest bidder, or when 19th-century political systems generate politicians and parties more interested in obtaining and keeping power than resolving issues essential to the human condition.

22

The Bush Bubble Comes to Ottawa

Canadians must bow to the inevitability of a new national-identity card for cross-border travel and they risk paying an economic price if the deadlines for implementation are missed, Prime Minister Stephen Harper warned yesterday.

— *Globe and Mail,* April 1, 2006, page A1

To live through President Bush's visit to Ottawa was to live through why those opposed to his policies have failed to make any impression on the walls around him. The rich and powerful have always been divorced from the common run — that is the nature of being at the top of the totem pole — but the extent of the bubble Mr. Bush dwells in is an amazing thing to see. It was as if the president was visiting a war zone instead of the federal capital of a friendly neighbor.

The center of the city was emptied of its residents for his 20-hour visit. Roads were closed. Trains and buses shut down or re-routed and residents advised to work from home. Thousands of police were mobilized. There were 56 black cars in his cavalcade from the airport to Parliament Hill. One of them appeared to be equipped with a missile launcher. You had to walk the eerie empty streets of a normally busy city, feel the presence of the helicopters thrashing overhead and the police in the streets to really seize the enormity of Mr. Bush's isolation.

The only people moving in the empty streets were demonstrators, and they were trapped between two impossible shores. If there was any violence, their protests would be dismissed as the actions of extremists and thus discredited. If their protests were polite and respectful, they would be dismissed as tepid and uninspired. In short there was no way to be heard by the hundreds of media covering the event, waiting for an "incident." Ultimately, the national media carried nothing but a few youngsters pushing down a temporary fence behind which were lines of police. Images of the great demonstrations at City Hall and Parliament Hill where thousands gathered carrying lighted candles to signal their solidarity with the victims of the American aggression in Iraq were never broadcast.

To be so fearful of attack or even criticism that it is necessary to shut a neighboring capital down, says more about the weaknesses of foreign policies than any protest. But the bubble around the president works in the short term, for critical questions have been effectively taken off the table. In this way, the Bush administration has been enormously successful.

What happened to all the questions around both Bush elections? The nations of the west got their knickers in a righteous twist because the exit polls in the Ukrainian elections differed from the published results. Exactly the same thing happened in the second Bush election. Thirty-seven percent of those who voted in the American election did so by touching a screen, using proprietary computer programs that were unverifiable. The computer programs used to count the votes were protected as the private property of Republican party supporters. Thus the counts of over one third of the votes cast were unverifiable, so it wasn't even possible to do recounts. The results in 26 counties in Florida alone contradicted both the exit polls and historical voting patterns.

The White House immediately cried foul in the Ukraine in similar circumstances, but what happened at home remained a non-issue. What's going on? What's going on is that people at all levels of society including Mr. W. Bush's political opponents are afraid to pursue things that really matter. These so-called opponents "for the good of the country" refused to ask for new elections with transparent, verifiable results. We got just a whiff of that fear when Mr. Bush came to Ottawa. I was obliged to stand in the square in front of City Hall for many hours in order to secure a space for a small stage for the protestors to speak from, otherwise they would have been shut out of City Hall for no other reason than for fear that something "might happen."

Happily that cornerstone of democracy — the freedom to assemble peacefully — finally overcame the fears City Hall security had of intruding on the Bush bubble, and the police left us alone with the little stage and thousands did come to protest in the square.

At the carefully screened invitation dinner that Mr. Bush spoke at, people clapped supportively. In the suburbs, people sat in their cars and waited patiently until roads were re-opened. People stayed home and didn't go to work. Fear is what the North American missile shield is about. Fear is what $900 million Canadian for four used submarines is about. Yet, how will four more submarines inching around the ocean make the planet a safer place? The naval yards of the old USSR are filled with rusting submarines.

The message that the people outside the bubble around Mr. Bush were trying to get to those inside the bubble was: we need more than a new emperor. We need new politics that care more about the fundamentals of civilized life (clean air, water, secure energy and food supplies) and the forces creating climate change and much less about submarines and missile shields. But the bubble Mr. Bush lives inside is so solid that there seems to be no way that it can be penetrated. It doesn't matter if protestors are polite as they were in Ottawa or provoke a tear gas confrontation as happened in Quebec City during the Free Trade of the Americas summit. Nothing penetrates the bubble.

I was immensely proud of the demonstrators in Ottawa. People gathered in thousands at City Hall and Parliament Hill to say "no" to the war in Iraq, and they did so with grace. On Parliament Hill they lit candles, and at City Hall there were even people who stayed behind to clean up.

After the US president left, the impression that remained the longest was the essential weirdness of it all. President Bush is a "saved" Christian — that means he divides the world into those that are "saved in Christ" and those that are not. He staffs the White House with graduates of "saved" Christian colleges. He believes "faith communities" should have a role to play in public education, in running jails and fighting wars that support their "values." He believes in "good guys" and "bad guys." In the global religious cleavage between those who believe in an "a priori" God and those who believe in a God which is internal to all life, Mr. Bush belongs with the "a priori" folks. He is a Christian extremist of fundamentalist persuasion.

Western nations spent centuries fighting horrific, internecine wars over religion. They were "wars without end" of unbelievable brutality. On St. Bartholmew's Day in 1572 in Paris, Protestant corpses were stacked along the banks of the Seine like firewood. Images from that day that have come down to us look little different from the Rwandan genocide. In Germany entire villages and towns were eviscerated for having the wrong religion. But the West finally did manage to bury their "wars without end."

After the Puritans, after Calvin, after centuries of Inquisition tortures and after the Catholic-Protestant wars, there emerged an idea that religion and the state should be separated. All of the leaders of the modern western democracies have understood this division: Benjamin Disraeli, Winston Churchill, Charles DeGaulle, Franklin Delano Roosevelt, Jack Kennedy, Lester Pearson, Pierre Trudeau. Who remembers who was a Jew, a Roman Catholic or an agnostic? The religious affiliations (or lack thereof) of these leaders did not intrude into political debate.

Pierre Trudeau was a devout, practicing Catholic. He died repeating the Lord's Prayer with a gentle and firm faith. But as the Prime Minister of Canada, he was also part of the government that enacted legislation to give equal opportunities for homosexuals, birth control choice for women and easier access to divorce. I do not understand why the current president of the West's leading nation uses words like "crusade" and expressions like "war without end." Does he not understand their significance? What happened to his education that he could not have a vivid understanding of the importance of dividing church and state? "Family values" have become just another stalking horse for returning to medieval religious conflicts between church and state.

What would President Bush have said or thought during the service at that little mosque that I and a couple of other politicians visited during the week of 9/11? Would he have been able to think, "these are my people. They are citizens of my city and country, and I am very glad to be here with them at this terrible moment?" If he could not think this, if he could not feel it in the very bottom of his soul, then we are back in the Dark Ages again with "my God" and "your God" competing to run the world. Except we now rely on aircraft carriers, guided missiles and tanks instead of cavalry and cannon. Religious war does not work. It hasn't in the past, and it won't now. These polarities are forces which favor physical and social entropy, not the continuation of human civilization.

23

Jean de La Fontaine

La raison de la plus fort est toujours la meilleure.
[Might makes right.]

— Jean de La Fontaine 1621–1695

WHEN I WAS FIRST LEARNING how to read, like millions of children before me I read the fables of Jean de La Fontaine. In my parent's house, these old stories were held in a big fat book, decorated with large, color illustrations of a fox trying to jump up and pull down some grapes hanging from a tree, rabbits racing tortoises and so on. These stories seemed more real to me than stories about people. The passage of years has not dulled my interest in the fables of La Fontaine. Unlike other stories from my childhood, they have grown more intriguing and beautiful with age. There is a sweet and complex wisdom to them that still makes me smile. The most famous is probably the one of the fox who couldn't quite reach the grapes hanging from the tree and then decided that it didn't matter anyway because they were surely sour.

I suspect La Fontaine used animals to tell his stories for the same reason Shakespeare chose distant cities like Venice as settings for his plays. Disguise was a foolproof method allowing each writer to say exactly what he wanted without fear of offending the court. The lamb could address the wolf as "your majesty" without the king and court finding an excuse to take it personally; this was a very real concern because people in France who offended the king often ended up in the Bastille. La Fontaine's stories were about crows and foxes, wolves and lambs, so who could take offence? It was La Fontaine's genius that he always found a way to end his fables so that the whole story bounced back to the human level and made the reader smile with self-recognition. The fox with his sour grapes has become a classic symbol of anyone who doesn't get what they want and then disparages their original ambition.

But there is one story that doesn't have any moralizing conclusion. It just ends. It's a story about a wolf who comes upon a lamb drinking in a stream at the edge of the forest. The wolf accuses the lamb of making the water dirty by the way he is drinking. The lamb replies reasonably that he is downstream from where the wolf drinks so he can't be harming his drinking water. Then the wolf complains that he was doing it last year, and the lamb replies that is impossible because he wasn't born last year.

"Then it was your brother," snarls the wolf.

"No," the lamb replies, "it couldn't be my brother because I don't have one."

The lamb always answers politely, deferring to this "seigneur" of the forest, referring to the wolf as "your majesty" and "sire," but he always has good reason and proves that the wolf is mistaken. The lamb has not done what the wolf accuses him of; he is always correct. The wolf is falsely accusing him. Finally the wolf in exasperation says "I don't care! You and your kind (referring to shepherds and dogs) have made my life miserable." He kills and eats the lamb without further discussion.

The wolf had been looking for his causus belli, couldn't find it and finally, losing patience, did what he wanted to do all along. You can think of many modern parallels; the invasion of Iraq would be a recent example. Clearly the British and the United States governments desperately wanted to invade Iraq and like the wolf searched mightily for a justifying reason, couldn't find one that was either substantial or satisfactory, and in the end did what they wanted to do anyway: invade Iraq for its oil fields.

La Fontaine has no clever moral comment at the end of his tale of the wolf and the lamb, except for the laconic observation that "la raison la plus fort est toujours la meilleure." The most frequent translation of this line is "might makes right," but the one I have always liked more is the literal one: "the reason of the strongest is always the best."

Perhaps Jean de La Fontaine gave this tale no clever moral conclusion because he could see no alternative to the wolf eating the lamb. In the 17th century, this was the way both the natural and the human worlds were composed. La Fontaine lived in precarious times and, like Shakespeare, he carefully removed his stories from anything that could be identified with the court. Shakespeare set his dramas and comedies in Italy or back in time; La Fontaine was even more cautious. He invented dialogues between talking animals. He was not an intimate of the king. In fact, it is recorded that Louis XIV did not like him. Not surprisingly, as La Fontaine grew older he began to spend much of his time far away from the court. A wise decision for it was not a healthy situation to have the king unkindly disposed towards one's person.

In 17th-century France when La Fontaine was writing his fables, an aristocrat could hang a peasant for poaching a rabbit on his land. The link between the wolf and the lamb is not hard to see. The king with a simple lettre de cachet could send anyone he was annoyed with into a windowless, damp hole underground in which the prisoner could not stand. The physical circumstances were so brutal that prisoners, if they couldn't arrange a quick release, died in a matter of days. It was rule of the wolf.

Jean de La Fontaine died of natural causes in 1695. A century later there would be a revolution in France, the aristocracy would be overthrown and the idea of running a country through laws created by democratically elected assemblies was introduced.

It's the alternative Jean de La Fontaine's fellow countrywoman Marie Lienemann would refer to instinctively when she described in ringing tones at Porto Alegre three centuries later that human beings were more than mere specks of dust in the universe, that they were not alone, they were citizens! Her confidence that, together as citizens, we could create something more complex and powerful than our own earthly voyage was inspiring. She was so sure that despair was nothing more than an individual conceit.

Perhaps if Jean de La Fontaine had known about democracy as a model for creating society versus a monarchy when he wrote his story of the wolf and the lamb, he could have found a small, clever moral to end his tale. For the greatest accomplishment of democracy has been the invention of a peaceful method of controlling the most powerful elements of society so that they have to sometimes bend their will to the concerns of the lamb.

◆ ◆ ◆

The interesting thing about La Fontaine's fables is the enduring nature of the dilemmas that they present and how little we are really removed from the essential situations they describe. Who has not seen someone disparage a formerly cherished desire when he or she fails to attain it? "Sour grapes" says it all. And the dilemma of the wolf and the lamb remains with us today. How do we serve the needs of the wolf and the lamb at the same time? The story presents a metaphor for irreconcilable differences. Maybe reconciliation can never be found between the wolf and the lamb, but it can be created in society by thinking and acting differently.

We are in a world now which requires us to think of ourselves not just as French or Japanese, Chinese or Indian, but as citizens of the planet. But how many people have made that switch in self-awareness and identity? Most of us are like La Fontaine was in the 17th century. He could not imagine a France without a king and aristocratic domains, just as we cannot imagine a planetary citizenship. So we are locked into 19th-century ideas like "preventive wars" and "missile shields."

Democracy was and remains a unique and powerful social invention. A democracy that works allows the lamb's view to be heard and sometimes upheld. Democracies that function have citizens, not customers. The differences between the two concepts are so broad and profound that it should be impossible to imagine the two words being used interchangeably. The overwhelming success of the private sector's colonization of the public sector is that many people now think it is reasonable to equate the two concepts of citizen and consumer. But consumer, client and customer are all commercial concepts. Whereas citizen is a political concept and refers to the role individuals play in a democratic society in electing and participating in the governance of their society.

The struggle to redefine local and world democracies in a way that responds to the planetary environmental crisis is the great struggle of our time because everything else depends on it. It is the struggle for a different kind of globalization, one that isn't about creating ever larger production units and ever smaller, cut-rate public services. It's the struggle to bring the human family into a connected political circle of citizenship that sustains the planet and its many peoples instead of finding new ways to exploit them. If the citizens of Porto Alegre can figure this out, so can everyone else.

If I have learned anything at City Hall it is that we do not lack for visionaries. We do not lack for good people. I believe in people. I believe in democracy, but a democracy that works. My wish for all activists is that they drop their favorite cause, their fervor for Medicare, public schools, whales, whatever and devote their considerable talents to political reform so we can get our cities and nations back.

It isn't rocket science. Abolish corporate funding from all political campaigns and get a form of representation that will return governments that reflect how people vote not how the vote splits. Do this and democracies will quickly develop new priorities and new solutions.

I would be prepared to believe President Bush's keen desire to drill for oil in Alaskan wildlife refuges was simply misguided if he hadn't been bankrolled by the oil industry. In the same vein I would be more inclined to believe President Bush's fear of Iraq's weapons of mass destruction was genuine if Iraq was not a major oil producer and his campaign had not been backed by the oil industry. I would also more readily believe his distaste for national healthcare was genuine if pharmaceutical companies (none of whom want to see a national health system realized) had not been major contributors to his campaign.

On all these issues, it is clear that ordinary citizens want the opposite of what the political system is actually delivering. Eighty percent of Americans want Medicare. A majority didn't believe the invasion of Iraq was justified, yet Mr. Bush was returned to office saying no to Medicare and yes to continuing the war. If citizens can't elect a government that will do what the majority wants, you have a democracy in name and symbol but not reality.

The Canadian democratic state is not much different. People cannot elect the government that they want. It takes two and ½ times the number of votes to elect a New Democrat as a Liberal. No wonder the party in power dives for cover every time the words "proportional representation" are used. Why should anyone in the political backrooms of the ruling parties that run the nation want to change an electoral system that keeps an imbalance that works in their favor?

The idea of sharing the federal and provincial tax revenues is another example of fundamental, meaningful change that never happens. It's been requested for decades by city leaders and never generates anything but tepid debate over a tiny increase in a gas tax transfer to the provinces, earmarked for cities. These little transfers may keep mayors quiet but don't address the fundamental problem: the basic imbalance in taxing powers between the three orders of government. It is only through changing the share of the great income and growth taxes that the way governments work will actually change. This will only happen when citizens make it an election issue.

And what about the worldwide "war on drugs?" It costs us billions every year that achieves nothing except the funding of organized crime. The war on drugs could be resolved tomorrow simply by decriminalizing drugs. You would think we would have learned with alcohol that criminalizing people's dependencies doesn't work. But when was the last time you ever heard a Prime Minister even breathe the thought out loud, "hey, I think we've got a solution here that doesn't involve jailing people?" Ever wonder why? Because we all know that decriminalizing drugs would instantly make our cities safer and less costly to administer than pouring more useless billions in the police and jail budgets. It costs more to keep one prisoner behind bars than I earn as a city councilor.

Democracy doesn't exist if people's votes can be manipulated so gravely that national voting becomes nothing more than a process of symbol setting rather than a call to action. There's a reason corporations are protected from any loss of profits or assets in Iraq with reparation payments paid for by the impoverished Iraqi people. The corporations own the government which is waging the war. So we have the horror of very large, very rich corporations getting "war reparations" while Iraqi children starve.

But no matter how badly twisted the electoral system becomes, no matter how many newspapers and television networks the corporations control, people will eventually choose what works. That's why the feudal system eventually creaked to an end; that's why the Soviet system crumbled, and that's why the present system will also. People will eventually figure out that reclaiming our citizenship and changing the human paradigm from occupying earth to sharing it is more important than a bigger bank account.

The only unknown is: will all this occur in time to save us from following the fantail of the cod? This is the great question of our times. Will the planet give us enough time to get it right? I don't know, but what I have learned as a city councilor is clear and unequivocal. There is nothing that doesn't connect. We are connected from the division of the first cell that ultimately creates a human being through to our shared history of cities and human civilization, to our mutual dependency on the planet's biosphere. To succeed today, we must remember how essential it is to make those connections work; and conversely we must remember what happens when we fail to connect the dots.

The Romans crumbled under their own inability to deal creatively with the possibilities that their vast empire created. Rome's frontier walls and the legions that guarded them were essentially dead ends just as the west's aircraft carriers and missile systems are dead ends today. There is only a technological difference between missile shields and Roman frontier walls. Both frontier walls and missile shields are driven by a culture of fear, and fear always collapses in on itself.

At the most basic level of our collective existence, it is as if we have learned nothing about the essentials of human survival since the first empires were put together along the Euphrates and the Tiber, since La Fontaine was writing about the wolf and the lamb. And this is the lesson we have not learned: the reason of the strongest is not always the best reason. Often it is the very worst.

"Might makes right" has been the cause of the rapid decline in the planet's biological and cultural diversity upon which humanity depends for life itself. Jean de La Fontaine sensed the importance of the lamb's sweet and reasonable responses to the wolf four centuries ago when he invented his magical conversation between the wolf and the lamb. But he did not have the governance construct to imagine the lamb having a place at the table instead of on it. We have that construct now. It's called democracy, but it has been stolen from us through our own greed and our own indifference to the consequences of the theft.

There are two great powers in the world. The second great power is the people, but the people have to decide that they want their citizenship back; that they want to be citizens first and consumers second; that they want to run the world for the needs of the many, not the power of a few. When people care enough about these issues, politicians also will care and the systems will change.

In reclaiming our citizenship, we can create inclusive governments with different priorities — priorities that reduce instead of augment the cleavages that divide society. Tragically government priorities are not reducing the fundamental cleavages which divide society; instead government priorities are feeding the forces which pry people apart into different camps.

Recent American governments have reduced planned parenthood programs domestically and internationally. Many developing countries have 40 percent of their populations below the age of 15. That age cohort is the most susceptible to organized and unorganized violence and poverty everywhere.

The same goes for the media. The media feeds the forces which promote social cleavages. It sells its products, newspapers and television news by focusing on and describing conflicts between people. The rise of hate/talk consumer-driven radio has further increased cleavages between people.

And relentless consumerism feeds climate change and the unequal distribution of goods and services. National tax cuts for the rich and reduction in common services have aggravated those cleavages. In these conditions it is hard not think of the American president at best as an inadvertent sociopath because his policies are rapidly moving the planet into decline by increasing the forces which are producing climate change, consumerism and unequal distribution of wealth.

One of the many wonderful things about national healthcare is that everyone — the poor, unwed mothers, the middle class, the rich — gets treated the same. National healthcare not only makes life more possible for more people; it does it in a way that creates bonds between people.

But in the end, whether creating the cleavages is deliberate or not hardly matters. Undoing the harm our present political system is creating is the most complicated task facing humanity. Yet each piece of the puzzle is simple enough. A laundry list of individual changes can be put together on one page. Most importantly, collectively the list is more than the sum of its parts. Collectively the changes we need will redefine what it means to be human and live in society such that even long-cherished beliefs about progress will be modified.

It can be done. That is the good news. We can elect governments more interested in saying no to terror with our voices instead of with armed might. We can reclaim our citizenship, stop the rape of the planet and give humanity a second chance. We are not the wolf and the lamb. We are men and women. We can find an accord and a way forward where La Fontaine's animals could not.

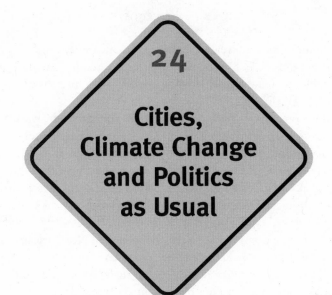

24

Cities, Climate Change and Politics as Usual

Partnership is an essential characteristic of sustainable
communities. The cyclical exchanges of energy and resources
in an ecosystem are sustained by pervasive cooperation....
In human communities partnership means democracy and
personal empowerment, because each member of the
community plays an important role.

— Fritjof Capra,
The Web of Life

REVOLUTION DOESN'T WORK. It's a revolving door that spins
society in a circle back to the starting point. Evolution takes individuals and society down a new track. When Lula da Silva was
running for the presidency of Brazil, he made this point many times.
Some accused him of losing his "commitment" to social justice issues. I heard him say several times, "with gray hair should come a little wisdom and I'm old enough now to accept that there is no
panacea. We've seen 'left' wing governments commit as many atrocities as right wing governments; both in the name of creating a better
society."

He was preaching the importance of moving in a new direction
but in an evolutionary way, not a revolutionary one. He was talking
about developing an inclusive national political philosophy that uses
language similar to that used by ecologists to describe how sustain-

able communities are created. The idea is to turn away from our present economic and political philosophies anchored in eternal competition. Our planet is a closed system, and our economic systems must reflect that reality.

As anyone who is paying attention now understands, we are depleting the substances upon which life depends faster than the biological systems of the planet can replenish them. Cities are the primary engines of this imbalance and are now the farthest out on the global plank. It will not take much to push them into a vertiginous meltdown. The only unknown is how, exactly, the eventual urban meltdown might occur. Will it be precipitated by a sudden violent climate event as has already happened in New Orleans — or will it come from the disappearance of enough water to provision a city? This is a very likely possibility for many great cities. Calgary, Canada and Lima, Peru are dependent on glacial fresh water melt from glaciers that will not exist in a few years. Where are six million people in Lima going to find their water when the surrounding glaciers are gone? It's difficult to imagine anything but an urban meltdown of the same proportions that saw the disappearance of ancient Rome.

An optimistic view is that the 21st century will be remembered for how city governments learned (in spite of national opposition) to grow their cities in energy conserving ways and how democracy was saved. This must be the scenario for the 21st century because right now, we hover on the edge of losing our national democratic governments. There is now no significant difference between the major Canadian and American political parties on all the priority-one issues: air and water self-sufficiency, food, oil and energy self-sufficiency and foreign policy. There are no significant differences because that's the way the North American political and corporate elite want it to be. The major political parties in both Canada and the US are like two mega-corporations which have fused their operating departments but maintained different public identities.

The political parties give the electorate the illusion of choice by focusing on "hot button" second-tier issues such as gay marriages and gun control, but the center of the Republican/Democrat, Liberals/Conservative platforms are virtually identical. The only way this can change is to change the electoral system so that parties like the Greens and the New Democrats can introduce some diversity of governance choice for the electorate. Electoral reform can make it possible for diverse parties to participate in government in a manner proportional to their electoral support. Canadian governments would then be true coalition governments, which is clearly what the electorate wants as there are presently six Canadian federal political parties.

In Canada the four "fringe" parties collectively have almost as many votes as the two main parties together and more than either alone; they also have very different mandates than the governing parties. With proportional elections, two-party rule or "politics as usual" would end immediately, and a new, more collaborative, consultative form of government would evolve both in Canada and the United States.

This is the kind of electoral system that all the European Nordic countries have had now for several generations, and their public priorities as a result are startlingly different from North America. Nordic countries are not only meeting their Kyoto requirement, they are exceeding them. Their attitude to promoting economic growth is also markedly different. It's not to slash taxes, starve government services and create a less equitable distribution of wealth. Instead, they fund robust public services, impose high taxes, distribute income more equitably and share tax revenues with municipalities on a one to one basis. It doesn't seem to hurt them a bit. Their populations are well served, prosperous and person by person much better off than North Americans.

North American governments remain trapped in an adaptive cultural gap, still using political systems that are leftovers from the horse and buggy era; so it should be no surprise that they are not responsive to the key issues of the 21st century. In North America we need to find the courage to force the governing parties into reforming the electoral system so true majority governments capable of representing diverse interests can be formed. Our survival depends on it.

◆ ◆ ◆

There's an old saying that an optimist sees the glass as half full and a pessimist sees it as half empty. I think it's the other way round. The optimist sees the empty part of the glass and wants to fill it up. By this measure, Al Gore is an optimist and Mr. Bush the pessimist. The pessimist sees only the part that is full and wants to enjoy the half of the glass where the water remains without worrying about the empty part. This little book has been written in the spirit of looking at the empty part of the human glass, trying to understand it and through that understanding to fill the glass up.

But understanding requires context. Facts without context are useless factoids. Unfortunately, fewer and fewer people have an education that has accomplished much beyond basic literacy and "skills training" for the marketplace. Hence even highly educated people have become technical specialists, knowledgeable about the tasks and techniques needed to accomplish their professional objectives but ignorant of the broad currents of the human voyage. History is not taught in schools. The study of language has been reduced to "communications skills" focused on PowerPoint presentations. Grammar — the common root of clear thinking, writing and speaking — is not taught. Fewer people study second or third languages. Literature has become an option.

Climate change is the ultimate context subject because it hasn't arisen suddenly from something that happened two weeks, two months or two years ago. It's been centuries in the making. Thus, much of this book has been about establishing the historical context from which the present governance crisis has arisen: from the recent invention of just-in-time global provisioning which now dominates what people purchase, to our definitions of success and progress buttressed each day by the singular corporate vision emanating from our cartel-controlled newspapers and television screens.[1]

Global warming has been made possible by technology, but it's rooted in political systems, social and philosophical beliefs about how society should function. Imagine if Al Gore were now the US president, not tripping around the world with a slide show on climate change. The reality is that he was the choice of the people. He lost by a judicial coup d'état made possible by an electoral system that no longer functions democratically. Yet very few people wish to champion the democratic reforms that could make sure a coup de juge would never happen again. You have to ask yourself "why?"

Seven years after his presidency was stolen, all Gore has said publicly about his defeat at the hands of the Supreme Court is that a revolution is the only protest possible against a Supreme Court ruling.[2] It is clear that Al Gore was not willing to risk that possibility. I understand that, but what I can't get my mind around is his unwillingness to even talk about the democratic deficit which stole his presidency.

It is unnerving when even the planet's most eminent victim of "power politics" cannot bring himself as a private citizen to talk about politics as a more important problem to be resolved than light bulbs. It's as if it has become a seditious act to even voice the thought that the political system is broken at a time of a grave ecological crisis. We can no longer afford to have political parties with very limited interests running nations any longer. Yet this is what continues to happen.

It's amazing to see the Canadian press faithfully reporting on Mr. Harper's first months as Prime Minister: how he is "winning" by re-profiling himself as a hero of middle-class Canada, with tax cuts, hanging out at Tim Horton's and visiting the troops. The "new" profile is a carbon copy of Mr. Bush with tax cuts, American flags everywhere and folksy Texas style. Mr. Bush has finally got a friend, Steve to the north of him; this is not surprising considering that the two men are running the same political franchise.

For both political leaders, governing is all about manipulating symbols and "photo ops" of the armed forces at war. Thus, Premier Charest's eco-tax on gasoline sales in order to meet Kyoto targets is characterized soberly by Mr. Harper as a "responsible exercise of provincial power," which he certainly supports. "Everyone should do their part." Sounds like a reasonable sound byte to me.

The reality is that Kyoto is an international responsibility of Canada's federal government. It's not primarily a provincial responsibility. It's become one because the federal government has refused to meet its international commitment. The justification for abandoning the Kyoto Protocol is that the political party the Conservatives replaced weren't meeting their Kyoto commitments anyway, so why pretend? Why not just get out of Kyoto, cut the environment budget as his "friend" Mr. Bush did? At least that's honest. Canada's prime minister is not saying one thing and doing another, and it plays well in the press.

Canadians are captives of the national governing parties. The reality is Canadian citizens, like Americans, don't have any real political choice. The reality is Mr. Harper is making immense decisions for a powerful G-8 nation based on 37 per cent of the popular vote. Two out of three Canadians did not vote for his party. Yet he is able to withdraw from Kyoto, participate in a war in Afghanistan and abandon a national daycare system, all on behalf of the one third of the population that elected him. The reality is this is neither democratic nor responsible government. But all this, like Mr. Bush's coup de juge election, appears to get lost in the game of power politics which Mr. Harper and Mr. Bush play very well. The stories in the media become who's "winning" this political game, not what the political parties are doing. It's ugly, ugly, ugly. What counts in 2006 is power and symbol manipulation in the media, not bad air in children's lungs.

By default, the key to braking global warming has become the responsibility of local governments, not national governments. Jane Jacobs said not long before she died that people have to take cities more seriously. I think she's absolutely right but the electorate, just like the national governments, remain locked into 19th century ideas of what cities and city politicians are all about.

I've been asked many times when I am going to run for a seat in the federal parliament. My response — drawn straight from Jacobs — is that I think city politics is more important, and people look at me as if I am slightly crazy. But it's not surprising people think this way: the federal government in both Canada and the United States is filled with men and women who used to be city councilors and have "moved on up" (can't blame them for doing so — the pay is better and so is the prestige). Unfortunately polls have consistently revealed that the majority of federal politicians quickly become disillusioned and frustrated with their ability to achieve anything but get elected.

"Act locally, think globally" was coined years ago to convince people to restrain their use of water, heat their houses more efficiently and so on. It's a sensible aphorism, and it also applies to local government. Local government is not perfect and I have spent considerable time documenting its imperfections, but it is by far the most responsive to the real needs of citizens; it's by far the most accessible; and it is the least controlled by the global provisioning corporations.

City wards are much smaller than the federal, state or provincial districts or ridings. This means that each elected official must have a much more intimate relationship with the people who elect her or him and the problems that are besetting them. It's much more difficult to play media and electoral games with municipal constituents. If you're a jerk, people tend to find out, and people — if they care to — can influence the political process. You don't have to drive to the state or provincial capital, you can just catch a bus, bicycle or drive down to City Hall. In our city, citizens can address their elected officials at committee meetings, and they have the same amount of time to speak as the city councilors that they elect. Collectively, usually more time.

I remember one of my supporters explaining to me about how she first began to get interested in city politics. She was a young mother. She lived near a park but there was no children's play area for her little girl. She began with some other young mothers to lobby for one and the next summer, she had one. Nothing like this had ever happened to her before. Dealing with other levels of government, it felt like she was yelling into a very deep well with nothing but the sound of her own voice ever returning. At the city she had spoken up, and a little children's park was created which is still there and still well used.

City councils across North America have been persuaded to respect Kyoto, to pass laws against purchasing sweat shop goods, to vote against the Iraq War, to put money into essential public services like daycare, transit and clean air initiatives when the federal and state or provincial governments were withdrawing money from those same services and spending it on Mr. Eisenhower's military-industrial complex. Cities continue to fight their own federal governments and the global provisioning systems with affordable local responses to crying needs.

The best way of resisting the rapacious maw of the global provisioning machinery is to empower — not enfeeble — local governments. A feeble local government becomes easy prey to national governments and multi-national corporations. Unfortunately in Canada we have a tradition where city governments were largely run on a semi-volunteer basis. It's often regarded as virtuous and useful to pay local elected officials very little, give them no pension and make them run for re-election so frequently it begins to feel like you're living in the middle of a constant referendum. This tradition creates governments where local politicians are always looking for something better.

Community activists, also, need more respect and more resources. At the moment they are expected to work on everything from planting trees to submitting briefs on the annual budget out of civic duty and goodness of heart. Local democracy can't work when it exhausts and exploits people of good will whether they are elected or volunteers.

So the first step on the road to recovery is to get control of your local government. Don't let your local government become a pawn for corporate and national party interests. Democracy costs money. Don't be afraid to invest in it. Big city politicians should be paid the same pay and resources as federal members of parliament. They work just as hard and have more responsibility. Sixty percent of the public services come from cities. That's virtually everything that people depend on to sustain life. The conversion of high energy lifestyles to low energy is largely the responsibility of city politicians; these responsibilities should be reflected in their wages.

Similarly, the efforts of citizens need to be recognized and rewarded. Local democracy works best when it becomes participatory instead of representational. It costs money to assemble people in local community halls and city arenas for the discussion of the city budget but it's money well spent because it means that people's tax money gets spent where they want it spent instead of where the back halls of city hall think it should be. In Porto Alegre when they introduced participatory budgets, daycares jumped from two to a 120 over ten years, transit grew quickly into an integrated rail, bus and minibus service that is considered state of the art and arterial road construction virtually ceased.

Taxes and politicians can do great things when they become part of the solutions instead of barriers to them. Remember the mantra that I began the book with: "knowledge is not the problem, politics is?" Part of the reason politics is a problem is that democracy is about a lot more than voting. Citizens hold elected officials accountable not just by voting them in or out of office. In four years a bad administration can do a hell of a lot of damage. You hold politicians accountable by participating with them in the process of governance, by helping them to set priorities and policies on air and water quality, green roofs, to manage parks and design streetscapes and public spaces. Good governments don't happen by accident.

Money has to be invested in the actual process of democracy just as it has to be invested in education and healthcare. The greatest engine for positive change is government. There are many great people, great ideas and great charities out there working for a better world, but their achievements are marginal when compared to the possibilities created by electing local and national governments that respond to the central issues of our time.

Human beings have a mandate to change the world. It's in our DNA. We are not like the buffalo who graze upon the prairie, whose manner of changing is so slow that they are rooted in earth's great, natural cycle of life. My Acadian grandfather changed the world without even thinking about it. He did it by building roads, cutting down trees, creating fields and pastures where there was only forest; raising houses, barns and children with my grandmother; each of these children in their own way went out and changed the world themselves. My English grandfather fought in the First Great War, pulled people out of bombed buildings in the Second War and became a social worker. We all change the world with our passing; we can't seem to help it, sometimes for the better and sometimes for the worse. Often the changes begin in such subtle ways that we are only aware of the original impetus many years after the moment has past. This is the way it has often been for me.

In ninth grade the view from my school desk was of construction workers ripping up the cross-city rail tracks to begin the great work of pouring the cement and asphalt needed to create a great new city expressway. That expressway was built right up to my school window. It was so close that if I leaned out the window I could have touched its steel barricade. To get across it, a caged pedestrian overpass was built for the students. It's still there and so is the expressway, which began the relentless process of sprawl that has dominated our city for 50 years.

Over the years, I have become obsessed by all this destruction in the service of the automobile. Even on European holidays, I find myself marveling more at a city's transit system than I do at its museums. In Strasbourg, France and Munich, Germany I look at the gorgeous old rail stations sitting in the city centers. They are built like turn-of-the-century stone cakes fronting magnificent plazas. And as I watch thousands of people hustling busily to and from the train station across the plaza to the streetcars I think to myself, "we used to have this in my city. We had all of this!" And I find my blood pressure rising at the stupidity of it all.

It's entirely possible to create a better world. I believe the world can have a full glass of water. It's all there in front of us waiting to be done. Creating more sustainable lifestyles are all absolutely achievable and have been documented in many books by many authors. But these books are frequently more about devising an individual eco-perfect existence, than they are about dealing with the political processes which make dealing with the rapacious consequences of our collective behavior possible.

The coming urban meltdown won't be resolved by country squires building ecologically perfect houses out of hay bales. Neither will it be resolved by celebs in Los Angeles who own eco-perfect houses in the Los Angeles hills or folks like George W. Bush who is snug as a bug in a Texas rug in his solar-powered house.

I'm sure that the authors of ecological house and garden stories mean well. No doubt they imagine that their eco-houses are inspiring the readers to live less carnivorously by demonstrating the many ingenious things that can be done to live better ecologically. I used to read these stories faithfully, but always with a vague sense of envy and unease. After all, if celebs, politicians and farmers can live comfortably with less drag on the planet, why couldn't I?

It took a walk in the ruins of a Roman hill town for it suddenly to click into place. Dougga was a Roman city in Tunisia. It was once a modest little market town of about 3,000 people in the Tunisian highlands. When I visited it on a wild spring day, the wind was gusting at gale force strength across the hilltops; just walking upright was a struggle. There were no other tourists about, nothing moving except the ghosts of the ancient inhabitants who had once attended the theater, shopped in the market place, bathed in the baths and attended their places of worship. It was empty of everything but the possibility of the life that had once been lived here.

Empty it seemed — until I discovered a shepherd grazing his sheep in the ancient graveyard on the hilltop just above the town. He had built an environmentally friendly house out of odds and ends just below the crest of the hill. It had a magnificent view of the ruins and the valley below. In his courtyard he had a donkey, a cart, a barking dog, some hens and his small flock of sheep grazing across the hill. True, he lacked a solar panel in the roof, but he had a battery-powered radio, a hand-dug well and a rainwater cistern. His house looked to me as eco-perfect as any of the fancier models.

A short walk away were the ruins of the town of Dougga. It was never a grand provincial city like Pompeii. It had always been a modest isolated place, but it still had a beautiful theater just inside the front gate of the town, the remains of 14 temples, a broad market place, municipal offices, two sets of generous public baths and many fine houses. The violent spring storm we found ourselves walking in had filled the drains of the town, which bubbled and gurgled as they escorted the rainwater under the streets safely down the hillside. I was fascinated that these ancient drains still worked and that they were so similar to modern ones. They had regularly placed manholes still in place for access. I think my companions were amused as I followed these city pipes in amazement along the streets, while they looked at the remains of once-graceful temples.

I joined my companions in the theater. It was startling how perfect the acoustics still were. Even with a wild storm blowing, my voice from the stage resonated upwards into every corner of the theater. It was like standing in the center of a bell when I was the clapper. Few modern theaters have such magnificent acoustics. Yet Dougga was just an African market town, nothing more substantial than a thumbprint on the old Roman landscape.

The only remaining inhabitant of Dougga was the shepherd and his family in his environmentally friendly house. It struck me with great force that this is exactly the way it will be if our present-day urban civilization collapses. The continuation of urban life requires more than eco-perfect housing. Having solar panels to generate electricity will mean nothing if there are no studios, performers, producers, technicians, engineers to maintain satellite networks or manufacture electrical appliances to make modern urban life, communications and travel possible. These are the accomplishments of a society, not just a few people living in comfortable ecological circumstances.

We will succeed or fail together in the 21st century just as the Romans succeeded and failed — together. The stories of ecologically perfect houses are destructive in that they give the illusion that we can build personal escape hatches from the perils of climate chaos and urban meltdown by investing in eco-perfect shelters. This is nonsense. Modern civilization requires — as the Romans did — a locally, nationally and globally coordinated effort of myriad skills and lives.

The Roman Empire was a connected society of cities just as ours is today. It had great factories and millions of skilled tradesmen employed producing the tiles that kept the buildings roofed; thousands of engineers, architects and maintenance workers to maintain roads and water works; transport fleets to ship spices for the kitchens, sculptures for the garden and books for the municipal libraries across the seas. The military ensured security efficiently and also integrated newcomers into Roman society by providing public career paths. The populace took their civic elections seriously, and the competition for local municipal officials was hot; city councils hired poets and actors to perform in their theaters; and most importantly people understood the primordial importance of public health. Their cities were clean, their piped water potable.

Twenty-first-century cities are more complex, requiring an even more widely coordinated combination of skills, resources and capacities. A few people living in eco-perfect houses will not be capable of preserving or replicating what has gone if our shared urban systems break down. The safety of the eco-house is as mythical as the basement bomb shelter was in the 1950s. The planet is our lifeboat, and we have to act accordingly. The keys to creating successful societies and a sustaining planet can be found in how we live together. The most powerful prescriptions for a stable planet are positive political and collective choices, not personal ones.

I am astonished that even Al Gore who understands climate change as well as anyone at the end of his film talks about changing light bulbs and driving small cars in order to combat climate change.

He didn't have one recommendation to address the democratic deficit which caused the theft of his own run for the presidency and resulted in the most ecologically destructive American administration ever to plague the planet.

If anything resonates from this book it is my hope that readers understand that people have been looking in the wrong places for the answers to arresting climate change. When you look back over the many attempts during the 20th century for new departures — the Sixties effervescence, the World Social Forum movement, the modern environmental movement to name just three — what stands out is the imperviousness of the political and corporate system to any substantive change. Individual politicians change but never the system. Without electoral changes, even bright, popular humanists like Brazil's President Lula da Silva can't accomplish much.

The changes needed to create a more secure environment are all about municipal collective action, political and justice reform. To stop fuelling climate change, we first must break the political chains that bind us.

◆ ◆ ◆

NATIONAL POLITICAL REFORM

Genuine democracy is not bought by corporations and then provided free of charge to the electorate. There is nothing "free" in life. The costs of elections must be assumed by the public purse, not by the corporations that can afford to pay.

There is no political will at the federal level to attack the issues that count and not enough resources at the local. We need to change the political division of authority and taxes to reflect the responsibilities and importance of the three levels of government.

National politicians and parties will be elected based on the proportion of the popular vote they receive, not on vote splitting. Governments must represent a majority of their citizens, and citizens need a genuine political choice. The only way this can be achieved is through genuine coalition governments based on a proportional voting system.

INTERNATIONAL POLITICAL REFORM

Just as cities need nations focused on sustainable environmental policies not corporate conquests, nations need an international level of government that is integrative and protective of the global commonwealth. The United Nations needs independently elected representatives empowered with the financial and policing authority to prosecute environmental and human rights criminals. No nation should have the right to pollute the air and water of another nation, but this is what happens every day. Parasite nations that produce less oxygen than they require for their populations to exist or pollute rivers other nations depend on must be called to account.

MUNICIPAL POLITICAL AND ENVIRONMENTAL REFORM

Municipalities need the political, legislative and financial authority appropriate to their responsibilities. They need more power and the other orders of government need less.

Cities need to create e-plans (environment plans) that are capable of redefining how we live, so how we live can continue without degrading everything we need to live.

All city streets shall be provisioned with trees shading the road and broad, safe sidewalks.

Buildings must have green roofs and be built to the Paris standard, i.e., no higher than seven stories, with the seventh set back. Elevators should be a luxury not a necessity. Buildings need to be small enough that residents can form communities and short enough to allow sunlight to reach the streets.

Electric public transit will be the first transportation priority.

Local farmers will be given public spaces for markets in city neighborhoods.

Parking lots must be taxed so that the real costs of running them are reflected in their construction and use. Sprawl malls are profitable because the costs of their parking lots are absorbed by society as a whole. Cities need to stop subsidizing parking lots.

The cost of car licenses should be related to engine efficiency. High fuel efficiency should result in low-cost licensing. Low fuel efficiency should be penalized through high-cost licensing.

Manufacturers must assume 360 degree manufacturing costs. No more dumping unrecyclable plastics which fill up city landfill sites.

Cities need to start profiting from their own municipal enterprise. Why should cities subsidize international corporations like Coca-Cola or Pepsi? If the public wants to buy bottled water, fine; but the profits should enrich the public purse, not the private. Let the cola companies stick to selling cola.

Cities need to create greenways that cross the entire city and are connected to national and international greenways so that animals and birds can travel safely from one region to another. Animals don't work on political jurisdictions; they work on natural landscapes. We've got to learn how to protect those landscapes and create passageways for them.

All waterways must be habitable for fish, frogs and human life.

Activities that compromise air quality will be taxed in proportion to the damage they create.

Companies that use the Swedish Natural Step method of procurement and production will be given preference for all public purchases of goods and services.

SOCIAL JUSTICE

The war on drugs has become a war on the poor, the disenfranchised and the sick. Criminalizing drug use is an annual, needless, billion-dollar burden for both Canadians and Americans. About one third of American prisoners are in jail for simple marijuana offenses, a drug that used to be legal and has about as much public violence associated with it as caffeine. The criminalizing of drug use has fed organized crime with billions of profit dollars that Al Capone could not have imagined in his wildest dreams, and it has simultaneously hammered the public sector with billions of police, justice and incarceration costs. This money is desperately needed for quality of life priorities such as health, education and transit — not jails. The only winners when we criminalize drugs are motorcycle gang executives. Everyone else loses. The war on drugs has also become an essential political distraction for the "politics as usual" governing parties. Whenever people's attention threatens to re-focus on such vital issues as air, water and energy self-sufficiency, or foreign policy based on a shared world view not on flag waving, the political cliques attack the moral fiber of their opponents and start preaching longer, tougher sentences for those people abusing drugs. How are air quality or adequate water supplies or neighborhood security or the prosecution of foreign wars related to how many years some unfortunate has been spending in jail for marijuana use or heroin illness?

NATIONAL AND INTERNATIONAL ENVIRONMENTAL BUDGETS

Federally, governments also need "green budgets" that make sustainable transportation, air quality, food and water supply a priority, not wars against "terrorists."

Internationally President Lula da Silva of Brazil is on the right track. We've got to start taxing the international flow of capital and eliminate tax havens. Then put that tax money into social and environmental justice initiatives. Everyone should pay their way.

These initiatives are not based on any grand break with the past. These changes do not require the rhetoric of revolution that we experienced in the 1960s. It is the stuff of evolution. The public willing, it can all be accomplished through and by our current political system but it will change the world more surely than the Paris barricades, the Mexico City student riots or the Port Huron Statement ever did — just as the simple choice to keep the electric streetcars going in Toronto benefited the city more than all the great demonstrations for a better world accomplished put together.

◆ ◆ ◆

If citizens begin by empowering their local democracies and investing in new Environment Plan priorities for their cities, great things
can be accomplished. The dots will finally begin to connect for positive, enduring change.

As much as I would like to think that the national governments
can be central players, they have become too large, too ponderous,
too removed from everything that counts to begin the shift that is required. The world has simply moved on, and national governments
haven't moved with it. In Canada and the United States cities generate 80% of the greenhouse gases, 90% of the taxes and house 90% of
the immigrants. The global solution is now local and urban. The future of the west now resides in our cities.

Yet these leftover governments from the 19th century have all
the power: financial, legislative, media access and organizational. It
makes no sense. One of the many things the federal leaders in both
the United States and Canada remain willfully blind to is that you
cannot add millions of people to cities without adding a whole lot of
very costly public infrastructure. Otherwise people retreat into religious and ethnic communities for the common services they require.
It's a natural enough response to an inadequate civil society. People
aren't dumb. They want the best schools and opportunities for their
families. In Calgary, Alberta, faith-based schools have largely replaced the public system. Calgary is the richest city in the richest
Canadian province. This is a destructive harbinger. Combine this
withdrawal from funding the civic sector with the growth of religious
fundamentalism of all stripes, and it's a recipe for local and national
instability.

North American communities have just lived through two of the
most prosperous decades the planet has ever seen, but where are the
new public investments which reflect those wealthy years? The
poster child for the puffery of nations and the skeletal condition of
cities is New Orleans. New Orleans sits in the deep, fabulously rich
bowl of the Mississippi Delta. It is a region loaded with oil and natural gas, refineries, magnificent ocean fishing and double-crop farming seasons. By all objective measures, the biggest problem for people
who live in Louisiana should be how to share their good fortune with
less blessed parts of the planet. Instead the only other state in the
American union which is poorer is Mississippi. How is it that, in a
land so laden with earth's bounty, the people and their communities
are so poor? The average annual income in some Louisiana towns is
as low as $5,000.

In New Orleans thousands of people died because they couldn't get on a bus and move a few miles before a hurricane struck. It wasn't just that individuals were poor; the city itself was impoverished with little capacity to react. The mayor became a figurehead reduced to making statements from a hotel suite while what was left of his police services operated out of vacant malls and pissed in tin cans hoping for some relief for themselves.

What has happened to the great wealth of the Mississippi Delta is very simple. It has been siphoned away by a long succession of national and state governments into the bank accounts of giant corporations who pay back the politicians at election time with "donations" for their campaigns. Only a tiny trickle of the Mississippi Delta's cornucopia comes back to cities like New Orleans, and what little does is used to build industrial infrastructure to assist the corporations to move the resource wealth that they are extracting from the ocean and the land to markets elsewhere which can afford to pay the prices they want.

The environmental decline of the Mississippi Delta is little different from the Niger Delta in Africa or the Mackenzie Delta in Canada. It seems that the greatest curse a country can have is oil. It brings political corruption and environmental degradation of every type. Norway is one of the very few countries that has been able survive the greed oil inspires. For most nations, oil creates a two-track society — the very wealthy and everyone else — while the country as a whole becomes a more fragile, polluted and sadder place to live.

Every city councilor knows that the neighborhoods which do best in bad times as well as good are the ones that have developed strong public infrastructure, ones that are blessed with robust neighborhood schools, libraries, community centers, health clinics, public transit, green parks, winter skating rinks and summer soccer pitches. These neighborhoods can survive a lot of tough going — ice storms, heat waves, hurricanes — absorb newcomers, adapt to change, self regulate and have low crime rates. The weakest neighborhoods are the ones that have little but pipes, pavement and police.

Nations are the same way. They need strong public infrastructure. Unfortunately we've spent the last 30 years divesting ourselves of it instead of investing. When I look into my crystal ball at the global future, I see both Americans and Canadians playing on the edge of an enormous abyss. The abyss is the fat tail curve of climate change without the necessary public infrastructure to deal with anything but business and politics as usual. But the future won't bring business or politics as usual. As described in the earlier chapters on biological and social phase transitions, the phenomenon of the fat tail curve isn't a gradual one. The curve suddenly spikes almost straight up. When the global fat tail explodes upwards, the weather will become too unpredictable to grow crops and the ordinary delivery systems of cities' heat, light and water will falter.

This doesn't have to happen. We can fill the empty half of the glass. The solutions are known, available and eminently possible. All we have to do is reach out and make them happen. But we have to first take the time to rejuvenate our civic cultures. Politics as usual hasn't been able to do it and can't. To defeat climate change, we need democracies that include people in the process of government, not devise ways to exclude them through the power party politics, corporately funded elections, gerrymandered districts and electoral counts that are impossible to verify.

The 21st century must be first about reclaiming our democracies and turning our cities into vibrant, low energy places with powerful effective public services. If the cities can get it right now the nations will follow, and together we can pull back from the climate change precipice. I have to believe this is all possible because the trend lines are clear. Without these political and environmental reforms, the dark age ahead scenario of Jane Jacobs is the one we will live: a global urban meltdown of too many people crushed into too small places without the necessary public and institutional resources to survive the resource shortages and price escalations that are an inevitable outcome of our present growth and consumption patterns.

Epilogue

It was the best of times, it was the worst of times, it was the age of wisdom, it was the age of foolishness, it was the epoch of belief, it was the epoch of incredulity, it was the season of Light, it was the season of Darkness, it was the spring of hope, it was the winter of despair, we had everything before us, we had nothing before us...

— Charles Dickens,
A Tale of Two Cities

A T NO TIME IN HUMAN HISTORY do those famous words apply better than today. Human beings have a genuine chance to create a global community, and it's happening all around us. The World Cup, the Olympics, the millions of arrivals and departures at the world's great airports, the creative clash of music, art and business happening every day in more ways than could have been dreamed of when Charles Dickens wrote the opening paragraph to *A Tale of Two Cities*. It is the best of times, it is the spring of hope, we have everything before us.

The irony is that the very accomplishments which are creating a genuine world society out of national and tribal ones have unleashed forces which threaten to pitch the entire human race into seasons of unprecedented misery. We are living on the bubble as we used to say when I was boy.

A big part of an old-fashioned Canadian winter is playing hockey. The best part is before you get organized into teams and arenas. It's about skating on a frosty day, your breath blowing steam, skates sending you flying over the ice on a creek bed, on a pond, on an icy driveway — any little sheet of ice will do. In St. John's, Newfoundland there was a marsh behind our subdivision. The frozen cattails protected the little pond in the center from blowing snow, so we would often have good ice there right into January. Everyone played —

boys and girls together. There were no distinctions. Someone's snow boots would form the posts for the goals and we would twirl back and forth on our little patch of ice.

If there is a heaven for me, it would be playing with my friends, twirling and swirling back and forth over ice on a winter's day. The sky is calm. There is no wind. It's quite warm and there is this sense of eternity as if we are all a little drunk on nothing but life. I can skate so much better now and have played hockey in great arenas, but nothing matches the magic of those long winter days, skating between the cattails with my friends when we weren't exactly sure what the rules of the game were, but felt a crisp accomplishment with each goal and groaned with each near miss between our rubber boot goal posts.

One day I went with some other kids on my street to try out for the St. John's Pee Wee All-Stars. Excepting Paul Thompson, none of us had ever played an organized game of hockey before; I didn't know a blue line from a red line, but we had skated a lot and someone said we should go. The St. John's All-Stars were going to fly to Halifax for a tournament, which was a trip that seemed as exciting as going to the moon. Howie Meeker, an ex-NHL star, was the coach.

We walked across town to the brand new arena, showing up with our skates and hockey sticks, ready to "try out." The whole place was amazing: the size of the building, the smoothness of the ice, the seats ranged upwards. Mr. Meeker had buckets filled with hockey pucks at the center of the rink. I had never seen so many pucks. We all got to play with one and just skate around like we did at home on the marsh. After a while Mr. Meeker and his assistants organized us into "drills". We would have to skate around little orange pylons stickhandling the puck as we cut by each pylon. Then there was a "one on one" drill when one boy was obliged to skate towards another with the idea of "deking" by him and then racing in on goal. I liked the drills, but as the practice went on I began to notice that there were fewer and fewer players on the ice.

A "coach" would tap a boy on the shoulder, say something to him and the boy would kind of slouch and then skate slowly away in the direction of the changing room. He wouldn't come back. It sent a kind of chill through me as I realized they were getting "cut." They weren't going to Halifax. More boys disappeared, until there was lots of room to skate. From our street, there was only Paul Thompson and myself left. I didn't know it at the time, but Paul and I were "on the bubble."

There are always a few outstanding players who are guaranteed to "make the team," but most are "on the bubble" — that's the place where the coaches consign players that they like something about but haven't quite decided yet if they will cut. Often it has little to do with how well you skate, shoot or play; instead it depends on the mix of players available to the coach. If the coach has got a lot of great skaters but few talented puck handlers, a fine skater can fall off the bubble in favor of a talented puck handler and vice versa. I fell off the bubble when we had to skate backwards in a circle.

I had never skated backwards in a circle in my life and could only fake some passing acquaintanceship with the movement. A coach came over and tapped me on the shoulder. It was over. I wasn't going to Halifax. I looked up at the man who had come to deliver the blow, knew it was futile but decided to try and stave off the execution anyway. "Why do I have to skate backwards in a circle?" I asked. "I'm a forward. I play right wing like Rocket Richard. I don't need to skate backwards."

It didn't work. Apparently, they needed forwards who could also skate backwards in circles. The good news is Paul made the team and went to Halifax and came back with a trophy which he showed all of us kids on the street. We were in awe.

◇ ◇ ◇

A lot of water has flowed under the bridge since those childhood days. We have lived through some amazingly prosperous times. Children now are outfitted with hundreds of dollars in hockey equipment. Skating among the cattails has disappeared. There is a parking lot where that pond once was; St. John's and its suburban Mount Pearl municipality have many indoor skating rinks. Flying to Halifax does not have the same importance either. We live in times when people routinely travel to hot beaches on Caribbean shores; visit the great cathedrals of Europe; cross continents for business, marriages or skiing. We have learned to take for granted what just a few years ago would have been extraordinary.

But amongst all this prosperity there has been growing peripatetic violence. Ordinary people on ordinary days in ordinary buses have seen their lives mangled and ended because they were in the wrong place at the wrong time. It's as if violence has become like the weather: unpredictable. "Terrorism" has become a junk political word which justifies more investments in the military, secret services and checkpoints as if more military hardware and checkpoints could solve the many problems confronting global society. Not surprisingly, there has been a growing sense that we are living on a bubble; that our wealth and amazing comforts are a temporary phenomenon; that our children will not enjoy the same comforts nor have the same security as we have had.

Even countries like Canada that used to be relatively immune from the violence virus are becoming infected. The Canadian government's response to our soldiers being unable to drive without being bombed between forts in Afghanistan has been to buy helicopters. The response has Vietnam written all over it. What have we learned? The quagmire has just become larger and more complex since Vietnam.

The sense of insecurity is also coming from the increasing costs of all the basic resources that sustain the fabric of daily life: water, oil, natural gas, electricity. Most observant people realize these steady increases in costs will begin to force a retreat from the constantly expanding lifestyles that we have experienced; and of course, there is climate change which hangs its muddy inclement skies over the entire globe.

◆ ◆ ◆

When I first arrived at Ottawa City Council in November of 1997, I was so intrigued by the world that I discovered there that I began to keep notes with the idea of creating a diary of a poet who goes to city council. Elements of this original idea can still be found throughout the book, but that original idea faded when faced with the complexities of the job. Two months after I was elected the city was hit with five days of freezing rain in January, the greatest ice storm the city had ever seen. Miles of giant steel hydro towers buckled like spaghetti. The ice storm hit the cities of Montreal, Ottawa and Kingston and covered all of eastern Ontario and western Quebec, which came to be known as the "black triangle" because this part of the country went dark.

As a neophyte city councilor I quickly became occupied with the nuts and bolts of personal and city survival: finding people blankets; trying to persuade the elderly to evacuate freezing houses; getting out emergency bulletins on safe water and heating procedures. It was my first introduction to climate change. It wouldn't be my last, and I began to understand that my experiences as a city councilor in Ottawa weren't unique, that the human race itself was "on the bubble." The more I thought about this and experienced the effects of climate change at the most visceral level of city management (keeping streets cleared, water and electricity flowing) the more I became convinced that climate change was the great axial issue of our age — that everything else was trivial.

My book began to be about climate change as well as the experiences of a city councilor, but writing about climate change proved to be much more difficult than skating backwards in a circle. One of the many problems that emerged was how fast events were unfolding. When I first began to write very tentatively about the heating of the oceans just to convince readers that it was really happening, force five hurricanes were a once-a-century phenomenon. Climate change theory had predicted force five hurricanes would become frequent as the super-heated waters of the Gulf of Mexico inflated modest tropical storms into killers, but it was an academic theory. Before I had finished the book, it was a reality for millions of people along the entire Gulf of Mexico coast.

When I first began writing *Urban Meltdown*, the disappearance of the polar ice caps was little understood outside the scientific and Inuit communities. Before I had finished *Urban Meltdown*, Al Gore was touring his film "An Inconvenient Truth" in which he showed graphic film images of glacier ice melt quickly eroding the land–based ice sheet itself and millions of cubic tons of ice collapsing into the sea. What I had spent much time thinking and writing about in the context of my city and thought of as new knowledge had become "old knowledge" before I had finished the book.

Politically, things are shifting just as fast. Mr. Bush and Mr. Harper have said they aren't interested in signing Kyoto or trying to meet its targets, but incredibly, city, state and provincial leaders are stepping into the gap saying: "Climate change is too important to allow the federal government to fumble the ball. We will meet the Kyoto targets even if the federal government won't." The Mayor of Seattle has devised a Climate Protection Agreement and has brought together more than 200 municipalities to sign on — regardless of what the federal government does — and has committed to meeting or exceeding Kyoto. The Canadian Province of Quebec is bringing in an eco-tax on carbon.

What this means is that the federal governments of both the United States and Canada no longer represent the citizens of their nations internationally on the dominant issue of our age. It is cities, provinces and states which do. The federal governments of both the United States and Canada remain preoccupied with "terrorism" which is a product, like climate change, of population pressures and inadequate integration of basic human needs, not the lack of armed men at border points. The result is the federal governments of both north and south of the border are becoming increasingly irrelevant to anyone except those involved in federal party politics.

How is it all going to play out? Will we fall off the bubble? I don't know. What I do know is that events at every level are moving so fast it's impossible for anyone to anticipate where it is all going to end. Who would have thought in their wildest dreams that a premier of Quebec would impose a tax on carbon emissions when the federal government wouldn't? Premier Jean Charest is a conservative politician who was elected on a platform of cutting taxes, not expanding them.

Will we make it? Will the human race continue to prosper for millennia? Or will we swept from the translucent bubble of earth's surface like grass caught in a prairie fire? I don't pretend to know, but I do know answers are to be found in our cities, among the people and the governments there.

Endnotes

Prologue

1. Bill Bryson. *The Life and Times of the Thunderbolt Kid: a Memoir.* Doubleday, 2006, p. 8.
2. James Howard Kunstler. *The Long Emergency: Surviving the Converging Catastrophes of the Twenty-First Century.* Atlantic Monthly Press, 2005.
3. This information has been calculated by a NASA-German satellite project to map changes in the planet's surface, reported in the New Yorker magazine in 2005.
4. Ibid.

Chapter 1

1. "From Restless Communities to Resilient Places: Building A Stronger Future For All Canadians." Final Report of the External Advisory Committee on Cities and Communities. June 2006. [online]. [cited September 22, 2006]. infrastructure.gc.ca/eaccc-ccevc/alt_formats/pdf/eaccc_rep_ccevc_rap_e .pdf.
2. See mayorsforpeace.org/english/
3. Coastal City Mayors Letter to President Bush and Signatories. [online]. [cited September 13, 2006]. www.ecobridge.org/content/g_wdo.htm.

Chapter 3

1. Roger Sauvé. "The Current State of Canadian Family Finances 1999 Report." [online] [cited September 14, 2006]. ivfamille.ca/library/publications/ state99.html.

Chapter 4

1. *In Between Friends: Perspectives on John Kenneth Galbraith* (Houghton Mifflin, 1999), Robert B. Reich describes how between 1950 and 1978, the rising economic tide lifted all boats and in fact it lifted the bottom fifth of the population fastest of all; but starting in the late 1970s and continuing until today, "the trend reversed itself." The median income which had steadily risen in the three decades after the Second World War stopped growing. By 1996 the fortunate (top) fifth commanded 47 percent of all money earned, up from around 40 percent in 1979. The topmost 5 percent took home 20 percent up from 15 percent in 1979, and the least fortunate fifth shared less than 5 percent from around 7 percent in 1979. In short, the American economic tide continued to rise, but it was now lifting only pleasure craft. The small rowboats were sinking. "Wealth became even more concentrated than income. In 1995, the richest 1 percent held half of all outstanding stock and trust equity, almost

two thirds of financial securities, and over two thirds of business equity. The top ten percent owned 82 percent" (Between Friends, pp. 92 and 93).

2. Ward is an old English term for a city political district. It has fallen into disuse in many American cities and has been replaced by the word district. Ward, though, is still used widely in Canada. Presently, I am an Ottawa City Councilor, and I represent Capital Ward which is a dense, complex, city-center ward with two universities, five distinct communities, a canal, a river, a freeway and a rail line cutting through it.

Chapter 5

1. Elliot Liebow. *Tally's Corner: A Study of Negro Streetcorner Men.* Little Brown, 1967.

2. Elliot Liebow. *Tell Them Who I Am: The Lives of Homeless Women.* Penguin, 1993.

Chapter 7

1. Jane Jacobs. *The Death and Life of Great American Cities.* Vintage, 1992 (original edition Random House, 1961).

Chapter 8

1. Eric Schlosser. *Fast Food Nation: The Dark Side of the All-American Meal.* Harper, 2002, p. 17.

Chapter 10

1. Dee Brown. *Bury My Heart at Wounded Knee: an Indian History of the American West.* Bantam, 1970.

2. For more on the worldview of North American's First Nations, see "Selected References to Creation Stories/Legends" and "Historical Perspectives" from the Royal Commission on Aboriginal Peoples, 1996; Boyce Richardson. *People of Terra Nullius: Betrayal and Rebirth in Aboriginal Canada.* Douglas and McIntyre, 1993 and Clive Doucet. *Notes from Exile: On Being Acadian.* McClelland and Stewart, 1999, p. 106.

3. Headline: Ontario to maintain lifetime welfare ban. "The five-member panel investigating the death of Kimberly Rogers concluded yesterday that the zero-tolerance crackdown on welfare cheats was 'devastating and detrimental' and should be scrapped. But Community Services Minister Brenda Elliott immediately poured cold water on the finding...." Toronto Globe and Mail, December 20, 2002, p. A11.

4. Roger Jones. "Selected References to Creation Stories/Legends" and "Historical Perspectives." Royal Commission on Aboriginal Affairs (RCAP) Hearings Infobase, page 73.

5. Personal recollection.

6. Roger Jones, op.cit.

7. Brian Goodwin. *How the Leopard Changed Its Spots: The Evolution of Complexity.* Princeton University Press, 1994, p. 181.

Chapter 11

1. Stuart Kauffman. *At Home in the Universe.* Oxford University Press, 1995, p. 233.

2. The British economist John Maynard Keynes correctly predicted that The Treaty of Versailles would be the first shot in the next war.

3. Sir Peter Hall. *Cities in Civilization.* Weidenfeld & Nicolson, 1998.

4. Joseph Heller. *Catch-22.* Simon & Schuster, 1961.

Chapter 13

1. The idea is that the soul of the individual is a shared facility — part of a plural, planetary construct that all humans share. The soul is something that we create through the conduct of our own lives together. The means through which we create our cities and wider societies is "mine," in the sense that I have navigated to these conclusions independently. But the concept of soul as a shared facility is not newly minted; it is echoed in the work of complexity scientists and in the spiritual understanding of aboriginal peoples.

2. Ilona Flutsztejn-Gruda. *Quand les Grands Jouaient A La Guerre.* Actes Sud Junior, 1999.

Chapter 14

1. Aristotle. *On Man in the Universe.* Walter J. Black Inc., 1943, p. xxxiii.

Chapter 15

1. "Quick Facts." Economic Development Corporation of Wawa Community Profile. [online]. [cited October 3, 2006]. edcwawa.ca/profile.pdf.

Part III

1. James Howard Kunstler. *The Long Emergency: Surviving the Converging Catastrophes of the Twenty-First Century.* Atlantic Monthly Press, 2005.

Chapter 16

1. Edward Gibbon. *The History of the Decline and Fall of the Roman Empire, volumes I, II and III.* Methuen, 1909.

2. The information about Roman urban design in this chapter is drawn from: A. Trevor Hodge. *Roman Aqueducts and Water Supply,* 2nd ed. Duckworth, 2002; Bejaoui Fathi. *Sbeitla, l'antique Sufetula.* Institut National du Patrimoine, Collection: Sites et monuments de Tunisie, 2004; Tunisia. *From the heroes of Carthage to the rulers from Rome.* Edition Regie 3/AMVPPC 2005; Alex Butterworth & Laurence Ray. *Pompeii, The Living City.* Weidenfeld & Nicolson, 2005; L.P.Wilkinson. *The Roman Experience.* Knopf, 1974.

Chapter 17

1. Malcolm X. *The Autobiography of Malcolm X.* Grove Press, 1966.

2. John Howard Griffin. *Black Like Me.* Signet, 1962.

3. E.F. Schumacher. *Small is Beautiful: Economics as if People Mattered.* Harper Collins, 1974.

4. Rachel Carson. *Silent Spring.* Fawcett Crest, 1964.

5. Herbert Marcuse. *One-Dimensional Man: Studies in the Ideology of Advanced Industrial Society.* Beacon Press, 1969.

6. Paul Berman. *A Tale of Two Utopias: the Political Journey of the Generation of 1968.* Norton, 1997.

Chapter 18

1. From a speech given at the University of Kansas, Lawrence, Kansas, March 18, 1968.

2. From a speech titled "Beyond Vietnam, A Time to Break Silence" given at Riverside Church in New York City, April 4, 1967. americanrhetoric.com/speeches/mlkattimetobreatksilence.htm

3. Eleanor Roosevelt. *The Autobiography of Eleanor Roosevelt.* Da Capo Press, 2000, p. 437.

4. Jane Jacobs. *The Death and Life of Great American Cities.* Vintage Books, 1992 (original edition Random House, 1961).

5. Jane Jacobs. *Dark Age Ahead.* Random House, 2004.

6. Susan Machum. "De-prioritizing Agriculture," in Parkland Institute, Roger Epp and David Whitson. *Writing off the Rural West: Globalization, Governments and the Transformation of Rural Communities.* University of Alberta Press, 2001, p. 73. Note also that "The perennial crop failures in the Soviet Union were attributed to a highly centralized system run by distant bureaucrats. Today the handful of agribusiness firms that dominate America's food production are championing another centralized system of production, one in which livestock and farmlands are viewed purely as commodities, farmers reduced to the status of employees and crop decisions are made by executive far away from the fields" (Schlosser, p.266) and "One of the fundamental misunderstandings underlying many of the so-called development programs is the notion that traditional farming practices based on biodiversity have low productivity. However when all the multiple yields of diverse crops, the value and outputs of biological systems are taken fully into account, agricultural practices based on diversity are more productive, produce higher nutrient value in food than monoculture farming and are sustainable" (Goodwin, p. 230).

7. Paul Berman. *A Tale of Two Utopias: the Political Journey of the Generation of 1968.* Norton, 1997, p. 99.

8. Berman, p. 120.

9. Personal recollection.

Chapter 19

1. See chapter 1.

Chapter 24

1. It is illegal in Canada for newspaper owners to also own a television network. This was regarded as an undesirable concentration of influence, and a federal competition or anti-trust law was passed in the 1960s to prevent such a concentration. At the time, it did not occur to federal legislators that television networks might also want to own newspaper chains so no law was passed to prevent this from happening. This is the loophole that has been used to concentrate the ownership of Canadian newspapers, television and radio into a couple of mega-corporations. Many Canadian provinces no longer have a single independent daily newspaper or television station. There is only one major daily in the entire country (The Toronto Star) which remains independently owned and not surprisingly, it is the most consistent and persistent critic of both government and industry.

The headline of Lawrence Martin's article on p. A19 of Toronto's Globe and Mail on January 23, 2003 was "It's not Canadians who've gone right, just their media. The article begins: "'You have a bit of a problem here,' a European diplomat was saying over lunch last week. 'Your media are not representative of your people, your values.'…Who could disagree? Witness Defence Minister John McCallum and his suggestion that Canada might fight a war alongside the United States even if the United Nations did not find reason for one. The media applauded the sentiment. As for Canadians themselves, a poll was taken: A piddling 15 percent favoured such an option.…"

2. Paraphrased from the end of his movie, "An Inconvenient Truth."

Bibliography

Adams, Michael. *Fire and Ice: The United States, Canada and the Myth of Converging Values.* Penguin Canada, 2003.

Aristotle. *On Man in the Universe.* Walter J. Black Inc., 1943.

Barber, Benjamin R. *Jihad vs McWorld: Terrorism's Challenge to Democracy.* Ballantine, 1996.

Berman, Paul. *A Tale of Two Utopias: the Political Journey of the Generation of 1968.* Norton, 1997.

Bohman, James and William Rehg, eds. *Deliberative Democracy: Essays on Reason and Politics.* MIT Press, 1997.

Brown, Dee. *Bury My Heart at Wounded Knee: an Indian History of the American West.* Bantam, 1970.

Buchanan, Mark. *Nexus: Small Worlds and the Groundbreaking Science of Networks.* Norton, 2002.

Buchanan, Mark. *Ubiquity: the science of history or why the world is simpler than we think.* Weidenfeld & Nicolson, 2000.

Capra, Fritjof. *The Web of Life: A New Scientific Understanding of Living Systems.* Anchor, 1997.

Carson, Rachel. *Silent Spring.* Fawcett Crest, 1964.

Carver, Humphrey. *Compassionate Landscape.* University of Toronto Press, 1975.

Chiasson, Remi. *Le père Joseph DeCoste, Curé de Saint-Joseph-du-Moine, Nouvelle-Écosse, Une appréciation personnelle.* A very simple and moving pamphlet describing the impact that Father DeCoste's career as a parish priest had on the village of Grand Etang written by one of his students.

Chomsky, Noam and Greg Ruggiero. *9-11.* Seven Stories Press, 2001.

Coleman, Alice. *Canadian Settlement and Environmental Planning.* Ministry of State for Urban Affairs, 1976.

Dallaire, Lt. Gen. Romeo. *Shake Hands with the Devil: the Failure of Humanity in Rwanda.* Random House Canada, 2004.

Doucet, Clive. *Canal Seasons.* Penumbra Press, 2003.

Doucet, Clive. *Looking for Henry.* Thistledown Press, 1999.

Doucet, Clive. *Notes from Exile: On Being Acadian.* McClelland and Stewart, 1999.

Dyson, Michael Eric. *I May Not Get There With You: The True Martin Luther King, Jr.* Free Press, 2000.

Elshtain, Jean Bethke. *Democracy On Trial.* Anansi, 1993.

Ferlinghetti, Lawrence. *These Are My Rivers: New and Selected Poems, 1955-1993.* New Directions, 1993.

Flutsztejn-Gruda, Ilona. *Quand les Grands Jouaient A La Guerre.* Actes Sud Junior, 1999.

Gervais, Marty. *Into a Blue Morning.* Hounslow Press, 1982.

Gibbon, Edward. *The History of the Decline and Fall of the Roman Empire, volumes I, II and III.* Methuen, 1909.

Goodwin, Brian. *How the Leopard Changed Its Spots: The Evolution of Complexity.* Princeton University Press, 1994.

Griffin, John Howard. *Black Like Me.* Signet, 1962.

Hall, Sir Peter. *Cities in Civilization.* Weidenfeld & Nicolson, 1998.

Hampton, Howard with Bill Reno. *Public Power: The Fight for Publicly Owned Electricity.* Insomniac Press, 2003.

Heaney, Seamus. *Opened Ground: Selected Poems, 1966-1996.* Faber and Faber, 1998.

Heller, Joseph. *Catch-22.* Simon & Schuster, 1961.

Iyer, Pico. *The Global Soul: Jet Lag, Shopping Malls and the Search for Home.* Random House, 2001.

Jacobs, Jane. *Dark Age Ahead.* Random House, 2004.

Jacobs, Jane. *The Death and Life of Great American Cities.* Vintage, 1992 (original edition Random House, 1961).

Jacobs, Jane. *The Nature of Economics.* Random House Canada, 2000.

James, Sarah & Torbjorn Lahti. *The Natural Step for Communities: How Cities and Towns can Change to Sustainable Practices.* New Society Publishers, 2004.

Kauffman, Stuart. *At Home in the Universe: The Search for the Laws of Self-Organization and Complexity.* Oxford University Press, 1995.

Kauffman, Stuart. *Investigations.* Oxford, 2000.

Kunstler, James Howard. *The Long Emergency: Surviving the Converging Catastrophes of the Twenty-First Century.* Atlantic Monthly Press, 2005.

Le, John B. *The Pig Dance Dreams.* Black Moss, 1991.

Liebow, Eliot. *Tally's Corner: A Study of Negro Streetcorner Men.* Little Brown, 1967.

Liebow, Eliot. *Tell Them Who I Am: The Lives of Homeless Women.* Penguin, 1993.

Malcolm X. *The Autobiography of Malcolm X.* Grove Press, 1966.

Mander, Jerry and Edward Goldsmith, eds. *The Case Against the Global Economy and for a Turn Toward the Local.* Sierra Club Books, 1996.

Marcuse, Herbert. *One-Dimensional Man: Studies in the Ideology of Advanced Industrial Society.* Beacon Press, 1969.

Nadasdy, Paul. *Hunters and Bureaucrats: Power, Knowledge and Aboriginal-State Relations in the Southwest Yukon.* UBC Press, 2003.

O'Connor, Honourable Dennis R. *Report of the Walkerton Inquiry: The Events of May 2000 and Related Issues.* Queen's Printer for Ontario, 2002.

O'Murchu, Diarmuid. *Quantum Theology: Spiritual Implications of the New Physics.* Revised and updated edition. Crossroad, 2004.

Orwell, George. *The Collected Essays, Journalism and Letters, Volume I. An Age Like This: 1920–1940.* Edited by Sonia Orwell and Ian Angus. Penguin Books, 1945.

Parkland Institute, Roger Epp and David Whitson. *Writing off the Rural West: Globalization, Governments and the Transformation of Rural Communities.* University of Alberta Press, 2001.

Paton, Alan. *Cry, the Beloved Country.* Scribner, 1948.

Putnam, Robert D. *Bowling Alone: The Collapse and Revival of American Community.* Simon and Shuster, 2000.

Rebick, Judy. *Imagine Democracy.* Stoddart, 2000.

Reich, Robert B. *Between Friends: Perspectives on John Kenneth Galbraith.* Houghton Mifflin, 1999.

Richardson, Boyce. *People of Terra Nullius: Betrayal and Rebirth in Aboriginal Canada.* Douglas and McIntyre, 1993.

Roosevelt, Eleanor. *The Autobiography of Eleanor Roosevelt.* Da Capo Press, 2000.

Saul, John Ralston. *Voltaire's Bastards: The Dictatorship of Reason in the West.* Penguin Canada, 1992.

Schlosser, Eric. *Fast Food Nation: The Dark Side of the All-American Meal.* Harper, 2002.

Schumacher, E.F. *Small is Beautiful: Economics as if People Mattered.* Harper Collins, 1974.

"Selected References to Creation Stories/Legends" and "Historical Perspectives." *Report of the Royal Commission on Aboriginal Peoples,* 1996.

Stone, I.F. *The Trial of Socrates.* Doubleday, 1989.

Urmetzer, Peter. *From Free Trade to Forced Trade: Canada in the Global Economy.* Penguin/McGill Institute, 2003

Walljasper, Jay, Jon Spayde and The Editors of the Utne Reader. *Visionaries: People and Ideas to Change Your Life.* New Society Publishers, 2001.

Index

About the Author

CLIVE DOUCET has been an urban activist all his life. He began as a student in Toronto with the successful Stop Spadina movement. His formal education includes an honours degree from the University of Toronto and a Masters degree from the Université de Montréal, both in urban anthropology.

He has worked for non-governmental groups as well as federal, provincial and municipal governments. At the Ministry of State for Urban Affairs, he was one of the authors of the Federal Urban Domain I-III; worked as a local government policy advisor for the Ontario Provincial Government and has been a city councillor in Ottawa since 1997. His columns on urban issues appear in the *Globe and Mail* and other Canadian newspapers and magazines.

His literary credits include novels, novellas, memoirs, poems and plays. Several are already considered Canadian classics. *My Grandfather's Cape Breton* — the Acadian Anne of Green Gables and has sold over 25,000 copies. *Notes from Exile* was one of the top 100 books chosen by McClelland and Stewart to celebrate a centenary of Canadian book publishing.

Clive Doucet is married with two children and two grandchildren: a son Julian who is an actor and writer, and a daughter Emma who works on native issues at Heritage Canada.

If you have enjoyed *Urban Meltdown* you might also enjoy other

BOOKS TO BUILD A NEW SOCIETY

Our books provide positive solutions for people
who want to make a difference. We specialize in:

Environment and Justice • Conscientious Commerce
Sustainable Living • Ecological Design and Planning
Natural Building & Appropriate Technology
Educational and Parenting Resources • Nonviolence
Progressive Leadership • Resistance and Community

New Society Publishers

ENVIRONMENTAL BENEFITS STATEMENT

New Society Publishers has chosen to produce this book on recycled paper made with **100% post consumer waste**, processed chlorine free, and old growth free.

For every 5,000 books printed, New Society saves the following resources:[1]

27	Trees
2,465	Pounds of Solid Waste
2,713	Gallons of Water
3,538	Kilowatt Hours of Electricity
4,482	Pounds of Greenhouse Gases
19	Pounds of HAPs, VOCs, and AOX Combined
7	Cubic Yards of Landfill Space

[1]Environmental benefits are calculated based on research done by the Environmental Defense Fund and other members of the Paper Task Force who study the environmental impacts of the paper industry.

---

*For a full list of NSP's titles, please call 1-800-567-6772
or check out our website at:*

www.newsociety.com

NEW SOCIETY PUBLISHERS